HANGING IN THE BALANCE

This book gives the first in-depth assessment of how justification functions when women are claiming their right to equality.

How can courts assess whether a proposed limit to women's equality is constitutionally justified? This question is rarely explicitly asked, with the assumption that well-established limitation frameworks, such as proportionality, are able to assess whether limits to women's rights are justified. However, delving into the theory and practice of justification reveals fracture points between the dominant approach to justification and women's rights to equality.

One of the book's distinctive characteristics is the question of whether any analytical entwining or unwinding of equality and justification enhances the protection of women's rights to equality in constitutional democracies. It proposes a novel asymmetric relationship between equality and justification that requires innovative methodological approaches that enrich the task of adjudicating limits to women's equality.

This is an intriguing, articulate and compelling examination of a question with real and applied significance to all those working on human rights and equality.

Hanging in the Balance

The Function of Justification in Achieving Women's Equality

Meghan Campbell

•HART•

OXFORD • LONDON • NEW YORK • NEW DELHI • SYDNEY

HART PUBLISHING

Bloomsbury Publishing Plc

Kemp House, Chawley Park, Cumnor Hill, Oxford, OX2 9PH, UK

1385 Broadway, New York, NY 10018, USA

Bloomsbury Publishing Ireland Limited, 29 Earlsfort Terrace, Dublin 2, D02 AY28, Ireland

HART PUBLISHING, the Hart/Stag logo, BLOOMSBURY and the Diana logo are trademarks of Bloomsbury Publishing Plc

First published in Great Britain 2025

A catalogue record for this book is available from the British Library.

A catalogue record for this book is available from the Library of Congress.

Library of Congress Control Number: 2025942486

ISBN: HB: 978-1-50996-787-2
ePDF: 978-1-50996-789-6
ePub: 978-1-50996-788-9

Typeset by Compuscript Ltd, Shannon

Acknowledgements

As SOMEONE WHO genuinely loves reading acknowledgements in books, it is a chance to see some of the person behind all those words and thoughts which follow, I will try to make these acknowledgements an insight into the richness of this experience.

Thank you to the British Academy for the Mid-Career Fellowship, as this book would not exist without the magic of protected and unbroken time for research and I'm very grateful to the British Academy for providing that magic. A similar thanks to Birmingham Law School as the sabbatical time they provided was instrumental in developing the ideas that resulted in this book.

Thank you to Sandra Fredman for constantly supporting my attempts at academic scholarship, convincing me that my loose ideas are worth it and patiently reading multiple draft chapters. There is a line from a Beach Boys song – 'God Only Knows What I'd Be Without You' – and when I think of my academic career, I have no idea where I would be without Sandy's love, care and support. I am so full of appreciation for it and for getting to work together on so many projects over so many years.

I have had the fortune to be part of Sandy's weekly Research Group for many years, and I want to give a big thank you to Justin Winchester, Sophie Treacy, Rawletta Barrow, Mandisa Shandu, Sfiso Nxumalo, Almas Shaikh, Anjali Rawat, Jinghe Fan, Monica Arango Olaya, Gautam Bhatia and Rishika Sahgal. Thank you for always asking the hard questions that I would much rather have ducked. This book is infinitely stronger for your friendship, inquisitiveness and rigour.

This book benefited from the insights from early readers, Fiona de Londras, Mairead Enright, Rosie Harding and Kate Bedford. When I blushingly think back on the early drafts, I am struck by how important their help and insights were and how fortunate to have a network of friends and colleagues who so generously give of their time and wisdom.

Thank you to Nomfundo Ramalekana, Rishika Sahgal, Judith Bauder and Gauri Pillai for reading multiple drafts of the chapters in the book and sharing their expertise, wisdom and knowledge. Their kindness is not only a model to strive for in academia but has enriched this book and made the process of writing it much more enjoyable.

Thank-you to Julie Suk, Jennifer Koshan, Aparna Chandra and Dhaya Pillay for there many insightful answers to my questions on women, equality and justification and for participating in the joy of RightsUp podcasting with me. Thank you to Sophie Smith for making us all sound so brilliant.

My favourite part of any project like this is to think about the cover. A joyful thank you to Jonathan and Alice Neve and Geoffrey Swenson and Francesca Ward for their help in designing the cover and for being amazing friends.

Throughout this project, I have been supported by my family. To my nephews, Ethan, Owen and Noah Hancox for always keeping my feet on the ground while doing scholarship and, I am sorry this book is not as exciting as getting to see each other on the Winnipeg Airport Hug Rug! To my brother-in-law, Keith Hancox, stepmother, Gillian Chase and my friend Zailey Ducharme, thank you for letting me talk through the ideas in this book and sharing their own thoughts and experiences on equality. And thank you to my Mom, Dad and sister Amy, thank you for the endless patience, love and support, always being proud of me even when I am not sure I was worth it and always providing the strongest examples on how to live the right to equality.

Thank you to Ben Warwick for always asking the questions this project needed and none of the ones it wanted. Thank you for metaphorically and literally holding my hand throughout all the anxieties of scholarship and for patiently listening to the highs and lows of working through the ideas in this book. You are the platonic truth of a friend–colleague and an even better friend.

And lastly to Silvia Pittner. On a rainy day in Edinburgh, when I was a nervous LLM student, Silvia non-chantingly said 'Of course you will write a book and you will obviously write more than one'. Thank you Silvia for believing in me at every step and in this book long before I ever believed that I could do this.

Meghan Campbell
May 2025

Contents

1

The Other Half of the Story

I. INTRODUCTION

THE CURRENT GLOBAL political climate is revealing the fragility of women's equality. Achievements in women's rights are being threatened, rolled back and demonised as immoral.[1] Women's equality has become a key battleground in the so-called 'culture wars' and a flash point for conservative populism.[2] Women have not been silent in the face of this backlash. On floors of legislative bodies, social media and in the streets, they are demanding the full guarantee and enjoyment of their equal rights. Women are also turning to the law. Domestic courts have a long history as sites of contestation over competing ideologies on the roles of men and women and on the rigidity of binary gender roles. The struggle for women's equal rights in the courtroom has seen pathbreaking victories and heartbreaking losses.

There is an unspoken assumption that the key struggle is establishing a transformative conception of what it means for women to be equal. There is frustration that courts have failed to embrace a substantive model of equality. Despite long-standing criticism,[3] courts continue to apply mechanical and formalistic notions of equality that fail to understand how inequalities manifest, operate and shape women's lives. Efforts to secure stronger constitutional

[1] UN Working Group on Discrimination Against Women in Law and Practice, 'Reasserting Equality, Countering Rollbacks' (2018) A/HRC/38/46; James FitzGerald, Nadine Yousif and Kayla Epstein, 'Trump Puts All US Government Diversity Staff on Paid Leave "Immediately"' (*BBC*, 22 January 2025), available at www.bbc.co.uk/news/articles/cgj288ywj23o.

[2] Elizabeth Corredor, 'Unpacking "Gender Ideology" and the Global Right's Antigender Countermovement' (2019) 44(3) *Signs: Journal of Women in Culture and Society* 613; Julie Mostov, 'Populism Is Always Gendered and Dangerous' (2021) 5 *Frontiers in Sociology* 1; Sahar Abi-Hassan, 'Populism and Gender' in Cristóbal Kaltwasser et al (eds), *The Oxford Handbook of Populism* (Oxford University Press, 2017) 426.

[3] Catherine MacKinnon, *Feminism Unmodified* (Harvard University Press, 1987); Kimberle Crenshaw, 'Demarginalizing the Intersection of Race and Sex' (1989) 8(1) *University of Chicago Legal Forum* 139; Cathi Albertyn and Beth Goldblatt, 'Facing the Challenge of Transformation: Difficulties in the Development of an Indigenous Jurisprudence of Equality' (1998) 14(2) *South African Journal on Human Rights* 248; Colleen Sheppard, *Inclusive Equality* (McGill-Queen's University Press, 2010); Sandra Fredman, *Discrimination Law*, 3rd edn (Clarendon, 2023); Ratna Kapur, 'Gender Equality' in Sujit Choudry, Madhav Khosla and Pratap Bhanu Mehta (eds), *The Oxford Handbook of the Indian Constitution* (Oxford University Press, 2016); Shrey Atrey, *Intersectional Discrimination* (Oxford University Press, 2019).

protection for women's right to be equal should, the thinking goes, be centred on refining doctrinal concepts and theories on substantive and transformative equality. Yet, focusing on equality only examines half of the story. The right to equality is not absolute and can justifiably be infringed. The constitutional structure in many jurisdictions, explicitly or through doctrinal innovation, allows limits on women's equality rights. Even if a violation of women's right to equality is established, it may be a permissible violation. To pursue other competing objectives the state can constitutionally treat women unequally. The other half of the story in using law to strengthen women's right centres on the part justification plays in either maintaining or dismantling women's inequality.

The relationship between women's enjoyment of equality and justification is overlooked, understudied and undertheorised. This might appear to be an odd or even impossible claim as both equality and justification have been extensively examined. On one track there is a rich corpus exploring women's right to equality, and on the other, there is a correspondingly abundant oeuvre on the theory and practice of justifying rights limitations. But these tracks run in parallel. Outside of a handful of outliers,[4] explored below, there is little awareness or attention to the function justification plays in adjudicating women's right to equality. The minimal scholarly engagement on the intersection between women's equality and justification is often mirrored in judicial practice. In many judgments on women's equality, which are lengthy and run to hundreds of pages, the justification assessment amounts no more than to a handful of paragraphs.[5] Women's equality and justifications for limiting women's equality are treated as hermetically sealed from each other. There is little explicit acknowledgment or any in-depth discussion on the relationship between assessing whether there has been a breach of women's equality rights and whether that breach can be constitutionally justified. Any pitfalls or strengths that are generated from the interaction between women's equality and justification remain hidden.

The lack of engagement on the intersection of women's equality with justification is unwarranted. The outcome of the case often hinges on justification. Courts will recognise there has been an inequality against women but then hold that inequality can be justified. A cap on the amount of social welfare benefits

[4] Beverely Baines, '*Law v Canada*: Formatting Equality' (2000) 11(3) *Constitutional Forum* 65; Sheilah Martin, 'Balancing Individual Rights to Equality and Social Goals' (2000) 80 *The Canadian Bar Review* 302; Harriet Samuels, 'Feminizing Human Rights Adjudication: Feminist Legal Methods and Proportionality Principle (2013) 21 *Feminist Legal Studies* 39; Vicki Jackson, 'Proportionality and Equality' in Vicki Jackson and Mark Tushnet (eds), *Proportionality: New Frontiers, New Challenges* (Cambridge University Press, 2017); Guy Lurie, 'Proportionality and the Right to Equality' (2020) 21 *German Law Journal* 174; Anna Nilsson, 'Same, Same but Different: Proportionality Assessments and Equality Norms' (2020) 7(3) *Oslo Law Review* 126; Jennifer Koshan and Jonnette Watson Hamilton, '"Clarifications" or "Wholesale Revisions"? The Last Five Years of Equality Jurisprudence at the Supreme Court of Canada (2023) *Supreme Court Law Review* 1.

[5] *Fraser v Canada (Attorney General)* [2020] 3 SCR 113; *SC and Others v Secretary of State for Work and Pensions* [2021] UKSC 26; *Bwanya v Master of the High Court* [2021] ZACC 51.

was held by the United Kingdom (UK) Supreme Court to be indirectly discriminatory against women, who due to their caring responsibilities disproportionately relied upon these benefits.[6] However, this breach was held to be justifiable as women's equality was outweighed by the state's need to generate fiscal savings and to reduce dependency on welfare benefits. Legislation that permitted delays in implementing equal pay for women in workplaces dominated by women was held by the Canadian Supreme Court to violate women's right to equality.[7] This inequality was justified as the state needed time to develop a methodology for correcting unequal pay that stemmed from gender occupational segregation. Establishing the inequality was only the first stage. The second stage, assessing whether it is justifiable to limit women's equality, was pivotal.

The value in examining justification holds true even for cases that hold the state cannot limit women's equality. In these cases, courts have found a breach but held that the breach cannot be constitutionally justified. Investigating how courts come to that determination gives glimmers on how the relationship between equality and justification can be operationalised to strengthen the protection of women's equality rights. By taking seriously the limitation analysis, it is possible to see how courts can flush out hard to detect gender inequalities when assessing justification claims, harms that may not be apparent when only assessing whether there has been a breach of the right to equality. Banning women from obtaining permanent commissions in the Indian army was a blatant violation of women's equality at work. The state argued that the ban was justified as it protected women from the harms of frontline service. The Indian Supreme Court, however, rejected this argument.[8] It explored how there was a lack of rationality between the state's objective and the ban as women had a long and successful history of serving in combat zones. Greater attention to justification shone light on limitation rationales that operated as a smoke screen for romantic paternalistic stereotypes. There were similar weaknesses in justifications for excluding de facto intimate partner unions from marital protection laws in South Africa. These exclusions were in place to protect individual choice. The South African Constitutional Court challenged the veracity of this limitation.[9] The Court pointed out that the measure was not rationally connected to enhancing autonomy as gender power relations in intimate relations meant that the law was only protecting and privileging the choices of men.

Recognising that claims for women's equality repeatedly turn on justification raises new questions and opens new avenues for exploration. Are justification frameworks inherently able to identify gendered assumptions that are embedded in limitation rationales? Are more probing, high intensity justification tests

[6] *SG and Others v Secretary of State for Works and Pensions* [2015] UKSC 16.

[7] *Centrale des syndicats du Quebec v Quebec (Attorney General)* [2018] 1 SCR 522.

[8] *The Secretary, Ministry of Defence v Babita Puniya and Others* (2020) Civil Appeal Nos 1127-28 of 2013, Civil Appeal No 1210 of 2020.

[9] *Sithole v Sithole* (2020) Case CCT 23/20.

more suited to limitations of women's equality? Are certain justification tests, such as proportionality, better suited to this interrogative function? However, courts using the same justification framework routinely come to diverging conclusions on the permissibility of limiting women's equality.[10] In many of the cases outlined above, there were strong dissents that used the same analytical framework but came to the opposite conclusion on the permissibility of limiting women's equality rights. This suggests that the ability of the limitation analysis to fetter out flaws is divorced from any specific justification test. Perhaps, what is required is a methodological shift to justification that cuts across the application of limitation criteria?

These questions themselves, however, are built on a belief that a rigorous justification analysis in the context of women's equality is needed. But a probing and searching limitation assessment might fail to recognise the hard choices that must be made in pluralistic constitutional democracies where numerous rights, interests and objectives must be balanced against each other. For example, limiting women's equality in response to a fiscal crisis may be a deeply regrettable economic necessity.[11] Is it dangerous to utilise a high intensity justification review to narrow the leeway needed for the state to pursue public interest aims that conflict with women's right to equality? Moreover, are courts institutionally competent to question these types of hard choices? At the same time, women's right to equality is of fundamental constitutional importance. Does failing to demand cogent, compelling and persuasive reasoning for limiting women's equality fail to respect the nature of the right? As Ramalekana and de Vos noted, equality 'is a unique obligation to protect the rights of the most vulnerable and marginalised members of society'.[12] The United States (US) and Canadian Supreme Court have explained that equality rights in constitutions are in place because statutes, regulations, policies, programmes have constructed 'headwinds' that deny the enjoyment of society's benefits to members of certain groups like racial identity groups, disabled persons and women.[13] Societies and communities have been legally built to disadvantage, demean, oppress and exclude, inter alia, women. Constitutionalising women's equality is a recognition that centuries and centuries of gender oppression must end. Law must be reoriented to undoing gender power hierarchies and needs to reflect the full humanity of women. Does a lower standard of review cut across and undermine the significance of women's equality? Does even the idea of permitting limits to women's equality operate to dilute that constitutional promise?

[10] *Nevada Department of Human Resources v Hibbs* 583 US 721 (2003); *A and B v Secretary of State for Health* [2017] UKSC 41; *Centrale* (n 7); *SG* (n 6).

[11] *Newfoundland (Treasury Board) v NAPE* [2004] 3 SCR 381.

[12] Nomfundo Ramalekana and Pierre de Vos, 'Erasure, Xenophobic Discrimination and Non-Citizen's Right to Equality and Work in South Africa: A Commentary on *Rafoneke v Minister of Justice*' (2024) *Constitutional Court Review* 1, 3.

[13] *Griggs v Duke Power Co* 401 US 424, 431–32; *Fraser* (n 5) [47], [53].

Or is there a middle ground, where the application of justification criteria can demonstrate respect for the significance of women's equality while also recognising there may be circumstances where that equality has to give way? Taking a step back, are there other nodes of synergy between women's equality and justification? Does justification shape how courts determine whether there has been a breach of women's equality rights? Can equality guide or enrich the justification assessment? These questions all indicate that there is much about how justification functions in relation to women's equality that is not understood.

The central inquiry of this monograph is to engage with these questions. Unravelling the relationship between equality and justification is of immense value in understanding the role of law in achieving women's equality. This unravelling brings to the fore unseen complexities, deeply embedded gendered value assumptions, nearly invisible patriarchal structures and rival visions of the court, the executive, and the legislative branches of government.[14] Justification is the missing half of the story and taking it seriously strengthens efforts to fortify constitutional guarantees of equality. The first aim of the inquiry is doctrinal. Little is known about the different facets of the relationship between women's equality and justification. The monograph unearths precisely: (i) how determining if there is a breach of women's equality is informed by the justification; and (ii) how assessing whether that breach is justifiable operates with respect to women's equality. It lays bare that any assumptions that equality and justification are two separate points of analysis is inaccurate. These assumptions obscure the interconnectedness in practice between finding a violation and whether that violation is justifiable. The doctrinal investigation also uncovers how there are a myriad of connections between women's equality and justification and diagnoses how these connections can both further and frustrate efforts to secure constitutional equality. Not giving attention to justification is only telling half of the story of how women's equality rights live or die in the courtroom. The doctrinal analysis in this monograph aims to tell the whole story.

The second aim is normative. Building on the clarity offered from the doctrinal analysis, the monograph develops the optimal relationship between women's equality and justification. It argues for an asymmetry in the role equality and justification play across assessing whether there has been a breach of right to equality and whether that breach is justified. The equality analysis should be hermetically sealed from justification. When assessing if there has been a breach of women's equality, the doctrinal analysis reveals that courts are borrowing from justification. Using justification criteria to assess the alleged violation. Limitation concepts or reasoning should not be deployed in this manner for two reasons. First, this is because justification

[14] Jackson (n 4).

concepts are analytically irrelevant to determining whether the right to equality has been breached and second, justification distorts the equality analysis, minimising the severity of women's inequality. Employing substantive equality to determine whether the right has been breached can protect against justification reasoning infecting the assessment.[15] While justification should play no role in assessing a breach of equality, equality can and should play a role in assessing whether the proposed rationale for limiting women's equality is constitutionally sound. There are two ways equality can positively shape the justification stage. First, it guides calibrating how closely courts should interrogate the veracity of limitation claims. It clarifies that the justification assessment must *always* be a forensic and rigorous analysis regardless of any countervailing factors that might seemingly push towards a more deferential justification review. To accept limitation rationale at face-value or subjecting them to a minimal level of scrutiny undercuts the significance of women's equality rights. Second, equality enriches the application of justification criteria. Equality can assist in determining whether proposed justifications are accurate, evidence-based and compelling. A new methodology for how equality can enrich justification in this manner is proposed.[16] Enriching justification with equality requires testing the limitation against the justification criteria in a way that is *relational* to the underlying breach of women's equality and *contextual* to a broader, substantive understanding of women's equality. Using substantive equality in a relational and contextual manner enhances the ability of the court to test where a limitation meets the required degree of legitimacy, rationality, necessity, balancing or other criteria as required by that jurisdiction's justification frameworks.

This chapter proceeds as follows. Section II sets out the parameters of this study. It explains the methodological choices with respect to the scope of the monograph, pins down in greater detail the lines of inquiry and defends the value of pursuing the doctrinal and normative aims through a comparative analysis. Sections III and IV proceed to investigate the building blocks of the monograph. Section III explores the conceptual boundaries of women's right to equality and section IV scrutinises justification. Both sections identify points of murkiness and ambiguity which create porousness and space for slippage between equality and justification. How slippages occur in the adjudication of women's equality and the normative value of these slippages is considered in the preceding chapters. Section V of this chapter examines the nascent linkages being drawn between equality and justification and Section VI concludes by mapping the inquiry undertaken in the remaining chapters.

[15] See chapter three.
[16] See chapter six.

II. ESTABLISHING THE PARAMETERS

A. Justifying the Limits on the Inquiry

The questions that animate this monograph are ambitious and could, without parameters, veer into unwieldy. This section outlines the methodological choices to give structure to the arguments and how those choices are geared towards generating meaningful insights into the relationship between women's equality and justification. In exploring how women's equality and justification *do* relate to each other and theorising on how women's equality and justification *should* relate to each other, the monograph only examines jurisprudence from the twenty-first century. The temporal cut-off has a pragmatic dimension, as it confines the relevant case law to a more manageable amount. It also has a more principled dimension. The concept of equality and justification have evolved over the years, and with many jurisdictions those evolutionary twists and turns have been non-linear and convoluted. Zeroing in on the past 25 years permits a more cutting-edge and up-to-date understanding of women, equality and justifications. Where required to make sense of a contemporary judicial decision, attention is paid to decisions prior to the twenty-first century.

A key parameter to the monograph is geographic. It focuses exclusively on the jurisprudence from apex courts from the twenty-first century from Canada, India, South Africa, the UK and US. Again, there is a practical dimension to this methodological choice as all of these courts adjudicate in English. There is also a principled dimension that is linked to the aims of the monograph. All these jurisdictions have constitutional commitments to women's equality, or in the case of the UK quasi-constitutional commitments and have accepted that equality rights can be limited. Courts in these countries have been crucial sites for the contestation of that commitment and the permissibility of limitations over the past 25 years. This has created a rich body of jurisprudence that through the analysis in this monograph generates pressing insights into women's equality and justification. The geographic boundaries are also harnessed to explore the inquiries central to this monograph through a comparative lens. This is explained further below.

Having established the 'when' and the 'where', it is also important to delineate the 'what' and the 'who' of this study. It is an investigation into women's equality rights focusing on the sex, gender, equality and justification. The aim is to unpack how sex and gender disadvantage, prejudice, stigmatise, oppression and marginalistion shape the relationship between equality and justification. As the analysis throughout the monograph reveals, there are unique features to women's equality that impact how justification should operate when assessing the permissibility of limits to that equality. The arguments developed, however, may still have salience for other grounds of discrimination. It also signals that further studies are needed, beyond this monograph, to uncover how the distinctiveness of other grounds relate to justification.[17] With respect to this investigation, there is another aspect to the 'who' question. The inquiry is centred on women. Pinpointing or defining women has become a fraught and politically controversial exercise. The judgments examined throughout the proceeding chapters centre around cis women as the jurisprudence argued on the basis of sex and gender equality has primarily been on cis women.[18] Trans women,[19] however, also experience inequalities rooted in patriarchy. Along with experiencing oppression based on perceived gender divergence, they experience subordination based on beliefs in the superiority of men and the inferiority of women.[20] The category of women in equality law must capture and take seriously the sex and gender-based inequalities faced by all who identify as women. Due to how claims have been litigated, the focus in this monograph is on cis women, but the arguments developed will have resonance for trans women and more broadly for those seeking to enhance protection for gender identity and expression.

With respect to the 'what' question, the monograph is restricted to jurisprudence where equality rights are at stake. The challenge is delineating what is or is not a decision on women's equality rights as equality is not merely a right but also a constitutional norm and an aspirational goal of the state.[21] Judgments where women's equality is argued on the basis of constitutional rights other than right to equality are excluded. The US jurisprudence on abortion is grounded in privacy not equality rights, despite women's equality, or resistance to that equality, permeating the US Supreme Court's reasoning.[22] Similarly, the Canadian Supreme Court's decision to strike down a series of provisions that criminalised elements of sex work was decided on the right to security of the person, although women's equality is laced throughout the judgment.[23] These cases are not included as the central aim is not to unpack how women's equality writ large is shaped by and shapes justification but how women's *right* to equality, and all the theoretical, conceptual and doctrinal nuances that entails, relates to justification. Only decisions where the right to equality was plead are included in the monograph.

[17] For a good analysis outlining justifying direct discrimination and different grounds, see Fredman (n 3).

[18] Cis gender is when a person's gender identity aligns with the gender assigned at birth; Sandra Duffy, 'Contested Subjects of Human Rights: Trans-and Gender-variant Subjects of International Human Rights Law (2021) 84(5) *MLR* 1041, 1044.

[19] Trans gender is when a person's gender identity differs from the gender assigned at birth; ibid.

[20] Katharine Jenkins, 'Amelioration and Inclusion' 2016 126(2) *Ethics* 394; Talia Mae Bettcher, 'Evil Deceivers and Make-Believers: On Transphobic: Violence and the Politics of Inclusion' 22(3) *Hypatia* 43; Robin Dembroff, 'Trans Women are Victims of Misogyny Too-and All Feminists Must Recognise This' *The Guardian* (19 May 2019), available at www.theguardian.com/commentisfree/2019/may/19/valerie-jackson-trans-women-misogyny-feminism.

[21] Jackson (n 4) 171; Vicki Jackson, 'Constitutional Law in an Age of Proportionality' (2015) 124 *Yale Law Journal* 3094.

[22] *Whole Woman's Health v Hellerstedt* 579 US 582 (2016); *Dobbs v Jackson Women's Health Organization* 597 US 215 (2022).

[23] *Canada (Attorney General) v Bedford* [2013] 3 SCR 1101.

However, the net is cast wide to capture decisions where another ground is a proxy for women's equality, such as the case for equality on the basis of marital status, as women's socioeconomic vulnerability is central to the judicial reasoning on equality and on justification. In a similar vein, decisions where the relationship between equality and justification are inverted from the traditional paradigm are included. Usually, the state breaches the right and seeks to justify that breach as a worthwhile intrusion into women's equality. But in some cases, it is the state seeking to statutorily protect and advance women's equality. Other individuals and groups then argue that this law breaches their rights to religious freedom or federalism principles. The state must justify giving greater priority to women's equality than these other rights and interests. There are a small handful of cases, mostly from the US, where this is the configuration between women's equality and justification.[24] These cases are analysed as they bring into sharper focus cross-cutting doctrinal trends which in turn crystallises where normative innovation is required.

For the majority of cases analysed, it is the constitutional right to equality that is at stake. In a handful of cases, mostly from the US, the 'what' doctrinal lens is expanded to include statutes that have a quasi-constitutional role or impact such as Title VII of the Civil Rights Act (US) or the Religious Freedom and Restoration Act (US). Again, this inclusion is both pragmatic and principled. Statutory cases have dominated the development of women's equality rights in the US jurisprudence. Moreover, these developments are drawn upon and are echoed back to the Fourteenth Amendment jurisprudence and they provide critical insights into the doctrinal and normative lines of inquiry.

And lastly, with respect to the 'what' parameter, it is rare for a judgment on women's equality from the five apex courts in South Africa, India, the US, UK and Canada to be unanimous. The points of fracture between majority, concurring and dissenting opinions often centre around justification. Gender discrimination in pensions or the constitutional validity of a federal law protecting against pregnancy discrimination all attracted dissents that use justification or justification-like arguments to deny women equality in employment.[25] Disentangling why the court is internally split on justification is of unparalleled value in considering the role of justification in achieving women's equality and the monograph gives equivalent analytical weight to majority, concurring and dissenting opinions. Furthermore, there is a high degree of trans-judicial dialogue and constitutional borrowing occurring between these courts.[26] A dissenting opinion in one jurisdiction can have echoes in a majority in another. Taking both types of decisions seriously thus brings into sharper focus patterns

[24] *Hibbs* (n 10); *Coleman v Court of Appeals of Maryland* 556 US 2012; *Burwell v Hobby Lobby* 573 US 682 (2014); *Little Sisters of the Poor v Pennsylvania* 591 US__(2020).

[25] *Fraser* (n 5); *Hibbs* (n 10).

[26] Sandra Fredman, 'Foreign Fads and Fashion? The Role of Comparativism in Human Rights Law' (2015) 64(3) *International and Comparative Law Quarterly* 631.

and tension points. It must be acknowledged that the scope of the monograph is not designed to be systematic or comprehensive. It uses the most relevant cases to untangle the overlooked relationship between women's equality and justification and to reflect on how these elements should relate to each other.

The women who have brought claims to apex courts in India, South Africa, Canada, the UK and US come from different backgrounds, have different experiences and possess an array of characteristics. These countries have radically different political, legal, social, economic and cultural histories and current realities. Despite these differences, the legal demands for women's equality in India, South Africa, Canada, the UK and US have a high degree of similarity; calls for equal pay at work, for a recognition of caring roles, and for including all forms of relationships in legal protections. These similarities create a jurisprudence that reveal common trends and patterns and steers the investigation away from seemingly obvious solutions to more nuanced answers.

At the same time, in investigating the doctrinal and normative lines of inquiry, the analysis plays close attention to intersectionality. Women's inequality cannot be exclusively collapsed into a single axis but must be attentive to how sex and gender intersect with other axes of disadvantage. Intersectionality theory arose in response to the subordination of Black women in the US. The racist and sexist oppression of Black women could not be captured solely through the lens of race or gender, rather their subordination had to be understood as unique, distinct, and synergistic.[27] The concept of intersectionality has evolved to take account of how a plethora of characteristics intersect to create reinforcing webs of inequalities for women.[28] The practice of equality law, however, has been critiqued for failing to incorporate the insights from intersectionality theory.[29] In exploring how justification functions when determining a breach of women's equality rights, attention is paid to how justification like reasoning can flatten and erase the intersectional nature of women's equality. In exploring how equality can guide and enrich assessing if a justification meets constitutional muster, the richness of women's identities and experiences informs the proposed relational and contextual methodological approach.

B. Establishing the Lines of Inquiry

Having established the parameters that guide the monograph, now it is possible to flesh out the doctrinal and normative lines of inquiry in greater detail. Starting with the doctrinal, the aim is to uncover, in the practice of adjudication, how women's equality and justification relate to each other. This relationship

[27] Crenshaw (n 3).

[28] Shreya Atrey and Peter Dunne (eds), *Intersectionality and Human Rights* (Hart Publishing, 2020).

[29] Atrey (n 3).

has to date been largely ignored. As outlined in the Introduction, justification is often determinative. There is some sort of connection being drawn between women's equality and justification. Little is known, however, about the different permutations of this connection. Uncovering what is happening in the courts constitutes a key advancement in understanding how law functions in achieving women's equality. It can be tempting to dismiss the doctrinal aim as merely recording what occurred in the judicial reasonings.[30] The doctrinal analysis, however, is much more than robotically transcribing how courts currently establish and shape the relationship between women's equality and justification. It is an intellectual exercise that evaluates, assesses and seeks to make sense of complex and often convoluted decisions.[31] This is because when apex courts make determinations on the breadth of women's equality rights or the permissibility of limits, they are not engaged in the mechanical application of legal rules. For example, in determining that protecting a centuries-old tradition was insufficient to justify violating women's equality rights, this required the Indian Supreme Court to utilise not only legal rules but also moral values, historical customs, constitutional and sociocultural norms and empirical evidence.[32] When the decisions are this rich and textured, a doctrinal analysis is not merely creating a compendium of legal rules.

While understanding what is happening in the decision is of value in and of itself, it also positively feeds into the second aim. The other aim of the monograph is to proscribe innovations to optimise the relationship between women's equality and justification. It is only in understanding how in practice justification is bleeding into determining breaches of the right to equality and how through various methodologies and techniques, justifications for limiting women's equality are repeatedly accepted at face-value, that this aim can be achieved. These doctrinal findings are used to craft targeted and precise measures that could effectively sharpen the practice of the apex courts in India, South Africa, Canada, the US and UK. As Kavanaugh recently explained, 'normative arguments must rest on descriptively adequate foundations'.[33] No bright line is drawing between the doctrinal and normative aims. The inquiries are pursued harmoniously. The doctrinal analysis uncovers how justification can make it more challenging to identify breaches of women's equality rights and how justification can be employed to shield from scrutiny limitation claims that are illogical, implausible, unfair and rooted in gender prejudice, stigma or oppression. It also identifies embryonic trends where courts are leaning towards an asymmetrical relationship between women's equality and justification. These

[30] Aileen Kavanagh, 'Keeping it Real in Constitutional Theory' (2023) 1(2) *Comparative Constitutional Studies* 244; Alan Bogg, 'Doctrinal Methods in Labour Law: Potential, Problems, Prospects' in Alysia Blackham and Sean Cooney (eds), *Research Methods in Labour Law: A Handbook* (Edward Elgar, 2023).

[31] Kavanagh, ibid 259.

[32] *Joseph Shine v Union of India* (2019) 3 SCC 39.

[33] Kavanagh (n 30) 259.

insights in turn support and strengthen the normative claims that any determination of the breach of women's equality must be protected and ring-fenced from justification reasoning and that equality can guide calibrating the intensity of review and enrich the application of justification frameworks.

There is one further point worth making with respect to the twin inquiries of this monograph. As canvassed below when exploring the theorising and conceptualising of justification, there are many proposed configurations between rights and limits, all holding to be the optimal relationship. In wading through the strengths and weaknesses, claims and counterclaims, and concluding that what is required is methodological innovations that are rooted in equality, the analysis rests upon its own foundational normative pillar: that women's right to equality is momentous, transformative and of the utmost significance. This understanding of women's equality motivates the doctrinal and normative analysis.

i. The Value in Comparing Women's Equality and Justification

The questions on how women's equality and justification should relate to each other are pursued through a comparative analysis examining the jurisprudence from the apex courts from the UK, US, India, South Africa and Canada. This subsection lays out the similarities and differences in the jurisdictional approaches to equality and justification as well as the strengths of comparative methodology in relation to the doctrinal and normative lines of inquiry.

These jurisdictions have intersecting and diverging understandings of women's right to equality and the permissibility of justifying incursions on it. All five jurisdictions have express guarantees on women's equality but differ in how they define or understand that right. In Canada and South Africa, the apex courts have consistently adopted a substantive understanding of equality in assessing breaches of women's rights.[34] Yet as demonstrated in chapter two, judgments from these courts are lapsing back into a more formal approach and draw on justification concepts to fill the conceptual holes that riddle formal equality. In India, the apex court is arguably slowly moving towards substantive equality.[35] On the other hand, the US and UK courts remain wedded to formalistic understandings of equality with only small glimmers in the case law of assessing whether women's equality rights have been substantively breached.[36] With respect to justification, Canada, UK and South Africa courts have textual

[34] *Andrews v Law Society of British Columbia* [1989] 1 SCR 143; *Harksen v Lane NO and Others* [1997] ZACC 12.

[35] *Lt Col Nitisha and Others v Union of India* [2021] 4 SCR 663; Rishika Sahgal, 'The Indian Supreme Court on Affirmative Action for the Upper Caste Poor-Part 1' (*OxHRH*, 30 January 2023), available at https://ohrh.law.ox.ac.uk/the-indian-supreme-court-on-affirmative-action-for-the-upper-caste-poor-part-i/.

[36] *Coleman* (n 24); Catherine MacKinnon, 'Substantive Equality: A Perspective' (2011) 96 *Minnesota Law Review* 1; *SG* (n 6); Meghan Campbell, 'The Austerity of Lone Motherhood: Discrimination and Benefit Reform' (2021) 41(4) *OJLS* 1197.

mandates that explicitly permit limitations of equality rights. These tests are unpacked more fully below but just to briefly canvas them here. Canada has committed to using the four-part proportionality test (legitimacy, rationality, necessity and balance) whereas the UK has shifted between rationality and proportionality.[37] The South African Constitutional Court has embraced the values of proportionality, and the text of the Constitution requires the Court to consider various limbs of the traditional proportionality test as well as additional factors.[38] In contrast, there is no limitation clause in the US or Indian Constitutions, yet the apex courts have developed limitation doctrines. India, much like the UK, moves between a rationality and loose proportionality framework.[39] The US has never fully embraced proportionality, but when evaluating whether differential treatment between men and women is constitutionally permitted, it utilises recognisable limbs of the traditional proportionality test.[40] These constitutional similarities and differences are layered over a range of other nodes of comparison including legal histories, institutional mandates and sociocultural attitudes.

The point of the comparative exercise is not merely to catalogue these similarities and differences, but as Fredman explains, comparativism aims to open up a 'vast array of new perspectives and insights'.[41] These insights can be harnessed to better understand the optimal relationship between women's equality and justification, an understanding that simply would not be possible by studying a single jurisdiction. Comparativism pierces through layers of complexities to expose deeper and harder to detect trends.[42] This in turn steers the arguments away from seemingly compelling solutions such as retooling the analytical frameworks for equality or justification. As the subsequent chapters argue, despite the array of textual and doctrinal differences across the US, UK, India, South Africa and Canada, there are striking similarities in how judgments establish the relationship between women's equality and justification. Despite different trajectories with respect to the right equality, judgments across the five jurisdictions use justification concepts to minimise the severity of women's inequality when assessing whether the right has been breached, to the point where the court

[37] *R v Oakes* [1986] 1 SCR 103; *SC* (n 5).

[38] *S v Makwanyane* [1995] ZACC 3; Stu Woolman and Henk Botha, 'Limitation' in Stu Woolman and Michael Bishop (eds), *Constitutional Law of South Africa*, 2nd edn (2013), available at https://constitutionallawofsouthafrica.co.za/.

[39] *Nitisha* (n 35); Vandita Khanna, 'Indirect Discrimination and Substantive Equality in *Nitisha*: Easier Said Than Done Under Indian Constitutional Jurisprudence' (2022) *International Journal of Discrimination and the Law* 74; Aparna Chandra, 'Limitation Analysis by the Indian Supreme Court' in Mordechai Kremnitzer, Talya Steiner and Andrej Lang (eds), *Proportionality in Action: Comparative and Empirical Perspectives on the Judicial Practice* (Cambridge University Press, 2020).

[40] *US v Virginia* 518 US 515 (1996).

[41] Fredman (n 26) 27.

[42] Jaakko Husa, 'The Traditional Methods of Comparative Law' in Mathias Siems and Po Jen Yap (eds), *The Cambridge Handbook of Comparative Law* (Cambridge University Press, 2024).

can no longer see violations. And although different justification frameworks are used, there are common patterns of isolating, decontextualising, misdirecting and misunderstanding limitation criteria to hide flaws, inflate the strength of the justification claims and camouflage value judgments on women's equality. Only comparing across different jurisdictions is possible to identify the granularity of these patterns which in turn provides a firm basis for the normative reconfiguration of the relationship between women's equality and justification proposed in this monograph. Importantly, comparativism is not employed to develop a definitive universal theory on the meaning of women's equality or the ultimate justification framework that should be applied by every court in every case. The arguments for an asymmetric relationship between equality and justification, developed from a comparative analysis, can be transplanted and adapted to each jurisdiction's unique legal and political context and textual and doctrinal distinctiveness.

There are challenges in deploying a comparative approach to the lines of inquiry in this monograph. How to analyse and even more basically, how to organise an analysis on women's equality and justification when the apex courts in this study approach the task of adjudicating women's claim for equality so differently. In Canada, the analysis broadly takes a two-stage approach. The first stage, the equality-stage, is a discrete evaluation into whether women have experienced harms that breach the right to equality in section 15 of the Canadian Charter. There is a distinct second stage. There is an explicit limitation clause in the Charter. Section 1 permits limits to rights when such limits are reasonable, are prescribed by law and 'can be demonstrably justified in a free and democratic society'. Under section 1, the court assesses whether the breach can be justified.[43] The UK also conducts a two-stage review. Under Article 14 of the European Convention of Human Rights (domesticated via the Human Rights Act), which prohibits discrimination in the enjoyment of Convention rights, the UK Supreme Court only investigates whether the law creates a difference or differential impact. There is minimal drilling into how or why that impact contravenes equality. The European Court of Human Rights has held that there is no discrimination if the distinction has 'no objective and reasonable justification'.[44] The second stage of the analysis in the UK Supreme Court is similar to Canada, and investigates if the difference can be justified.[45] South Africa is slightly more complicated. The first step in the equality analysis, under section 9(1) of the Constitution which guarantees equality before the law, is to assess whether the law creates irrational classifications.[46] This first step is more akin to a rationality review, a common feature among justification tests, than a dive into why the law breaches the right to equality. The second step then

[43] *Fraser* (n 5).
[44] *Carson v UK* (2010) 51 EHRR 369 [61].
[45] *SG* (n 6).
[46] *Harksen* (n 34); Cathi Albertyn and Beth Goldblatt, 'Equality' in Woolman and Bishop (n 38).

proceeds to examine whether the differentiation is fair or unfair discrimination which is a searching and substantive evaluation into the equality wrongs potentially embedded in the law. The third step is then an assessment under section 36 of the Constitution, which looks at whether the breach of the equality rights can be justifiably limited if the limit is 'reasonable and justifiable in an open and democratic society based on human rights, equality and freedom'.

The US and Indian approach to the adjudication of women's equality is slightly different, arguably reflecting the fact that neither respective constitution has an expressed limitation clause. After establishing that the law creates a distinction between men and women under the Fourteenth Amendment, in the US, the Supreme Court will then assess whether that distinction is justified, evaluating whether the state has a compelling purpose in pursuing that distinction and whether that distinction is substantially related to that purpose.[47] There is no dedicated stage where the Court explicitly determines whether the gender-based classification violates the equality guarantee of the US Constitution. The Indian Supreme Court echoes this approach to adjudication. In assessing whether there has been a breach of Article 14 of the Indian Constitution, which protects the right to equality, it tests whether a difference was an intelligible differentia and whether that difference had 'reasonable nexus with the object the law sought to achieve'.[48] The jurisprudence from the US and Indian Supreme Court may refer to this as an equality assessment, notwithstanding the thrust of the analysis is assessing whether the law is justified.

This variety of approaches to adjudication that echo, refract and diverge from each other presents challenges in how to comparatively explore the doctrinal and normative lines of inquiry. For ease of analysis, the monograph looks past names courts might place on the nature or purpose of the analysis and considers what the analysis is geared towards assessing. When the investigation is directed towards assessing why the law breaches the normative concept of equality, it is classified as the equality-stage and when the investigation seeks to assess the defence of the law, it is classified as the justification-stage. As mentioned above, the paradigm can also be inverted. The state can seek to advance women's equality through legislation, and other stakeholders argue that this advancement infringes, for example, federalist boundaries or the religious freedom rights of others. In these scenarios, the other stakeholders are arguing women's equality should be burdened or restricted and the state must justify why it has chosen to prioritise women's equality over these other rights and interests. For the purposes of this monograph, this is categorised under the rubric of the justification-stage as the state seeks to defend its choice to guarantee women's equality. These classifications may not be how judges, lawyers or scholars in

[47] *Virginia* (n 40).

[48] Tarunabh Khaitan, 'Equality: Legislative Review Under Article 14' in Choudhry, Khosla and Bhanu Mehta (n 3) 701.

those jurisdictions refer to them, but it creates a logical organisational structure that facilitates the aims of the monograph.

III. THE DIFFICULTIES OF EQUALITY

Having established the parameters that shape the doctrinal and normative lines of inquiry, it is now possible to examine in more detail the two concepts that form the core of this monograph: equality and justification. These next two sections explore the theorising on the meaning and purpose of women's equality and justification while also sketching out how these concepts have been developed by the apex courts of South Africa, Canada, the UK, India and US. It identifies theoretical and doctrinal points of tension and ambiguity. It is these points that are harnessed by courts, as argued in the preceding chapters, to dilute the seriousness of women's inequality and to inflate the value of measures that limit women's equality. The relationship between women's equality and justification can be re-oriented so that equality protects, guides and enriches all stages of adjudicating women's equality. The first step in this reconfiguration is to grapple with the meaning of women's equality and how that meaning relates to justification.

Equality is bemoaned by judges as inherently or particularly difficult.[49] This is because it is perceived to be an elusive concept that evades easy or simple definition. Albertyn pertinently observes that 'the plasticity of equality means that it [is] always open to different interpretation by the executive, legislature and … courts'.[50] Equality is rarely defined in a constitutional text, leaving the matter of interpreting women's right to equality largely with the courts. A running thread through much of the jurisprudence on women's equality is the seemingly never-ending tension between formal and substantive equality. When assessing whether women's equality rights have been violated, should courts investigate whether the law treats women in an identical manner or should courts explore whether the law is inconsistent with the normative values that underpin a substantive approach to equality? This question has dominated equality law, but it also matters for justification. To date little attention has been paid to how the conceptualisation of equality impacts or shapes the relationship between women's equality and justification. In fact, Canadian feminists have repeatedly noted the absence of any meaningful investigation between these elements.[51] Chapter two marks an important step forward as it argues that the emptiness

[49] Beverley McLachlin, 'Equality: The Most Difficult Right' (2001) 14 *The Supreme Court Law Review* 17; *DA and DS v Secretary of State for Works and Pensions* [2019] UKSC 21 [20].

[50] Catherine Albertyn, 'Contested Substantive Equality in the South African Constitution: Beyond Social Inclusion Towards Systemic Justice' (2018) 34 *South African Journal of Human Rights* 441, 442.

[51] Sonia Lawrence, 'Critical Reflections on Fraser: What Equality Are We Seeking?' (2021) *Constitutional Forum* 43; Beverley Baines, 'Contextualism, Feminism, and a Canadian Woman Judge' (2009) 17 *Feminist Legal Studies* 27, 38.

of formal equality creates space for justification to distort adjudicating whether women's equality rights have been breached. Substantive equality, on the other hand, can not only be directed to protect the equality-stage from this distortion but it can also guide and enrich the justification-stage.

A. The Limits of Formal Equality: Justifying Treating Women Like Men

Formal equality has a long lineage with origins in Aristotelian philosophy. It is premised on sameness-difference. Individuals 'who are alike should be treated alike' and individuals 'who are unlike should be treated unlike'.[52] This is a seemingly simple and straightforward formula.

Individuals who are similarly situated are treated identically, similarly or consistently and individuals who are different are treated differently. Under this model, courts explore whether women are similar enough to men to warrant similar treatment or whether there are material differences that legitimate differential, and invariably, worse treatment.[53] It is this reasoning, for example, that explains why the US Supreme Court in *Nguyen v Immigration and Naturalization Service (INS)* concluded that differential treatment between men and women in naturalising children born outside of marriage was not a breach of the Fourteenth Amendment.[54] Women give birth where men do not and the different citizenship rules were a natural consequence of these biological differences. Identifying similarities and differences between women and men can, however, obscure how stereotypes had infected the law. In the case of *Nguyen*, the differences between men and women masked how the law drew a false relationship between giving birth and having caring responsibilities. As many have pointed out, the formal conceptualisation of equality is simply unable to excavate how facile similarities and differences have been used to cement traditional gender roles.[55]

This critique of the formalistic approaches to adjudicating women's equality is nothing new. Yet as analysed in chapter two, formal equality continues to exert a gravitational pull on judicial reasoning. The aim here is not to retread the cogent arguments on the flaws of formal equality but to consider why the sameness-difference paradigm matters to the relationship between women's equality and justification. Courts use justification criteria to identify sameness-difference and in doing so, the equality-stage collapses into a covert limitation analysis that only analyses the defence of the law not why the law contravenes the conception of equality. Justification plays this role because there is no

[52] Peter Westen, 'The Empty Idea of Equality' (1982) 95 *Harvard Law Review* 537, 539–40.
[53] *SC* (n 5) [59].
[54] *Nguyen v Immigration and Naturalization Service (INS)* 553 US 53 (2001).
[55] MacKinnon (n 3); Sandra Fredman, *Women and The Law* (Oxford University Press, 1997).

mathematical formula for identifying salient similarities and differences.[56] Why are different rules needed with respect to citizenship because men do not give birth? Why can't the same rules apply to men and women? While there are good arguments on why naturalisation rules should be consistently applied between women and men,[57] in different contexts it is argued that for women to be equal they must be treated differently. Pregnant women should not be treated the same as every other employee but must be given accommodation at work when medically advised not to undertake employment tasks that involve heavy lifting.[58] The innovation of 'treating likes alike and differences differently' offers little guidance to courts on assessing whether there is a breach of the right to equality when citizenship rules treat men and women differently or when the law treats pregnant women the same as everybody else. Rather than filling the vacuum of formal equality by reaching for more substantive normative principles, courts are drawing on justification reasoning and concepts. To test whether women should be treated similarly or differently, courts employ concepts like rationality or legitimate purpose. This means the equality-stage is not an investigation that squarely confronts the wrongness of inequality or whether the law perpetuates those wrongs in the lives of women, but a justification of why the law is worth pursuing. This distorts the equality-stage as there is no investigation into gendered harms, only an account of how the law seems to draw similarities and distinctions that are sensible or laudable.

An example helps illustrate this point. In *Nguyen*, the majority of the US Supreme Court argued that the differences between men and women were rational as they flowed from biological realities and were therefore not in breach of the equality provisions in the US Constitution.[59] Rationality is a core feature of the justification-stage, discussed in further detail below, and in *Nguyen* it was utilised to fill the emptiness of formal equality. The reasonableness of treating biological difference differently explained why it was permissible to have gendered naturalisation rules. This justificatory logic, however, failed to contend with the long legislative history of citizenship laws that had alleviated men of responsibility for children born outside of marriage and how the naturalisation rules were a continuation of this gendered stereotype. The equality analysis became a defence of tying legal rules to biological differences. In a similar vein, the legal systems in Canada and South Africa treated marriage and de facto intimate partner unions differently, excluding the latter from a range of legal protections. Judgments from these jurisdictions undertook formalistic assessments seeking to identify similarities and differences between intimate relations

[56] Fredman (n 3) ch 1; Westen (n 52).

[57] Sulini Sarugaser-Hug, 'Article 9' in Patricia Shulz, Beate Rudolf and Marsha Freeman (eds), *CEDAW: Commentary* (Oxford University Press, 2022).

[58] *Young v UPS* 575 US 206 (2015); Joanna Grossman and Gillian Thomas, 'Making Pregnancy Work: Overcoming the Pregnancy Discrimination Act's Capacity-Based Model' (2009) 21 *Yale Journal of Law and Feminism* 15.

[59] *Nguyen* (n 54) 68.

and then drew on justification reasoning to explain why this differential treatment was not in breach of constitutional equality guarantees.[60] The aim of the exclusion, the state argued, was to protect the autonomy of those who had chosen not to marry and this was held by judges in the Canadian Supreme Court and South African Constitutional Court as an aim that was so legitimate, so worthy, so socially desirable, there was no breach of equality rights. The importance or properness of the law's objectives, the initial step of the justification-stage in both Canada and South Africa, was the determinative factor at the equality-stage. Utilising justification concepts to explicate why differential treatment was not in violation of equality shielded from view how the law failed to account for gendered constraints on women's autonomy in intimate partner unions. These two examples illustrate how the porousness or emptiness of formal equality, its inability to answer when sameness and when difference is required, creates space for justification to seep into the determination of whether there has been a breach of women's equality rights. And in doing so the equality-stage analysis becomes an investigation into reasons the law draws gendered distinctions and ignores what the law actually means to women and how it impacts on their lives.

The other relevant ambiguity revolves around identifying the relevant points of comparison of sameness and difference and this murkiness can indirectly shape the limitation analysis. In assessing whether a restriction on accessing abortion funding across different parts of a federalist or devolved state breaches the right to equality, should the court assess the similarities and differences based only on geography? Or is the synergy between gender, socioeconomic status and geography at stake when analysing whether the restriction breaches equality rights? Inequality, as intersectionality theory points out, is rarely located within one identity characteristic, but a range of identities, positions, circumstances and experiences underpin women's inequality.[61] The formula of treating likes alike and treating differences differently provides little guidance in grappling with these layers of similarities and differences. Formal equality has been heavily criticised for narrowing the points of comparison and inaccurately collapsing complex identities into unidimensional experiences.[62] Again, this insight into the limits of formal equality is not novel but it has yet to be considered how this pliability impacts justification. Courts can construct or restrict the points of similarities and differences under a formalistic assessment in a way that erases gendered inequality. This in turn can radically shape the justification burden. Rather than defending why the law burdens the equality rights of women, the analysis can be centred around a much more benign question, such as defending internal geographic distinctions within the state. By bleeding gender out of the

[60] *Nova Scotia (Attorney General) v Walsh* [2002] 4 SCR 325 [38], [40], [43], [48]–[50], [57], [62]; *Quebec v A* [2013] 1 SCR 61 [259], [262]; *Volks v Robinson* [2005] ZACC 2 [88], [93].

[61] Crenshaw (n 3); Atrey (n 3).

[62] ibid.

equality-stage, the court can construct a justification-stage that tips the analysis towards permitting the limit.

This is what happened in *A and B v Secretary of State for Health*.[63] At the relevant time, abortion was criminalised in Northern Ireland. Northern Irish women and girls would travel to England for an abortion. All other women and girls who normally reside in England could access abortion services freely in England while Northern Irish women and girls would be charged for abortion services performed in England. A and B argued this breached Article 14 of the European Convention on Human Rights. The UK Supreme Court exclusively framed the abortion funding restriction as a breach of equality because it treated individuals who were similarly geographically situated (all women seeking abortions in England) differently (women and girls from Northern Ireland were charged when seeking abortion in England). The equality analysis failed to engage the gendered harms of the restriction. For example, that it forced Northern Irish women and girls who could not afford abortion services to remain pregnant or risk criminalisation, missing the intersection of gender, poverty and sexual and reproductive health.[64] This thin equality analysis eased the justificatory burden. In this case, the state argued the funding prohibition was in place to protect devolution, a power-sharing arrangement between England, Scotland, Wales and Northern Ireland. The Court then had to determine whether it was justified to impose geographic differences to protect a political structure that itself was based on geography. Unsurprisingly, the limit was justified as the breach of equality and the justification pulled in the same direction. The formalistic equality-stage elided the more challenging question that a richer equality analysis would have promoted the justification-stage to ask: was it justified to impose intimate and long-ranging costs on women and girls to protect the constitutional architecture of the state? The lack of direction formal equality provides with respect to nodes of comparison of similarities and differences can indirectly shape the justification-stage.

It can be tempting to conclude that these formalistic flaws correlate with jurisdictions, like the US or India, that seemingly do not have a dedicated step that requires courts to investigate why a law contravenes equality rights. In both these jurisdictions, the courts are meant to ascertain whether the law draws a distinction and then supposed to assess, in the case of the US, whether the law has a compelling interest and whether the distinction is substantially related to that interest, and in the case of India whether that distinction has an intelligible differentia and is rational. The UK is similar. The courts should investigate whether the law perpetuates differential treatment before proceeding to assess whether that difference is justified. All these tests centre around the sameness-difference paradigm and in many judgments the flaws identified

[63] *A and B* (n 10).

[64] Committee on the Convention on the Elimination of Discrimination Against Women (CEDAW), 'Inquiry Procedure: Northern Ireland' (2018) CEDAW/C/OP.8/GBR/1.

above are evident. The merging of women's equality and justification, however, is not confined to jurisdictions that construct analytical frameworks along the lines of formal equality. As argued in chapter two, judgments from the Canadian Supreme Court and the South African Constitutional Court which have a more sophisticated equality-stage, similarly employ formalistic reasoning and fill the vacuum of formal equality with justification. These cross-jurisdictional trends point to the need not to tinker with equality tests or frameworks but the deep need to consign formal equality to the past.

B. The Protecting, Guiding and Enriching Function of Substantive Equality

The strength of substantive equality over formal equality is a well-trodden argument. Substantive equality seeks to transcend the problems of formal equality and infuses it with a normative underpinning, recognising that men and women for historical, biological, social and cultural reasons are not the same and, at times, different treatment may be required to achieve equality. It is less well understood how substantive equality can positively shape justification. Subsequent chapters argue that it can protect the equality-stage from being warped by justification reasoning. This is not the only way that equality matters to the justification-stage. It is also instrumental in guiding the intensity of review courts should employ when scrutinising limitation claims and can enrich the application of justification criteria. This subsection maps out the theoretical and doctrinal meanings given to substantive equality to both lay the necessary groundwork for the investigations in later chapters and to argue that the precise meaning given to substantive equality is irrelevant to how it can strengthen equality's relationship to justification.

The concrete normative aims of women's substantive equality have alluded easy capture. Some argue that it should be collapsed into a single value, although there is no consensus on what that value should be, while others argue that substantive equality should be defined in a multidimensional way.[65] On one hand, MacKinnon focuses on social hierarchy. Substantive equality must undo notions that men 'are intrinsically more worthy than women'.[66] The analytical lens needs to be directed toward power relations and systems of hierarchical domination and subordination in whatever form they manifest.[67] In a similar vein, Kapur argues that substantive equality questions 'whether the practice … contributes to the subordination of the disadvantaged group'.[68] Other prominent

[65] Denise Reaume, 'Discrimination and Dignity' (2003) 63(3) *Louisiana Law Review* 645; Iyiola Solanke, *Discrimination as Stigma* (Hart Publishing, 2017).

[66] Catherine MacKinnon, 'Substantive Equality: A Perspective' (2011) 96 *Minnesota Law Review*.

[67] Catherine MacKinnon, 'Substantive Equality: A Rejoinder to Sandra Fredman' (2017) 15(4) *International Journal of Constitutional Law* 1174.

[68] Kapur (n 3) 744–45.

values are dignity, disadvantage and stereotyping. Collapsing substantive equality into a single norm has been critiqued for failing to give equality the desired breadth and weight.[69] On the other hand, there is an emerging consensus that substantive equality must be understood as multi-layered, as this more accurately mirrors the deeply embedded reasons for women's inequality and the varied experiences of patriarchy. Sheppard argues that substantive equality must be attentive towards 'overlapping layers of contextualism' particularly to 'individual experiential knowledge of inequality, institutional barriers to inclusion and larger socio-structural constraints to equality'.[70] The harms of multi-layered inequalities against women are broadly drawn including economic, social, psychological, physical, and political disadvantage or exclusion.[71] Fredman argues women's substantive equality pursues four aims: breaking cycles of disadvantage; eliminating stigma, stereotyping, prejudice and violence and promoting the dignity and worth of all; amplifying marginalised voices in all political and social decision-making spaces; and dismantling structures constructed upon dominant norms and transforming institutions so that difference is not only accommodated but valorised.[72] Building upon these multi-layer and dimensional approaches, Albertyn holds substantive equality must also account for substantive freedom. There needs to be a transformation of background conditions, so women can freely exercise agency and choice.[73] Uniting all of these models is a deep commitment to moving beyond a technical, sterile or mechanical legal analysis and a more substantive approach that is deeply attuned to the context and impact of the law.

The apex courts of the US, UK, South Africa, India and Canada mirror the diversity of arguments on the meaning of substantive equality. The Fourteenth Amendment of the US Constitution guarantees equal protection of the law and predominantly this has been developed in formalistic terms, as outlined above. There are glimmers of a more substantive understanding of the Fourteenth Amendment centred on how legal distinctions perpetuate gendered based stereotypes against women.[74] Article 14 of the European Convention on Human Rights domesticated by the UK Human Rights Act guarantees non-discrimination in the enjoyment of all Convention rights. The UK Supreme Court examines whether the law perpetuates a difference in treatment or has a disproportionality prejudicial effect on a particular group.[75] Article 14 of the Indian

[69] Sandra Fredman, 'Substantive Equality Revisited' (2016) 14(3) *International Journal of Constitutional Law* 712; Rory O'Connell, 'The Role of Dignity in Equality Law: Lessons from Canada and South Africa' (2008) 6(2) *International Journal of Constitutional Law* 267.

[70] Sheppard (n 3).

[71] ibid 62–63.

[72] Fredman (n 3) ch 1.

[73] Albertyn (n 50) 467–68.

[74] Cary Franklin, 'The Anti-Stereotyping Principle in Constitutional Sex Discrimination Law' (2010) 85 *New York Law Review* 83.

[75] *SG* (n 6) [7], [8], [13].

Constitution also guarantees equality before the law and equal protection of the law. Although the evolution of this provision has been centred on assessing the strength of reasoning for justifying the classifications the law creates, there are also steps toward a more substantive equality approach that examines whether the law reinforces, perpetuates, or exacerbates disadvantage.[76] This evolution in Indian equality law was borrowed or transplanted from the Canadian Supreme Court.[77] Section 15 of the Canadian Charter of Rights and Freedoms guarantees equality before and under the law and equal protection and benefit of the law without discrimination. The Canadian Supreme Court from the beginning has confirmed that the Charter protects women's substantive equality and currently conceptualises section 15 as premised on disadvantage, with it broadly defined in line with Sheppard's 'overlapping layers of contextualism' approach.[78] The Indian Supreme Court has also drawn on Fredman's multidimensional approach and in judgments on women's equality explores not only disadvantage but also stereotyping, stigma and prejudice, institutional structures and agency.[79] Lastly, section 9(3) of the South African Constitution prohibits the state from unfairly discriminating and the South African Constitutional Court has embraced a multidimensional model of substantive equality when examining unfairness. It will explore the past patterns of disadvantage and the position of the complaint in society; the nature of the discriminating law; and the extent the law impacts on dignity.[80] At first glance, this seems to incorporate criteria from the justification-stage, the purpose of the law, but as argued in chapter three, the Court has used this criteria when adjudicating women's claims to equality to explore the historical context the law operated in.

Substantive equality has been subject to criticism with these concerns rooted in the perceived amorphous nature of the concept. With sceptics arguing that with all these meanings and counter-meanings it is 'an empty concept that operates as an undisciplined rhetorical device by which courts may privilege … their own policy preferences'.[81] Even advocates express concern that substantive equality may be unable to confront gender disadvantage with questions on how it can effectively respond to a rapidly warming climate or a changing political economy.[82] These concerns, while important, are not detrimental to building an asymmetric relationship between women's equality and justification. This is because the ability of substantive equality to ring-fence, guide and enrich justification is not contingent on a certain model, conception or definition of substantive equality. It is not that the dignity conception of substantive equality is better placed to ring-fence justification from the equality analysis or that

[76] *Nitisha* (n 35) [46].
[77] *Fraser* (n 5) [5], [27]–[31].
[78] ibid [76].
[79] *Nitisha* (n 35) [44].
[80] *Harksen* (n 34) [52].
[81] *Fraser* (n 5) [146].
[82] Lawrence (n 51) 43.

the disadvantage model is ideal for enriching the application of justification criteria. All that is required is that courts shift away from searching for similarities or differences and undertake a substantive analysis that centres on the impact of the law and its context in the lives of women.[83] Regardless of how the jurisdictions understand substantive equality, it provides the courts with sufficient analytical tools at the equality-stage such that resort to justification criteria to analyse whether an inequality exists is not necessary. With respect to the justification-stage, there is no one model of substantive equality that is needed to guide the calibration on how intensely the courts will interrogate a limitation claim nor is one version more optimal than another in enriching the application of justification criteria. The fluidity of substantive equality, its open-textured nature, its ability to continually evolve in response to new power hierarchies, is a strength. It permits the protecting, guiding and enriching function to be sensitive to the myriads of forms of inequality against women, to nascent and stubborn obstacles to equality and to the unique factual-legal circumstances of the claim.

While the monograph does not argue for one model of substantive equality over another in building an asymmetric relationship between women's equality and justification, there is one requirement to using substantive equality in the adjudication process. Courts must undertake a searching and probing analysis to determine whether there has been a breach of women's substantive equality rights. A full account of the equality harms before preceding to the limitation analysis ensures that substantive equality can positively guide calibrating the intensity of review and provides the tools needed to enrich testing the legitimacy, rationality, necessity and balance of limitation arguments. For example, skirting over the gendered equality harms in restricting access to social benefits at the equality-stage made it more difficult to detect how the justification for the restriction – spurring individuals into paid work – was premised on stereotypes that women in poverty were work-shy welfare queens.[84] In contrast, with respect to a law that excluded domestic workers from a workplace injury compensation scheme, a robust substantive equality analysis explored the stigmas and structural biases against domestic workers and connected the legal exclusion to the broader context of gender, race and class. The sophisticated substantive equality analysis strengthened the justification-stage. It guided and clarified that very persuasive reasons would be needed to justify an exclusion that conceptualised poor Black women domestic workers as lesser. And it enriched the limitation analysis by flushing out how the purpose of exclusion lacked any degree of legitimacy as it was premised on gendered and racist beliefs.[85]

[83] *Fraser* (n 5) [42].
[84] *SG* (n 6); also see chapter two.
[85] *Mahlangu v Minister of Labour* [2020] ZACC 24.

IV. THE DIFFICULTIES OF JUSTIFICATION

At the justification-stage, courts must determine if it is permissible to put limits on women's right to equality to achieve some competing objective. This differs from the equality-stage. Courts are not determining why the law runs afoul of equality, but assessing whether the public reason-orientated justification is sufficient to permit a limitation.[86] Determining if women's right to equality can be limited is also not an easy feat. The justification-stage raises difficult questions on the purpose of justification, what justification reveals about the nature of rights and the role of the courts in ascertaining whether the justification is sufficient to limit rights. Much of the theorising and doctrinal developments with respect to the justification-stage has been done either in the abstract or against other rights. Bomhoff observes that despite claims on the optimal potential of proportionality, one of the most prominent justification frameworks, little is known on its 'functionality and effectiveness in promoting rights protection'.[87] There are assumptions on how rights work, about how justification works, about what courts should or should not be doing that do not hold true when evaluating potential limits to women's equality rights. Many of these assumptions also falter against the actual practice of adjudicating limits on women's equality. Grappling with women's substantive equality destabilises dominant thinking on justification and can address flaws in the mechanics of the justification-stage. The chapters within Part II propose new ways of orienting the relationship between women's equality and justification. When calibrating the intensity of review it guides the justification-stage towards a probing and searching justification assessment regardless of any other potential countervailing factors. When applying justification criteria equality can enrich this process and protect women's equality from being limited based on arguments that do not have the strength to meet the justification criteria.

A. Reorienting the Relationship between Women's Equality and Justification

With the exception of a few absolute rights, the majority of rights, including women's right to equality, can be limited. Theorists have sought to untangle what the permissibility of limiting rights reveals about the nature of rights and what this in turn means for justification. In the competing framings of the rights-justification matrix, women's equality is starkly absent. This absence may appear unproblematic as various theories on the rights-justification matrix are

[86] Alec Stone Sweet and Jud Mathews, *Proportionality Balancing and Constitutional Governance* (Oxford University Press, 2019); Aharon Barak, *Proportionality: Constitutional Rights and Their Limits* (Cambridge University Press, 2012).

[87] Jacco Bomhoff, 'Proportionality in Comparative Law' in Jan Smits and others (eds), *Elgar Encyclopaedia of Comparative Law* (Edward Elgar, 2023).

rarely referred to in the actual jurisprudence of apex courts. Yet this framing is foundational as it directly shapes calibrating how intensely the courts will interrogate limitation claims and how courts will apply justification criteria. Bringing women's equality into this matrix can positively reorient the relationship between women's equality and justification and have positive knock-on effects for the adjudication process.

On one line of thinking, rights are fundamental such that even the possibility of justification prompts considerable consternation. Rights should act as virtual trumps or firewalls to block the pursuit of any law or policy that violates those rights notwithstanding how desirable or important that law or policy is.[88] Women's right to equal pay is so important that nothing could possibly outweigh protecting it. This is an attractive conceptualisation as it offers the strongest protection as nothing could possibly outweigh guaranteeing women's equality rights. This, however, would be a dangerous development. Chapter two argues that in the practice of adjudication justification bleeds into the equality-stage and does so in a way that minimises the gravity and severity of inequality against women. Seeking to pitch the relationship between women's equality and justification at the level of de facto absolute right would likely result in the equality-stage becoming a covert justification assessment. In modern, liberal constitutional democracies hard decisions do have to be made between women's equality and other rights and interests. By foreclosing an open and transparent assessment to deprioritise women's equality, there is no analytical space to defend those hard choices. To fill this vacuum, given the current practices uncovered in chapter two, it is likely the equality-stage would devolve into a defence of the law. Lurie in his study on the relationship between justification and equality writ large and not just women's equality, in Canada, South Africa, Germany and Israel, similarly noted that rolling justification concepts into equality could potentially metamorphose the right to equality into an absolute right that can never be justifiably violated.[89] He leaves unanswered whether this merging would enhance the adjudication of equality rights.[90] Chapter two directly engages with whether women's equality and limits on that equality should be assessed within a single analytical step. It argues that this would be dangerous as there would be little to no space devoted to establishing whether the law breached women's equality. This analytical imbalance would lead to a failure to develop the content of a right that is already criticised for being too vague and would also tip the scales towards never finding a breach of the right. The evaluation would be primarily focused on the strengths of the competing law or policy and there would be no accounting for how it negatively impacted on women's lives. Permitting justifications, when those justifications met the established threshold, is vital in protecting the equality-stage.

[88] Ronald Dworkin, *Taking Rights Seriously* (Harvard University Press, 1977).
[89] Lurie (n 4).
[90] ibid 195.

Rights as trumps is not the only framing of the rights-justification matrix. On another line of thinking, pioneered by Alexy, is that rights are not shields but are better understood as optimisation principles.[91] At the justification-stage, the aim is to optimise rights and other public interests 'to the greatest extent possible given the legal and factual possibilities'.[92] Conflict between rights and interests are resolved through balancing. Alexy explains that 'the determination of the appropriate degree of satisfaction of one principle relative to the requirements of the other principles is brought about by balancing'.[93] The level of optimisation of women's right to equality can be reduced so as to increase the optimisation of other interests. Women's equality is not given any special eminence in the balancing exercise as justification seeks to ensure after 'all things considered' the highest level of optimisation of both rights and interests. The precise weight attached to women's equality or competing public interests at the outset is not pre-determined and fluctuates depending on the totality of the circumstances. This sits oddly with the constitutional importance assigned to women's equality. As Ramalekana and de Vos argued, equality rights are unique in that they are rights that are specifically targeted towards the powerless.[94] Equality rights give constitutional tools for the most marginalised to demand legal recognition of their personhood. Women's constitutional right to equality was a recognition that law has been weaponised to subjugate women to men and a legal promise to transform gender power hierarchies.[95] Equality rights are simultaneously unique and of fundamental importance. A justification analysis that at the outset draws an equivalency between women's equality and the competing aim, and then seeks, in all of the circumstances, to optimise each to the maximum level possible, undercuts and undermines the role equality rights play in the constitutional order.

The third prominent configuration is seeing rights as triggers to justification. The claim advanced here is that the core function of rights is to empower individuals to demand reasoned and evidence-based justifications from the state.[96] The court is then to assess the strength of the proffered 'reasons that justify the infringement'.[97] Kumm puts significant value on a justification analysis, observing that in evaluating the quality of limitation claims, courts can 'challenge existing power relationship by insisting that those relationships be susceptible to justification in terms of public reason'.[98] Möller,

[91] Robert Alexy, *A Theory of Constitutional Rights* (Oxford University Press, 2002) 47.

[92] ibid.

[93] Robert Alexy, 'Proportionality and Rationality' in Jackson and Tushnet (n 4).

[94] Ramalekana and de Vos (n 12) 3.

[95] *Indian Young Lawyers Association v State of Kerala* (2019) 11 SCC 1 Part A (concurring opinion of Justice Chandrachud); *Bhe v Khayelitsha* [2004] ZACC 17 [71].

[96] Mattias Kumm, 'The Idea of Socratic Contestation and the Right to Justification: The Points of Rights-Based Proportionality Review' (2010) 4 *Law and Ethics of Human Rights* 140, 150.

[97] ibid.

[98] Mattias Kumm, 'Is the Structure of Human Rights Practice Defensible? Three Puzzles and Their Resolution' in Jackson and Tushnet (n 4) 65.

goes a step further, arguing that almost the entire catalogue of rights could be collapsed into a type of meta-right of justification.[99] The substantive meaning or content of rights themselves are not particularly analytically relevant to the justification-stage as the right primarily serves a gate-keeping function to justification. Rights as triggers is premised on the belief that justification claims or arguments are wholly disconnected from the precipitating breach of the right. The reasons why rights could be limited have nothing to do with the right itself. This creates a sharp divide between determining a breach of the right and whether that breach can be constitutionally justified. This assumption does not reflect the practice of adjudicating limits on women's equality. As outlined above, with respect to *A and B*, the analysis of the breach of women's equality rights can be constructed to ease the justification burden and tilt the analysis towards permitting limits. This is explored more fully in chapter two. Furthermore, the reasons for the limit can be intimately entwined with the violation of the equality rights and the broader context of women's equality. Assessing whether legislation that creates a civil remedy for gender-based violence validly contravenes the federalist structure of the state requires understanding whether gender-based violence impacts intra-state commerce.[100] This in turn requires a deep appreciation for how gender-based violence impacts women's lives. As a further example, the claim that prohibitions on women dancing in bars is justified as it would channel women away from exploitative work can only be assessed with a greater understanding of the reality of women's employment opportunities.[101] Women's equality is not irrelevant or divorced from the justification-stage. It can offer rich tools for testing the strength of limitation claims.

A reorientation between women's equality and justification is needed. These competing conceptualisations weigh too heavily and too lightly women's equality rights. Women's right to equality is not a trump but neither is it an optimisation principle nor a trigger. Rather, women's equality should be conceptualised as mattering to justification. Women's equality is highly relevant to the justification-stage. This mattering respects both the significance of women's equality while recognising the complexities of decision-making in pluralistic democracies that are connected to a highly globalised world. Mattering is not a claim to an overarching theory on rights or justification but a more narrowed argument that women's equality can methodologically guide and enrich justification processes. It can be drawn upon to guide calibrating the intensity of review and to enrich the application of justification criteria. These points are explored further below.

[99] Kai Moller, *The Global Model of Constitutional Rights* (Oxford University Press, 2012).
[100] *US v Morrison* 529 US 598 (2000).
[101] *State of Maharashtra v Indian Hotel and Restaurants Association* (2013) 8 SCC 519.

B. Women's Equality Guides Calibrating the Standard of Review

Before conducting a justification assessment, courts must calibrate the standard of review. That is, they must determine whether it will rigorously interrogate the claim that women's equality should be limited or whether it will only subject those claims to a light-touch review. At times, this calibration is overt but more often than not, this analysis is not made explicit. There is no universal methodology for calibrating but an approach that examines an array of factors has become dominant.[102] There is no agreement on which factors are relevant. Broadly, the factors can be grouped, on one hand, those that would pull towards a searching standard of review, such as the nature of the rights violation and on the other hand, those that push towards a lower standard, such as whether the claim involves a controversial area of life, such as decriminalising sex work or regulating assisted dying. Crucially, this factorial approach does not assign any specific weight to any specific factor. Echoing Alexy's optimisation approach to the justification-stage, the non-weighted approach to calibration treats the nature of the violations of women's equality in the same manner as any other calibration factor. At the outset, women's inequality is given no special or significant weight. Proponents argue that this gives courts much needed flexibility and permits the justification-stage to be attuned to the specific factual-legal circumstances of the claim.[103] Moreover, at a more foundational level, a non-weighted factorial approach addresses long-standing debates on the role of courts. There are fears that courts, which have neither the democratic mandate nor the competence to second guess the decision-making of executive and legislative bodies, are overstepping their institutional role when assessing whether the limit is constitutional or not.[104] There are also fears that executive and legislative bodies will fail to respect, protect and fulfil the rights of minority groups, like women.[105] By examining a wide range of push and pull factors in a non-weighted manner, the justification-stage can simultaneously protect rights and respect institutional boundaries. While this approach enjoys broad acceptance, there are multiple instances where it is ill-suited to calibrate the justification-stage when assessing the permissibility of limits to women's equality.

Echoing the concerns articulated above, the non-weighted approach fails to respect the fundamental importance of women's constitutional right to equality. There is a dissonance between, for example, treating evidence on the extent of

[102] Aileen Kavanagh, *The Collaborative Constitution* (Cambridge University Press, 2023) ch 9; Cora Chan, *Deference in Human Rights Adjudication* (Oxford University Press, 2024) ch 1.

[103] Kavanagh, ibid ch 9; Jeff King, *Judging Social Rights* (Cambridge University Press, 2012) ch 5.

[104] For a summary of these arguments, see Alison Young, 'In Defence of Due Deference' (2009) 72(4) *MLR* 554; Jeff King, 'Institutional Approaches to Judicial Restraint' (2008) 28(3) *OJLS* 409.

[105] Rosalind Dixon, 'The Core Case for Weak-Form Judicial Review' (2017) 38(2) *Cardozo Law Review* 2193.

the legislative debates on the law in question with the same weight as a breach of the constitutional promise to end women's inequality.

The doctrinal analysis uncovers how, in practice, courts are overamplifying push factors that lower the standard of review while downgrading and trivialising pull factors. These principled and practice-based concerns require a new approach to calibration when women's equality is at stake. To be more faithful to the normative significance of the right, chapter four argues equality guides the calibration to a weighted approach. Women's equality is a powerful and overriding factor that pulls the intensity of review towards a rigorous and interrogative standard regardless of the push of any countervailing factors. At the justification-stage, women are being asked to endure equality harms – economic precarity, patriarchal sociocultural norms that ignore, demean and stigmatise them, oppressive structures and constraints on their agency – the analysis must respect the magnitude of these harms by applying limitation criteria in a ruthlessly searching manner. Regardless of any other factor, women's equality should pull the justification-stage to the highest degree of scrutiny. A weighted approach does not require courts to overstep their constitutional role. It does not mandate that the courts impose their own purely subjective views on where constitutional priorities should lie. It does, however, demand that courts assess how the executive and legislative bodies have decided on the constitutional ordering by forensically applying accepted justification criteria. Courts are not overreaching their role in the separation of powers by having inquisitive minds to claims that women's equality should be limited. All that is required is that courts not accept limitation claims at face-value and that any justification argument be rigorously interrogated for its veracity, strength and persuasiveness. Moreover, the doctrinal analysis reveals a pattern where many of the factors that would pull towards a searching standard are misapplied and those that push towards a lower standard of scrutiny are employed in an inaccurate manner inflating democratic legitimacy concerns. A weighted approach can correct these mischaracterisations and misuses of pull and push factors.

Examining in greater detail the factors in the non-weighted approach, this further supports the arguments for a weighted approach. The conceptualisation of many push and pull factors sits jaggedly with women's equality. Using them to calibrate the justification-stage can result in the justification-stage being wrongly calibrated. On the pull side, the more serious the violation of the right, the higher the degree of scrutiny that should be employed at the justification-stage.[106] This assumes that violations of women's equality can be neatly segmented between serious and non-serious. Ordinary and everyday decisions, such as who is responsible for collecting the children from school, have serious and negative legal impacts for women, limiting their ability to access

[106] Mark Elliott, 'From Bifurcation to Calibration' in Hanna Wilberg and Mark Elliott (eds), *The Scope and Intensity of Substantive Review* (Hart Publishing, 2015).

social benefits or pensions.[107] Patriarchy is a totalising force, warping virtually every aspect of life, and trivial instances of women's inequality underpin and maintain more grave and serious ones.[108] Trying to draw distinctions as to the severity of women's inequality for the purposes of calibration is conceptually wrong. Downplaying the infringement of women's equality to push towards a light-touch review misunderstands how women's inequality is a highly interconnected reinforcing web of norms, practices, standards, policies, regulations and law. This can be corrected through a weighted approach that reflects the seriousness that attaches to all breaches of women's equality.

On the push side, there are two factors that are repeatedly drawn upon in the jurisprudence and each of these factors misunderstands women's equality. A distinction is drawn between the matters that are within the legal realm and should attract a higher degree of scrutiny, and those within the political realm and which should out of respect for institutional boundaries attract a lower degree.[109] Women's equality straddles law and politics. For example, negative cultural attitudes towards women's sexuality become codified in laws that criminalise adultery.[110] Is this law a legal matter or is it a political matter? Trying to untangle the law-politics distinction against the backdrop of women's inequality is conceptually incoherent. This is because patriarchy itself is political and, at the same time, it is legal as law has a prominent role in maintaining patriarchy.[111] Moreover, the law-politics categorisation is not a neutral assessment but is informed by decades, if not centuries, of excluding women from the constitution.[112] Branding care as a political rather than legal matter reflects gendered ideologies that demean and exclude matters that remain of primary concern to millions of women from constitutional protection.[113] Determining the claim is too political for a high intensity justification analysis can continue to perpetuate the invisibility of women from constitutional norms, values and rules. This can be corrected through a weighted approach that does not seek to impose artificial or exclusionary boundaries. Weighing women's inequality as the overriding factor eschews asking irrelevant, incoherent and deeply gendered questions on whether it is legal or political inequality. In a similar vein, the dominant thinking is that if a breach of women's equality is contentious or controversial, this should push the court to a lower standard of review at

[107] *SG* (n 6); *Fraser* (n 5).

[108] Sylvia Walby, *Theorising Patriarchy* (John Wiley and Sons, 1990) ch 1.

[109] *SC* (n 5) [119]–[129], [208].

[110] *Joseph Shine* (n 32).

[111] Carole Pateman, *The Sexual Contract* (Stanford University Press, 1988); Fredman (n 55).

[112] Donna Greschner, 'Can Constitutions Be for Women Too?' in Dawn Currie and B MacLean (eds), *The Administration of Justice* (University of Saskatchewan Social Research Unit, 1986); Jill Hasday, *We the Men: How Forgetting Women's Struggles for Equality Perpetuates Inequality* (Oxford University Press, 2025).

[113] Sandra Fredman, 'Care as a Constitutional Value' (2024) *International Journal of Constitutional Law*; Ruth Rubio-Marin, *Global Gender Constitutionalism and Women's Citizenship* (Cambridge University Press, 2022) ch 1.

the justification-stage. This factor fails to comprehend that women's equality is inherently disputed, particularly when a claim reaches an apex court. Women's equality challenges and destabilises long-held beliefs and norms on how men and women should think and behave.[114] Using this factor in the non-weighted approach automatically condemns limits on women's equality to minimal scrutiny as claims of this nature are invariably radical and disruptive. The weighted approach, however, recognises a core characteristic of women's right to equality rather than framing it as aberrant.

Women's equality should guide the calibration of the intensity of review at the justification-stage. The proposed weighted approach assigns powerful and overriding weight to the seriousness of women's inequality and the importance of women's equality such that it pulls the court towards a searching, rigorous and probing justification assessment. In turn, this ensures that any limits are not based on speculative, flimsy, illogical or inaccurate claims. This approach is also more consistent with the nature of gendered inequality and lived experiences of women and prevents the calibration exercise from being distorted by factors that ring hollow in the context of women's equality.

C. Women's Equality Enriches Justification

The guiding function is not the only way women's equality can be beneficial to the justification-stage. It can enrich the application of justification criteria. Courts can test justification claims by bringing the argument that the limitation is legitimate, rational, necessary or balanced in relation to the precipitating breach of women's equality and in the broader context of women's equality. Before outlining how this proposed methodology can work in practice, this subsection begins by canvassing the differing justification frameworks employed in each jurisdiction.

Much like the equality-stage, there are overlapping and diverging analytical frameworks for assessing whether limits to women's equality are permissible. Canada and the UK adopt the four-limb proportionality test. There are slight variations between these jurisdictions. The Canadian Supreme Court examines whether:

(i) there is an objective that is pressing and substantial in a free and democratic society;
(ii) there is a rational connection between the law and the objective;
(iii) the means used to achieve the objective impair the right as little as possible; and
(iv) the beneficial effects outweigh the deleterious effects on women's equality.[115]

[114] Patricia Smith, 'Introduction' in Patricia Smith (ed), *Feminist Jurisprudence* (Oxford University Press, 1993) 10.
[115] *Oakes* (n 37).

The UK Supreme Court assesses whether:

(i) the measure has a legitimate aim sufficient to justify the limitation of a fundamental right;
(ii) the measure is rationally connected to that aim;
(iii) a less intrusive measure has been used; and
(iv) bearing in mind the severity of the consequences, the importance of the aim and the extent to which the measure will contribute to that aim, has a fair balance been struck between the equality rights of the individual women and the interests of the community?[116]

The UK Supreme Court, however, has deviated from the proportionality test and applied the manifestly without reasonable foundation test.[117] This only requires that the Court assess whether the justifications for breaching women's equality have a basis in reasonableness.

The South African Constitutional Court's limitation analysis is strikingly similar to the four-limb proportionality analysis but expands upon it. Per section 36 of the Constitution, the South African Constitutional Court assesses the:

(i) nature of the right;
(ii) importance of the purpose of the limitation;
(iii) nature and extent of the limitation;
(iv) relation between the limit and its purpose; and
(v) less restrictive means to achieve the purpose.

As mentioned above, the Indian Supreme Court has historically employed a rationality review testing whether the law is non-arbitrary and makes reasonable classifications.[118] There has been a shift towards adopting the four-part proportionality justification test, but this shift is embryonic.[119] The US Supreme Court examines whether the law has (i) a compelling purpose and (ii) whether the difference the law creates is substantially related to that purpose.[120]

Much of the debate on justification has centred on the legitimacy and efficacy of these tests. Similar to the fears and trepidations that animate calibration, there are concerns that justification tests, like proportionality, are too unstructured, too loose, too rule-less. Sceptics worry that proportionality only offers a 'myth of mathematical precision'.[121] How can the courts logically and

[116] *Tigere v Secretary of State for Business, Innovation and Skills* [2015] UKSC 57 [33].
[117] *SG* (n 6); *DA v Secretary of State for Work and Pensions* [2019] UKSC 21; Jed Meers, 'Problems with "Manifestly Without Reasonable Foundation" Test' (2020) *Journal of Social Security Law* 12.
[118] Shreya Atrey, 'Feminist Constitutionalism: Mapping a Discourse in Contestation' (2022) 20(2) *International Journal of Constitutional Law* 611, 622.
[119] Chandra (n 39).
[120] *Virginia* (n 40).
[121] Stavros Tsakyrakis, 'Proportionality: An Assault on Human Rights?' (2009) 7(3) *International Journal of Constitutional Law* 468; Yun-chien Chang and Xin Dai, 'The Limited Usefulness of the Proportionality Principle' (2021) 19(3) *International Journal of Constitutional Law* 1100.

coherently balance women's equality against religious freedom? Or women's equality and a sound fiscal budget? The argument goes that any attempt to answer these questions is nothing more than the constitutional imposition of individual judicial preferences, biases, idiosyncrasies and ideologies.[122] Critics believe justification tests, like proportionality, unduly elevate the court at the expense of the legislative and executive branches of the state.[123] Another line of criticism is that these tests collapse the justification-stage into a mechanical exercise that fails to grapple with the moral and political dilemmas at stake when deciding whether it is permissible to limit rights.[124] Defenders of justification tests like proportionality argue that its strengths lie in its ability to foster a culture of reflective, transparent and deliberative justification.[125] It requires 'courts to acknowledge and defend-honestly and openly-the policy choices that they make when they make constitutional choices'.[126] These debates are unresolved. Although there is an ever-growing global consensus on proportionality, there remain passionate critiques and defences of the different limitation and analytical frames.

What is less understood is whether these debates have any salience to adjudicating limits to women's equality.[127] Chapter five argues that the fault lines of these debates, the desire to avoid accusations of using the justification-stage to impose personal preferences on the appropriate constitutional ordering, result in courts isolating, decontextualising, misdirecting or misunderstanding the application of justification criteria. In *A and B*, the UK Supreme Court employed the four-part proportionality analysis to assess whether the funding prohibitions on abortion access for Northern Irish women and girls seeking abortion in England were justified.[128] This required the Court to balance the benefits of protecting devolution, the purpose of the prohibition, against the harms of the prohibition on Northern Irish women and girls. This was not an easy assessment. Rather than squarely confronting these challenges, the Court avoided the complexity of balancing by examining the breath and scope of abortion protection in international human rights law.[129] The extent to which the UN Convention on the Elimination of All Forms of Discrimination Against Women guarantees access to abortion is analytically irrelevant to balancing the importance of the prohibition against the severity of its effects on Northern Irish women and girls.

[122] For a good summary of the problems with judicial balancing, see Stephanie Barclay, 'Constitutional Rights as Protected Reasons' (Forthcoming) *University of Chicago Law Review*, available at https://papers.ssrn.com/sol3/papers.cfm?abstract_id=4740989.

[123] Tsakyrakis (n 121).

[124] ibid.

[125] Anne Peters, 'A Plea for Proportionality: A Rely to Yun-Chien Chang and Xin Dai' (2021) 19(3) *International Journal of Constitutional Law* 1135.

[126] Stone Sweet and Mathews (n 86).

[127] Talya Steiner, Andrej Lang and Mordechai Kremnitzer, 'Introduction: Analysing Proportionality Comparatively and Empirically' in Kremnitzer, Steiner and Lang (n 39) 6.

[128] *A and B* (n 10) [32].

[129] ibid [34]–[35].

In *Burwell v Hobby Lobby*, the US Supreme Court had to decide whether it was justified to require employers to include contraception in the employer group health plan despite the religious objection of corporations to this inclusion.[130] The state had to justify why it chose to prioritise women's equality over protecting religious pluralism. This required the Court to ascertain whether the state had a compelling interest and whether the Government had pursued that interest in a way that least restricted the right to freedom of religion and belief. Justice Alito, in *obiter* for the majority, questioned why the state itself did not just fund contraception, as this would have accomplished the state goal without intruding on the religious beliefs of others.[131] At first glance, this might appear progressive, but placing this claim in the context of women's equality in the US would reveal the idea that the federal Government would fund contraception is not the least restrictive measure but is a chimera. Conservative politicians and lobbyists had repeatedly frustrated, defunded and killed legislative efforts to enhance access to contraception such that it is entirely unrealistic to hold that fully funding contraception through federal funds would be a measure that would achieve the state's compelling interest.[132] The misdirecting and decontextualising in *A and B* and *Hobby Lobby* simplifies the justification-stage and protects courts from the criticism it would attract if it were to squarely and transparently apply justification criteria. It avoids balancing the harms between devolution and women's sexual and reproductive health or calculating the necessity of access to contraception notwithstanding the impact on the religious rights of corporations. But this comes at a steep cost. Women's equality rights are limited on the basis of untested claims. There is an uncritical acceptance that women's equality must be limited as courts have failed to ensure that the limits meet the required justification thresholds. This is not to mean that women's equality cannot be limited but limits can only be in place after the courts have rigorously tested whether the claims are flimsy, dubious, inaccurate and illegitimate.

Equality can enrich the application of justification framework to redress the current doctrinal problems with adjudicating limits to women's equality. Courts can explore whether a limitation is sufficiently legitimate, rational, necessary or balanced by bringing the limitation into a *relationship* with the underlying breach of women's equality and each limitation claim can be examined within the broader *context* of women's equality. The current flaws that riddle the doctrine can be redressed not through reinventing a new justification framework nor through advocating that jurisdictions adopt a specific analytical test, but by adopting a relational and contextual methodology that is anchored in women's equality. This approach aligns broadly with feminist legal methodology as it requires courts to use women's equality to 'look beneath the surface' of

[130] *Burwell v Hobby Lobby* 573 US 682 (2014).

[131] ibid 41–45 (concurring opinion of Justice Alito).

[132] Frederick Gedicks, 'One Cheer for Hobby Lobby: Improbable Alternative, Truly Strict Scrutiny and Third-Party Employee Burdens' (2015) 38 *Harvard Journal of Law and Gender* 153, 157.

justification claims.[133] It can flush out flaws and problems with the justification claims that can otherwise be difficult or near impossible to detect.[134] Jackson in her work on equality and proportionality in the context of the US, advocates for a 'conscientiously applied' proportionality framework as she argues that this can 'generate insights into the nature and structure of inequality that might otherwise elude judges'.[135] The arguments in this monograph breathes concrete life into the call for a consciously applied justification test. It takes each justification claim and explores its meaning in light of the specific breach of women's equality rights and tests the claim out against the historical, political, economic, social and cultural equality of women. Using the cases referred to above, a contextual understanding of women's equality in the US, the legislative antagonism towards sexual and reproductive health, can test claims that the state has not adopted the least restrictive measure. Or a relational approach to balancing would weigh up the strengths of devolution against the equality harms imposed by the funding prohibition. A relational and contextual methodology directs the court to the aspects of women's equality that can shine a spotlight on whether the justification claim has met the constitutional threshold it is required to meet.

As another example, protecting long-standing sociocultural traditions appears a sufficient, pressing and important purpose to form the basis for a constitutionally permissible limit to women's equality. Yet a relational and contextual methodological approach to the application of the justification criteria shows otherwise. A relational assessment does not explore the legitimacy of an abstract sociocultural tradition, but explores the objective of the law in relation to the breach of women's equality. Preserving culture by legally exempting a man from criminal sanction when he sexually assaults a girl who he is married to and who is between the ages of 15 and 18 is not a legitimate aim. Drawing on the broader context of gendered sexual violence and the early forced marriage of girls, it is also apparent that the value of preserving these traditions is not balanced against the harms it imposes on girls. A relational and contextual approach is to be pursued harmoniously rather than a distinct and separate analysis. The Indian Supreme Court in *Independent Thought v Union of India* implicitly adopted this methodology when it concluded the exemption to the Indian Penal Code was not justified.[136] In other judgments across the Indian Supreme Court, the Canadian Supreme Court and the South African Constitutional Court, there are glimmers of the examining justification claims in relation to the specific breach of women's equality and in the broader context of women's equality, but this methodology has yet to be fully applied by these courts. Chapter six strengthens and crystallises these nascent trends.

[133] Katherine Bartlett, 'Feminist Legal Methods' (1990) 103(4) *Harvard Law Review* 829, 843.
[134] Samuels (n 4) 49.
[135] Jackson (n 4) 171.
[136] *Independent Thought v Union of India* [2017] 13 SCR 821.

Lastly, this enrichment also operates to deflate fears that courts overstep institutional boundaries in adjudicating on the permissibility of limits on women's equality. This is because it enhances transparency, shining the analytical light on weaknesses in claims and arguments, which in turn marks out the institutional appropriateness of courts employing justification frameworks to assess if women's rights should be limited.

V. TELLING THE OTHER HALF OF THE STORY

This last section concludes by mapping the remaining chapters in the monograph. Part I explores the role of justification in shaping how courts reason through whether there has been a breach of women's equality.

Chapter two argues that justification should not matter to the equality-stage. Canadian legal feminists have identified slippages between equality and justification in the Canadian Supreme Court.[137] Pointing out that it is analytically irrelevant to use justification concepts to answer the question of whether women's equality rights have been breached. However, a comparative analysis reveals more worrisome patterns on how justification is perverting the equality assessment. It does so in two ways. First, chapter two identifies how justification concepts – legitimacy, rationality, necessity, balance – are used to assess breaches of women's equality. When justification is used in this manner, it dilutes and minimises the severity of inequalities to such an extent that the court can no longer identify a breach of women's equality rights. Second, courts conduct the equality-stage analysis in the shadow of justification. Courts brush over the inequality against women, fail to interrogate the nature and breadth of that inequality, which operates to lower the justificatory burdens at the justification-stage. Without a meaningful assessment as to why the right to equality is breached, there is nothing to draw upon to interrogate the claims that limiting women's equality is worth it. In both cases, the warping of the equality-stage tracks with formalistic reasoning.

Chapter three makes the case for stripping out justification from the equality-stage of the claim. Substantive equality can protect the integrity of the equality-stage. It provides a complete analytical tool set to determine whether there has been a breach of women's rights such that there is no need to resort to justification concepts or reasoning. There is no requirement to adopt a specific model of substantive equality, it can function to protect the equality-stage regardless of the precise meaning the court assigns to it. Courts must move away from mechanical, technical or abstract assessment and explore on a substantive basis whether the law breaches women's equality. This will protect the equality-stage

[137] Baines (n 4); Martin (n 4); Koshan and Watson Hamiliton (n 4).

for becoming a surreptitious justification-stage. There is, however, one requirement. The substantive equality analysis must be robust. Without comprehensively identifying whether the law perpetuates inequalities against women via a comprehensive substantive equality analysis, there is a paucity of counterarguments to bring in relation to the strengths of the limitation arguments. A robust substantive equality analysis prevents justification claims being accepted at face-value and positively feeds into the enriching of the justification-stage through a relational and contextual approach. The arguments in chapters two and three support a distinct equality-stage and a separate justification-stage. Not all jurisdictions studied in this monograph adopt this approach, but these arguments can be drawn upon to further support nascent jurisprudential developments in these jurisdictions, to argue for a dedicated equality analysis that ascertains the equality wrongs of the impugned law and policy.

Part II then turns to the justification-stage, arguing for an asymmetric relationship between equality and justification. Where justification should be irrelevant to assessing a breach of women's equality rights, equality guides and enriches assessing the constitutional permissibility of limiting women's equality.

Chapter four makes the case that women's equality guides the calibration of the intensity of review at the justification-stage. At the outset, courts must determine how closely they will interrogate claims that women's equality should be justifiably limited. Calibration is challenging as courts must traverse competing imperatives. On one hand, it must respect the hard choices executive and legislative bodies make and, on the other, it must ensure that women's equality rights are not eroded simply because these bodies deem it expedient or worthwhile. The push and pull factors that courts use to resolve this tension, however, fail to appreciate the nature of women's equality.

Calibration orthodoxy is embedded with assumptions that do not correspond with the realities and experiences of patriarchy nor with the constitutional weight assigned to women's equality. And in practice, many factors automatically condemn women's claim to a light-touch application of justification criteria, making it permissible to limit women's equality on the basis of untested claims. A deeper appreciation of women's substantive equality guides the calibration of the justification-stage to a searching, forensic and rigorous review. Rather than conceptualising this as an anti-democratic, judicial usurpation of policymaking, it is a recognition that assigning less moral worth to women guides the court to be inquisitive and not accept justification claims at face-value.

Chapter five reveals unseen patterns and trends on how justification functions in the adjudication of women's equality rights. Justification is being hollowed out and women's inequality is being justified on the basis of dubious, speculative, irrelevant and stigmatic arguments. There are three trends to this hollowing out both likely rooted in a desire to avoid criticism that the court is utilising justification to impose judicial beliefs, ideologies and biases. First, courts outrightly misdirect justification criteria. Instead of directing the analysis to what the justification criteria requires, such as whether a gendered prohibition against entry to a temple is non-arbitrary, the courts direct the analysis to an assessment that is entirely irrelevant to assessing if the limitation meets criteria, which in the case of the prohibition was whether there were other temples women could enter.[138] Second, court apply justification criteria in an isolated and decontextualised manner. This shields from judicial scrutiny flaws in the limitation arguments, often gendered assumptions and stereotypes embedded in the limitation arguments and operates to inflate or overamplify the justification claims. For example, claims that imposing income poverty on women to incentivise them into the formal labour market appears legitimate when assessed without reference to the broader context of the demonisation of gendered welfare dependency.[139] Third, some courts are leaning into a relational approach to justification – assessing a limitation claim in relation to the breach of – but they misunderstand women's equality rights. This hides errors in the limitation claim.

Chapter six argues these doctrinal flaws can be redressed through enriching the justification-stage with a relational and contextual approach that is anchored in women's substantive equality. Women's equality can be used to test whether the limitation claim meets the constitutional requirements for a permissible justification. In practice, courts can latch on to inaccurate relations and irrelevant contexts. The relational and contextual methodology directs courts towards aspects of women's equality that are precise and pertinent to testing the limitation claim: the relationship between the limit and the specific breach of women's rights and the meaning of the limit in the broader context of women's equality. There may be other relations and contexts that are illuminating but the relations and contexts anchored in women's equality are always relevant. This methodology respects the momentous nature of women's constitutional equality and by assessing it acknowledges the burdens that law seeks to impose on women. This enriching does not require the adoption of one specific justification test or another. Courts can test using the framework unique to their jurisdiction. What is required is that they test whether the proposed justification meets the required veracity, cogency and persuasiveness required by the framework by exploring the limitation claims in relation to the breach of women's equality rights and in the context of women's equality in the state. Chapter six reflects on how feminist relational theory and contextual approaches to law can be transplanted to enrich the justification-stage and explores how this methodology can be deployed in the praxis of courts.

VI. CONCLUSION

Despite the pivotal role that justification can play in using law to advance women's equality, the relationship between women's legal right to equality and

[138] *Indian Young Lawyers Association v The State of Kerala* [2018] 9 SCR 561.
[139] *SG* (n 6); Campbell (n 36).

justifications for limiting that right is poorly understood. By examining the jurisprudence of the US, Canada, UK, India and South Africa, this monograph offers doctrinal clarity on how courts are conceptualising this relationship and, building on this clarity, offers normative prescriptions on how this relationship can be optimised and reconfigured. Women's equality and justification should be conceived of as an asymmetric relationship. Determination of whether there has been a breach of women's equality should be conducted without any reference to justification. Women's equality, specifically substantive equality, can protect the equality-stage from justification. While equality and justification should be sealed off from each other at the equality-stage, equality matters to the justification-stage. It should guide and enrich the justification-stage. To ensure the justification-stage accurately captures the reality of gendered equality and to fully respect the constitutional importance of women's equality rights, courts should deploy a high intensity review to any claims that it is permissible to limit women's equality. Enriching the application of justification criteria with a relational and contextual methodology anchored in women's substantive equality, the justification-stage ensures that any limits imposed are not illogical, implausible, unfair or rooted in patriarchal attitudes and systems. This guiding and enriching function does not require courts to inappropriately cross institutional boundaries or competencies but only requires courts to squarely apply accepted justification criteria in a searching manner. Nor does it foreclose limiting women's equality, it simply requires that justifications are of a high degree of accuracy, cogency and persuasiveness. Women's equality informs both sides of the story and should be understood as instrumental to both the equality and justification assessment.

Part I

The Equality-Stage

2

Diluting Equality Through Justification

I. INTRODUCTION

WHAT DOES IT mean for women to be treated equally? This question has perplexed apex courts for decades. A range of overlapping normative concepts – consistency, dignity, stigma, systemic oppression, disadvantage – have been used to test what it means for a law or policy to perpetuate an inequality against women. Each of these concepts has been the subject of much debate on whether it is the right normative value to explain equality and have led many judges to bemoan the difficulty of the right.[1] The challenges in determining what constitutes an inequality have led some courts to both implicitly and explicitly look to the justification-stage. An inequality against women exists when, for example, the law does not have a proper purpose or if the law is irrational.

Courts turn to core justification concepts to explicate the scope and breadth of women's legal right to equality.

This entwining of equality and justification is most evident in jurisdictions where there is a clear demarcation between the equality and justification stages, such as in the United Kingdom (UK), Canada and South Africa. Others have observed this bleeding of justification into the equality-stage, particularly in the Canadian context.[2] There is a worry that this trend makes the justification-stage redundant or inadvertently puts the evidentiary burden on women, who must not only prove a violation of their equality rights but must also demonstrate why the impugned law does not meet justification criteria. But there is also something more sinister happening when justification creeps into the equality-stage. It imports analytically irrelevant concepts and directs the court away from grappling with the wrongness of women's inequality. This trend is most pronounced

[1] Beverley McLachlin, 'Equality the Most Difficult Right' (2001) 14 *The Supreme Court Law Review* 17; *Law v Canada* [1999] 1 SCR 497 [2].

[2] Guy Lurie, 'Proportionality and the Right to Equality' (2020) 21 *German Law Journal* 174; Denise Reaume, 'The Relevance of Relevance to Equality Rights' (2006) 31 *Queen's Law Journal* 696; Sheilah Martin, 'Balancing Individual Rights to Equality and Social Goals' (2000) 80 *The Canadian Bar Review* 302; Jennifer Koshan and Jonnette Watson Hamilton, '"Clarifications" or "Wholesale Revisions"? The Last Five Years of Equality Jurisprudence at the Supreme Court of Canada (2023) *Supreme Court Law Review* 1.

when courts revert to a formal equality-like analysis. To fill the emptiness of the sameness–difference paradigm, courts reach for justification concepts. However, the purported legitimacy, suitability, necessity or balanced nature of the law does little to identify the inequality a stake. Identifying that marital property laws aim to enhance individual autonomy does not identify how the exclusion of de facto intimate partner unions from these laws ignores gender power relations, devalues care work within the home and cements women's economic vulnerability on relationship breakdown. By focusing on justification when assessing the wrongness of inequality, the courts minimise the gravity and severity of women's inequality. This conceptual bleeding is not neutral as to the outcome of claim. It increases the likelihood that the courts will not find a violation of women's right to equality even in circumstances where there is overwhelming evidence that the law disadvantages, stigmatises, oppresses and excludes women. When justification enters the equality-stage, the court is focused on the defences of the law, and these reasons shield from judicial scrutiny how the law perpetuates and exacerbates women's inequality.

This is not the only way that justification impacts the equality-stage. Courts also assess the nature of women's inequality in the shadow of justification. It is possible to trace how the requirement to justify shapes how courts understand the nature of women's inequality. When the equality-stage brushes over the inequality, when the courts fail to interrogate the nature and extent of the equality harms against women, the analysis is tipped in favour of limiting women's equality rights at the justification-stage. This is because without a robust equality-stage, there are no counterclaims or arguments to challenge that it is permissible to breach women's rights. Ignoring the way gendered poverty constrains women's agency at the equality-stage strengthens, despite strong evidence to the contrary, the state's justification claims that restricting social benefits is a logical way to get women into paid work. By glossing over the equality-stage, particularly ignoring the gendered dimensions of the claim, the court alleviates the burden of the justification-stage. It forecloses an enriched approach to the justification-stage and shifts the limitation analysis to a sterile and technical analysis. Claims that the justification is constitutionally valid are assessed in the abstract and flaws in limitation claims remain hidden when the courts fail to meaningfully excavate why the law is unequal against women. Giving fleeting attention to the equality-stage tilts the justification-stage towards limiting women's equality regardless of the flimsiness or implausibility of justification claims. Again, this trend is most pronounced in jurisdictions like the UK, that have a clear demarcation between equality and justification. However, this chapter also holds relevance to jurisdictions like India and the United States (US), that do not consistently articulate the wrongness of inequality. It marks out the dangers of jumping straight to the justification for the law and not pausing to investigate why that law is a breach of equality. Ultimately, this chapter stands as a warning against any normative desire to entwine equality and justification at the equality-stage.

II. ANALYSING INEQUALITY AGAINST WOMEN WITH THE TOOLS OF JUSTIFICATION

There is a conceptual distinction between evaluating whether the right to equality has been violated and whether the violation can be justified. Adjudicating an alleged breach of women's equality requires courts to interpret the breadth and scope of equality. It must determine what is morally, normatively, and constitutionally wrong about how the law conceptualises, treats, and impacts on women. This task is complicated as equality is deeply contested and inequality is complex. Sheliah Martin, writing before her appointment to the Supreme Court of Canada, explained that 'equality rights rest on comparison, competing characterizations and larger social, political, historical and economic contexts, they are enjoyed by individuals but may involve connection to groups and collectivities'.[3] These challenges are steep and require courts to have a deep appreciation for not only the impugned law but also an understanding of the expressive function of the law, the history of the law in this area of life and how the law actually operates in women's day-to-day lives.

To navigate these challenges, courts are simultaneously reverting to the seeming simplicity of formal equality, assessing whether women are entitled to similar or different treatment and then turning to justification concepts to assess whether consistency is warranted and if there is a breach of the right to equality.

Is this something to be worried about? On one hand, the merging of equality and justification may be critiqued for being analytically untidy, blurring the distinction between rights and limitation of rights.[4] Concerns on this bleeding could be brushed off as just being pernickety. Some have even implied that this should not be conceptualised as a problem. Theorists have argued for a broad, or even loose, understanding of rights, as rights are mere triggers for justification, so skipping over how precisely the law breaches equality rights is not as important as assessing whether the law is justified in doing so.[5] Importing justification reasoning into determining a breach of women's equality rights would not under this line of thinking raise any concerns. On the other hand, Canadian legal feminists have marked this as a troubling development in the context of equality rights. Beverley Baines expressed concern that shifting the limitation test to the equality-stage means the state will never have to explain the interference with equality rights.[6] Martin warned that justification concepts are useless in explaining why the law is in breach of equality rights and further that is illogical to allow justification to seep into the equality-stage as it is irrational to

[3] Martin, ibid 301.

[4] ibid 304.

[5] Mattias Kumm, 'The Idea of Socratic Contestation and the Right to Justification: The Point of Rights-Based Proportionality Review' (2010) 4(2) *Law and Ethics of Human Rights* 141; Kai Möller, 'The Right to Justification and the Culture of Justification' in Neha Jain and Mila Versteeg (eds), *The Oxford Handbook of Comparative Human Rights Law* (Oxford University Press, 2025).

[6] Beverely Baines, '*Law v Canada*: Formatting Equality' (2000) 11(3) *Constitutional Forum* 65.

require women, who bear the burden under section 15, the equality right in the Canadian Charter, to prove why the law does not meet the justification criteria.[7] Watson and Hamiliton are similarly anxious that the presence of justification reasoning at the equality-stage shifts the burden of proof to women.[8] Their fears are well-founded but this chapter argues that there is something more ominous occurring when justification bleeds into equality.

This is because when justification concepts are imported into the equality-stage it operates as a diluting agent. Using limitation concepts to evaluate whether an inequality exists masks the gravity and severity of inequalities against women. For example, if the court uses a legitimate purpose as the touchstone for the equality-stage, a law with a good purpose, regardless of the extent of the negative impact of the law on women, will be held not to breach equality rights. This dilution is particularly pronounced in claims of indirect discrimination against women. Conceptually, in cases of indirect discrimination, the law does not explicitly mark out women for differential treatment and the equality-stage is meant to be directed towards the impact and effect of the law. Courts, however, sidestep an effects-based analysis by zoning in on whether the law has a proper or ameliorative purpose. Whether the law has a purpose that is significantly important enough to justify the hardships imposed on women is a question for the justification-stage. However, when the same question is asked at the equality-stage it misdirects the analysis away from the impact of the law on women's lives. The suffering and hardship the law imposes on women is ignored because a law with a salutary aim cannot be in breach of equality rights. If the court uses rationality, the equality-stage can fail to unearth how gendered inequalities can have a veneer of logic or challenge the rationality of institutions, structures and norms built around men's living patterns. Whereas if the court uses necessity to explicate inequalities against women, the equality-stage devolves into demonising women for making absurd claims that upend the 'natural' ordering. Lastly, when balancing works its way into the equality-stage, the scales are tipped as the court only considers the strengths of the competing public policy interests but fails to account for the harms to women.

At the equality-stage, justification concepts result in courts ignoring how laws perpetuate and exacerbate disadvantage, stigma, negative cultural attitudes, constraints on voice, agency and participation and the design of oppressive gendered institutional structures. Despite strong and overwhelming evidence of gendered hardships, asking if the law is legitimate, rational, necessary or balanced at the equality-stage, shields this evidence from judicial scrutiny. And thus, the migration of justification into the equality-stage is a worrisome development.

[7] Martin (n 2) 311, 305 citing in *Miron v Trudel* [1995] 2 SCR 418, 485–6.
[8] Koshan and Hamilton (n 2) 15–17.

Others have correctly observed that merging justification and equality alleviates any obligation to defend the decision to burden women at the justification-stage, the analysis in this chapter brings greater texture to this observation and more precisely identifies the problem. When courts use justification concepts to test whether an alleged inequality breaches the constitution, the courts typically latch onto *one* concept at the equality-stage. The court determines there is no breach of the right by, for example, only assessing whether the law has a proper purpose without assessing further whether that purpose is rationally achieved, whether there are other means to achieve that purpose or whether the benefits of the purpose outweigh the harms towards women. This not only dilutes the equality-stage from grappling with the wrongness of women's inequality but also eases the burden of justification as the law must only meet an abbreviated justification test. By only using select justification criteria at the equality-stage, the courts stealthily reduce the stringency of limitation tests and ultimately give constitutional imprimatur to a normative ordering that deprioritises women's equality without ensuring that order meets constitutional requirements.

To demonstrate how justification functions in this manner, this section uses the traditional four-part proportionality framework. Examining how the courts use: (i) legitimate aims; (ii) rational connection; (iii) necessity; and (iv) fair balance to determine if there has been a breach of women's right to equality. Although, as outlined in chapter one, proportionality is not the ubiquitous standard of review for justification, its limbs echo in the limitation analysis across the jurisdictions in this study and offers a logical framework for analysing how the equality-stage is diluted with justification reasoning.

A. A Good Law is an Equal Law

The purpose of the law is the cornerstone of most justification assessments. After establishing the legitimacy, significance, properness, pressing or substantiveness of the law, courts then explore whether that law meets the remaining justification criteria employed by that specific jurisdiction.

When the purpose of the law is used as an analytical tool at the equality-stage it performs a different function. The goals of the law are dispositive of whether the law violates women's right to equality. The objectives are framed as worthy and laudable, and this praiseworthiness is sufficient in resolving women's claims for equality. The law cannot exacerbate or create women's inequality when the law has a good purpose. Since it is relatively easy to identify a salutary goal, women's claim for equality tends to be defeated when the purpose of the law creeps into the equality-stage, notwithstanding the evidence that the law, as marked out in the cases analysed below, pushes women into economic precarity.

i. Purpose Hides Gendered Financial Precarity

The courts are drawing a straightforward relationship between the worthiness of a law and the existence of inequality against women. This was most evident in a series of cases on marriage equality from the Canadian Supreme Court and the South African Constitutional Court. In *Nova Scotia v Walsh*, in the Canadian Supreme Court, Susan Walsh argued that the Nova Scotia Matrimonial Property Act (MPA) violated the equality provision, section 15, of the Canadian Charter of Rights and Freedoms.[9] Unlike married spouses, there was no automatic presumption that individuals in intimate partner unions were entitled to an equal division of property upon the breakdown of the relationship. *In Quebec v A*, A argued that the exclusion of unregistered intimate partner unions from family patrimony and spousal support from the Civil Code of Quebec (CCQ) was a breach of section 15.[10] And in *Volks v Robinson*, Ethel Robinson claimed that the exclusion of the surviving partner of a permanent intimate partner union from the Maintenance of Surviving Spouses Act (MSS) was unfair discrimination under section 9(3), the equality provision, in the South African Constitution.[11] The equality-stage in all of these decisions myopically directed the equality analysis to assessing whether the law had a salutary purpose and in finding a legitimate aim concluded that the law could not be in breach of the right to equality.

Identifying how the purpose of laws that excluded de facto intimate partner unions diluted the equality-stage, it is necessary to set out the equality and justification architecture in Canada and South Africa. At the time of deciding *Walsh*, the Canadian Supreme Court had equated section 15 equality rights with dignity and held that, inter alia, if the law had an ameliorative purpose or effect for disadvantaged groups, it was unlikely the law would violate dignity and was unlikely to breach section 15.[12] Or to put it differently, if the law was targeted at breaking cycles of disadvantage for those historically or contemporaneously excluded, demeaned or oppressed, the law was unlikely to be in violation of the right to equality. The ameliorative effect or purpose of the law strongly echoed the first limb of the proportionality test for justification. Under the section 1 limitation clause of the Charter, equality rights can be 'subject to only such reasonable limits prescribed by law as can be demonstrably justified in a free and democratic society'. The first step of the influential *Oakes* proportionately test that breathed life into section 1 of the Charter, centred on determining if the state had an objective that was sufficiently 'pressing and substantive' to justify limiting rights.[13] Both the equality-stage and the justification-stage explored whether the law had a proper purpose. Pressing, substantive and ameliorative

[9] *Nova Scotia (Attorney General) v Walsh* [2002] 4 SCR 325.
[10] *Quebec v A* [2013] 1 SCR 61.
[11] *Volks v Robinson* [2005] ZACC 2.
[12] *Law v Canada (Minister of Employment and Immigration)* [1999] 1 SCR 497.
[13] *R v Oakes* [1986] 1 SCR 103.

were overlapping concepts and were conceptually blurred in *Walsh*.[14] The majority of the Supreme Court of Canada repeatedly stressed that the aim of excluding de facto intimate partner unions from marital property laws was directed at protecting agency, autonomy and self-determination and thus could not be in breach of the equality guarantee in the Charter.

Canadian equality law is never static and when *Quebec v A*, a case very similar to *Walsh*, was decided, the equality framework under the Charter had shifted. The analysis no longer centred on dignity, nor was it meant to examine the ameliorative effect of the law. The breach of equality was located in disadvantage.[15] If the law perpetuated or widened disadvantage, the law was unequal. The Canadian Supreme Court was internally split on defining disadvantage in *Quebec v A*. Justice LeBel for the majority judgment held it manifested as prejudice and stereotyping. He used the legislative objectives of the Quebec Civil Code to test whether these recognition harms had materialised.

This synergy between justification and equality also echoed in South Africa. In *Volks*, the South African Constitutional Court had to determine whether the exclusion of the surviving partner of a permanent intimate partner relation from marital property law was unfair discrimination in violation of section 9(3) of the Constitution. Much like the Canadian framework, one of the factors to assess unfairness was whether the law's purpose was 'aimed at achieving a worthy and important social goal'.[16] Albertyn and Goldblatt observed that there was a significant overlap between the equality-stage and the section 36 limitation analysis.[17] Much like section 1 of the Charter, section 36 of the South African Constitution held that rights can be limited 'if this is reasonable and justifiable in an open and democratic society that is based on human dignity, equality and freedom'. Section 36(1)(b) explicitly directed the South African Constitutional Court at the justification-stage to evaluate the 'importance of the purpose of the limitation'. Justice Ngcobo in his concurring judgment in *Volks* also stressed that the laws providing for surviving married spouses had a good and important purpose so the exclusion could not be unfair discrimination.

Diving more deeply into the cases, the overlap between equality and justification was most evident in the leading judgment of Justice Bastarache in *Walsh*. The core aim of the MPA, he held, was to protect the choices of individuals. Spouses, by choosing to get married, were presumed to consent to an equal economic partnership and were correspondingly entitled to the legal presumption of equal division of property upon the relationship breakdown.

[14] Martin (n 2) 332; Jamie Cameron, 'A Work in Progress: The Supreme Court and the Charter's Equation of Rights and Limits' in Debra McAllister and Adam Dodek (eds), *The Charter at Twenty: Law and Practice* (Ontario Bar Association, 2002) 31.

[15] *R v Kapp* [2008] 2 SCR 483.

[16] *Harksen v Lane* [1997] ZACC [50].

[17] Cathi Albertyn and Beth Goldblatt, 'Equality' in Stu Woolman and Michael Bishop (eds), *Constitutional Law of South Africa*, 2nd edn (2013), available at https://constitutionallawofsouthafrica.co.za/.

Individuals in intimate partner unions had not performed any legal ceremony and there could be no presumption that they had chosen an equal property arrangement. The differential treatment between marriage and intimate partner unions signalled respect for the autonomous decision not to marry. Despite the Supreme Court of Canada's commitment to substantive equality and the veneer of this reasoning in *Walsh*, Justice Bastarache was in fact reverting to formalistic reasoning, analysing whether the law should treat unmarried persons the same or different as married. He filled the emptiness of formal equality with justification. According to Justice Bastarache, given the commendable goals of the Act, there could be no violation of the right to equality.[18] There was nothing demeaning, undignified or unequal in the law's intentions to protect choice and self-determination and thus the unmarried could be treated differently. It was impossible that a law that aims to respect personal autonomy could 'perpetuate the idea that unmarried couples are less worthy of respect or valued members of Canadian society' because they are excluded from the law.[19]

Eleven years later, these arguments were largely repeated by Justice LeBel in *Quebec v A*. He used the purpose of the exclusion to conclude there was no breach as the purpose did not disadvantage anyone by replicating prejudice and stereotyping. Much like *Walsh*, he held that excluding unregistered intimate partner unions from the CCQ was designed to protect 'autonomy of the will'.[20] Again, this was a reversion to formal equality as the analysis was centered on the sameness–difference paradigm and again justification was used to fill the vacuum. He observed that protecting individual choice, the aim of the law, was 'a key factor in the determination of the scope of the right, and not only in the justification of a limit on that right'.[21] This was a direct acknowledgment that limbs of the section 1 *Oakes* limitation analysis were analytically relevant to the section 15 equality assessment. As the aim of the law was to protect self-determination which in turn is tied to self-worth, confidence and respect, the exclusion did not perpetuate prejudice nor was it based on stereotypical assumptions. It is not 'wishful thinking' to conclude that matrimonial matters were premised on autonomy of will and that differential treatment that sought to protect that autonomy was not a breach of equality.[22]

Justice Ngcobo in his concurring judgment in *Volks* employed similarly reasoning to his Canadian counterparts. He explained that 'one of the factors that is relevant to the determination of unfairness is the purpose sought to be achieved by the law [Maintenance of Surviving Spouses Act]'.[23] The point of the law was to protect the economic interests of the surviving spouse and the aim

[18] *Walsh* (n 9) [38], [40], [43], [48]–[50], [57], [62].
[19] ibid [62].
[20] *Quebec v A* (n 10) [36].
[21] ibid [262].
[22] ibid [271].
[23] *Volks* (n 11) [88].

of limiting the maintenance obligation to spouses was to protect the choices of individuals to take or not take on the legal duties that correspond to marriage.[24] Extending the Act to permanent intimate partnerships would be to undermine autonomy and Justice Ngcobo concluded that this would be unfair. The analysis centred on the differences between married and permanent intimate partner unions and he used the purpose of the law to delineate those differences. The exclusion, which aimed at protecting those who have chosen a certain legal arrangement, did not impede equal worth, dignity or perpetuate any unfairness for those who have not chosen this arrangement. The objectives of the law, a limb of the justification-stage, was the lynchpin for analysis at the equality-stage and determinative that marital property laws in South Africa did not breach the constitutional guarantee of equality.

There are a number of features that are striking in mining the relationship between equality and justification in these marriage equality cases. First, most notably is what is missing from the analysis at the equality-stage. There was no examination of gender within intimate partner relations, the expressive function of the exclusion, the economic impact on the lives of women or any understanding of how real people navigate the messiness of intimate relation dynamics and the law.

No meaningful consideration was given to the fact that relationship breakdown, be it marriage or intimate partner union, greatly increases the risk of economic precarity for women.[25] The gendered structures of the labour market and the burden of unpaid care work within the home and its role in trapping women in relationships of financial dependence was given short shrift. These harms were either ignored when considering the inequality or were written off as the regrettable conduct of individual men and not the result of legal institutions that privilege certain forms of relationship.[26] By applauding the objective, protecting choice, the equality-stage was directed away from the gendered impacts of the law. Without an automatic presumption of a joint division of assets on separation or maintenance upon death of a partner, the law continued to ignore women's economic vulnerability and devalued caring work simply because it was performed by women who were not married. When legislative purpose bled into the equality-stage, it became impossible to fully grapple with the gendered harms of the law. The majority decisions of the Canadian Supreme Court and South African Constitutional Court were blinded by the laws' ameliorative purpose, however, the dissenting opinions in *Walsh*, *Quebec v A* and *Volks*

[24] ibid [93], [94].

[25] Margot Young, 'Blissed Out: Section 15 at Twenty' (2006) 33 *Supreme Court Law Review* 45, 62–63; Elsje Bonthuys, 'A Duty of Support for All South African Unmarried Intimate Partners Part 2: Developing Customary and Common Law and Circumventing the Volks Judgment' (2018) 21 *Potchefstroom Electronic Law Journal* 1, 4; The CEDAW Committee, 'General Recommendation No 29 on the Economic Consequences of Marriage, Family Relations and their Dissolution' (2013) CEDAW/C/GC/29.

[26] *Volks* (n 11) [59].

centred the legal analysis on the impacts, paying close attention to the gendered impacts of the exclusion. These decisions and how they used substantive equality to protect the equality-stage from justification is explored in greater detail in chapter three.

Second, the equality analysis in *Walsh, Quebec v A* and *Volks* rested upon an untenable presumption that the aim of the law, respecting choices, accurately reflected reality. Feminists have long argued that the decisions on marriage are not individualised but are made synergistically between the people in the relationship.[27] Gender inequalities, particularly economic power imbalances in relationships, can heavily influence the choice to marry or not to marry. While the purpose of the law may have been to protect autonomy, by failing to account for women's vulnerability and oppression within intimate partner relations and the constraints on their agency within and outside the home, the laws operated to protect men's choices. As Justice Sachs, in dissent in *Volks*, put it, women's choices may be 'between destitution, prostitution and loneliness on the one hand, and continuing cohabitation with a person who was unwilling or unable to marry them on the other'.[28] By examining the purpose in the abstract and assuming that purpose matched on the ground realities, the courts failed to understand how the law really operated. The uncritical acceptance that the aims of the law were achieved, and consequentially that no inequality existed, is precisely why justification should not seep into the equality-stage.

Third, the equality frameworks in both jurisdictions echoed analytical features of the justification-stage. This merging was harnessed to dilute the inequality against women. Despite the Canadian and South African courts' strong commitment to substantive equality, there was a reversion to formalistic reasoning. The judgments broadly established that the law treated married and non-married people differently and then plugged in the worthiness of the law to hold that this difference was not a breach of equality. In both cases, the purpose of the law elided any more substantive analysis on the equality impacts and harms of the exclusion. *Volks* and *Walsh*, thus, stand as a warning of the dangers of conceptually bleeding between equality and justification in the design of equality analytical frameworks.

Fourth, when justification bleeds into the equality-stage, it is an abbreviated form of justification, further concealing women's inequality and the flimsy reasoning to cement that inequality. Neither section 1 of the Canadian Charter nor section 36 of the South African limitation framework end at identifying the pressing and substantive objective or the importance of the law. This is because the seriousness and gravity of women's inequality cannot be justified simply because the law has a good purpose. Using the Canadian cases as an example,

[27] Natasha Mukhtar, 'A Feminist Critique of *Quebec v A*: Evaluating the Supreme Court's Divided Opinion of Section 15 and Common Law Support Obligations' (2017) 30(1) *Canadian Journal of Family Law* 129.

[28] *Volks* (n 11) [225].

under a fully-fledged *Oakes* proportionality justification assessment, the state would also have to defend the rationality of using the law to protect individual choice. This limb of proportionality would bring to the surface how women's decisions on relationship formation and breakdown are not unencumbered but are shaped by patriarchal norms, structures and constraints. For many women the decision not to marry is not a conscious or deliberate choice but is reflective of gendered power differentials in the relationship.[29] Accounting for women's experiences would destabilise the logic of the exclusion as the law is not rationally connected to choice but to preserving men's financial control over women.[30] By only using select justification concepts at the equality-stage, it is possible to skirt around the rigors of a fully-fledged justification assessment that would have exposed the tenuous rationality of excluding intimate partner unions.

ii. Purpose Expunges Gendered Structures and Bias in Pay, Promotion and Pensions

A majority opinion from the US Supreme Court and a series of dissenting opinions from the Canadian Supreme Court on women's equality at work also drew on the purpose of workplace policies and equal pay laws to hold that there was no inequality against women. The aims of the policies and laws at stake in these cases, unlike the marriage equality case law, were explicitly designed to strengthen women's equality. While these high-level aims were commendable, they were not unequivocal proof that no inequality against women existed. Justice O'Connor, from the US Supreme Court, explained 'the fact that a discriminatory policy embodies the good intention of "seek[ing] to foster" the opportunity for something beneficial to happen is of little relevance in itself to whether the policy substantially furthers the desired occurrence'.[31] This echoes the concerns on the disjuncture between the aims of marriage equality and women's realities of intimate partner relationships. The dissonance between legal objectives and gendered experiences came again to the fore in the jurisprudence on women's equality at work. Women's inequality in employment is maintained through an intricate web of norms and structures and undoing that web is not a simple feat. Legal measures that are designed to promote women's equality can fail to account for the complexity of that web and inadvertently retrench women's disadvantage, stereotypes, exclusion and oppression. Relying solely on justification concepts, such as legitimate, proper or ameliorative purpose, to determine whether these measures breach women's equality masks how the law operates

[29] Beth Goldblatt, 'Regulating Domestic Partnerships: A Necessary Step in the Development of African Family Law' (2003) 120 *South African Law Journal* 610; Koshesayi Madzika, 'Dawn of a New Era for Permanent Life Partners from *Volks v Robinson* to *Bwanya v Master of the High Court*' (2020) *De Jure Law Journal* 393.

[30] Mukhtar (n 27).

[31] *Nguyen v Immigration and Naturalization Service (INS)*_533 US 53 (2001) 87.

in women's lives. Women are being told there is no inequality as the goal of the measure is women's equality, regardless of how little that goal matches their experience.

The US Supreme Court used the objectives of an employment policy to deny women's inequality in pay and promotion. In *Wal-Mart v Dukes*, Wal-Mart had a formal, high-level umbrella employee policy prohibiting sex discrimination which 'impose[s] penalties for denials of equal employment opportunity'.[32] Notwithstanding this policy, women in Wal-Mart were underpromoted and underpaid. This inequality stemmed from Wal-Mart's decision to grant local managers broad discretion in awarding pay and promotions. Dukes brought a class action, arguing that this discretion was a discriminatory employment practice in breach of Title VII of the Civil Rights Act. This provision prohibited discrimination on the basis of sex in employment practices unless the practice could be justified as a bona fide occupational qualification. In determining whether to certify the class action, the US Supreme Court had to assess if there was a common experience of discrimination uniting the class action claims. In concluding that the claim did not have the required degree of a common experience of discrimination, Justic Scalia did not draw on any theories of inequality, nor any empirical evidence of how the grant of managerial discretion operated. He examined the aims of the umbrella non-discrimination policy. This approach was more akin to a justification analysis as the focus was on defending Wal-Mart's policy choices.

Justice Scalia concluded that there was no common experience of discrimination as Wal-Mart had a workplace policy forbidding sex inequality.[33] Examining the employer's laudable aims echoes the 'important governmental objective' analysis the US Supreme Court uses when assessing whether the state has made a constitutional gender-based classification under the Equal Protection Clause of the Fourteenth Amendment of the US Constitution.[34] In *Wal-Mart*, this purpose analysis was a complete answer to whether there was a common experience of inequality against women at work. Justice Scalia opined that 'left to their own devices most managers … in a corporation that forbids sex discrimination would select sex-neutral, performance-based criteria' for promotion.[35] Women cannot be unequal at work because the employer said they should not be unequal at work. The circularity of this argument was both insidious and a form of legal gaslighting. High-level corporate policies on women's equality were a smokescreen for everyday workplace practices that denied women equal pay and promotion. The statistical, sociological, and experiential evidence that the

[32] *Wal-Mart v Dukes* 564 US 338__(2011).

[33] ibid.

[34] *US v Virginia*__518 US 515 (1996) 533; Leslie Goldstein, 'Gender, Sex and the US Constitution' in Mark Tushnet, Mark Graber and Sanford Levinson (eds), *The Oxford Handbook on the US Constitution* (Oxford University Press, 2015).

[35] *Wal-Mart* (n 32) 355.

local managers had created a company culture steeped in bias towards women was dissected and discarded as irrelevant.[36] There was no acknowledgment that discretionary pay and promotion systems were well-documented breeding grounds for repeated patterns of gender bias when evaluating women's skills, competence, commitment and leadership.[37] Justice Scalia framed any manager who did misuse their discretion as individualised and isolated acts of discrimination and not evidence of systemic inequality that would warrant a class action.[38] By restricting the equality analysis to an examination of the importance of the objective of the high-level employment policies, the claimants were unable to show the commonality required to be certified as a class action and the claim was dismissed.

The dissenting judgments in two equal pay cases from the Supreme Court of Canada adopted similar reasoning to the US Supreme Court in *Wal-Mart* and demonstrate how justification concepts, such as pressing and substantive purpose, dilute the equality-stage. Quebec required that employers conduct periodic equal pay audits and prospectively correct any unequal pay identified by the audit. There was no duty to remedy unequal pay between the periodic audits. In *Quebec v Alliance du personnel professional et technique de la santé at des services sociaux*, the dissenting judgment of Justices Côté, Brown and Rowe held there was no breach of women's section 15 equality rights, stressing that the law was designed to remedy women's inequality.[39] At this point in time, consistent with the analytical framework employed in *Quebec v A*, the equality-stage was meant to test whether there was a breach of substantive equality by assessing whether the law widened disadvantage.[40] The ameliorative purpose of the law, which so strongly mirrored the pressing and substantial limb of the *Oakes* justification test had been jettisoned from the equality-stage.[41] Despite this doctrinal shift, the dissent in *Alliance* collapsed the disadvantage analysis into the assessment of the law's purpose and in doing so minimised the negative impact of periodic pay audits on women's equality. According to the dissent, the equal pay laws 'do not reinforce the idea that women can be paid less simply because they are women' since 'the Act's objective is to permanently eradicate pay inequities by establishing a maintenance mechanism'.[42] There was a direct equation drawn between the ameliorative purposes of the law and the non-violation of women's

[36] ibid 369–72.

[37] Deborah Eisenberg, '*Wal-Mart Stores v Dukes*: Lessons for the Legal Quest for Equal Pay' (2012) 36 *New England Law Review* 229, 256–59; Melissa Hart, 'Learning from *Wal-Mart*' (2006) 10 *Employee Rights and Employment Policy Journal* 355.

[38] *Wal-Mart* (n 32) 353.

[39] *Quebec v Alliance du personnel professional et technique de la santé at des services sociaux* [2018] 1 SCR 464.

[40] *Fraser v Canada (Attorney-General)* 2020 SCC 28 [76]; Jonnette Watson Hamilton and Jennifer Koshan, 'Equality Rights and Pay Equity: Déjà vu in the Supreme Court of Canada' (2019) 15 *Journal of Law and Equality* 1.

[41] *Kapp* (n 15).

[42] *Alliance* (n 39) [99].

equality rights. There were ameliorative features in the equal pay laws including placing positive duties on the employer to identify and prospectively remedy unequal pay. Justices Côté, Brown and Rowe concluded that these features indicated that the law aims to 'address the problem of systemic discrimination', so 'how can it be argued, the Act has widened the gap between [women] and the rest of society or that the Act perpetuates discrimination?'[43] This question ignored the impact of the prohibition on retroactive pay. Women were legally permitted to be paid unequally for prolonged intervals. The overarching aims of the law, ending unequal pay, were dispositive that the law did not breach equality, and the impact of the specific provision was ignored, concealing, as the majority concluded, that the law breached women's equality.

The same reasoning was apparent in *Centrale des syndicats du Quebec v Quebec* which was released at the same time as *Alliance*.[44] The dissenting judgment of Justices Côté, Brown, Wagner and Rowe used the overall ameliorative purpose of the law, addressing women's inequality at work, to hold that the law was not in breach of section 15. In *Centrale*, Quebec had delayed implementing equal pay in workplaces dominated by women. The province struggled to design a methodology for assessing equal pay when there was no male comparator. The Quebec legislature had set up a scheme to redress systemic inequality, tackling the link between unequal pay and gender job segregation. It sought to narrow the gaps between women working in industries dominated by women and 'the rest of the society'.[45] From this Justice Côté for the dissent concluded that 'the Act has an ameliorative effect and does not have the effect of perpetuating systemic discrimination'.[46]

Under this line of thinking, it was impossible for a law to disadvantage women in contravention of constitutional equality rights when the law has a good purpose, even when that law continued to tolerate women's unequal pay for years. The aim of narrowing gender disadvantage was sufficient to answer whether the law was unequal or not. The law was 'designed to enhance substantive equality' and it 'should be encouraged and praised' regardless of the impact of the law on women'.[47]

The goals of a pension scheme were central to the dissent's conclusion in *Fraser v Canada* that the design of that scheme was not in violation of women's equality rights. The Royal Canadian Mounted Police (RCMP) allowed for certain gaps in employment to be treated as fully pensionable through a buy-back process. The RCMP also had a job-sharing scheme, predominantly used by women with childcare responsibilities. The job-sharers, however, were not entitled to buy back pension credits. The claimants argued that this was a form

[43] ibid [92].
[44] *Centrale des syndicats du Quebec v Quebec* [2018] 1 SCR 522.
[45] ibid [142].
[46] ibid [140].
[47] ibid [140], [142].

of indirect discrimination against women, contrary to section 15 of the Charter. This required an assessment of whether the buy-back restriction perpetuated gendered disadvantage against women. Justices Brown and Rowe, however, examined the aims of the job-sharing scheme. The RCMP had created the job-sharing scheme 'to provide flexible working arrangements in recognition of the burden women face in pursuing a career due to the unequal distribution of children'.[48] Women could remain connected to work and keep their skills up to date. From this the dissent concluded that

> In the present case, the Plan ... does not contribute to women's systemic disadvantage; nor does it reinforce, perpetuate, or exacerbate the pre-existing disadvantage of women in the workplace which arises in part from unequal distribution of parental responsibilities. Rather, it seeks to ameliorate (although without eliminating) the effects of that pre-existing disadvantage on women's careers in the RCMP by providing employment options which allow them the flexibility to continue to pursue their careers while raising children.[49]

The pension plan could not breach the right to equality because job-sharing was directed towards alleviating women's disadvantage. Much like *Wal-Mart*, *Alliance* and *Centrale*, the dissent did not investigate the specific impugned provision, the prohibition on buying back pension credits, but the overarching objective of the measure, the purpose of job-sharing. This shifting hid the disadvantageous economic impact on women, which was part of a systemic pattern of designing pensions around men's traditional employment patterns, and per the majority of the Court constituted a breach of section 15.[50] Justices Brown and Rowe due to their exclusive use of justification concepts at the equality-stage appeared incredulous that the majority could find a breach of the Charter. They were critical that 'this case is an instance of that inherent malleability [of substantive equality] being deployed so as to strike down a scheme which was, after all, designed to be ameliorative'.[51]

Much like the marriage equality cases, there are common features across jurisdictions in how justification is used when assessing breaches of women's equality at work. In *Wal-Mart*, *Alliance*, *Centrale* and *Fraser*, the judgments from the US and Canadian Supreme Court either examined the purpose of the overall law or the purpose of a different policy rather than the purpose of the specific legal provision or the impugned policy that formed the core of the claim. This made it easier to identify a worthy purpose which in turn made it easier to conclude there was no breach of equality rights. For example, it is easier to identify an ameliorative purpose to equal pay laws that seek to shift accountability burdens to the employer than to identify a laudable objective in restricting

[48] *Fraser* (n 40) [142].
[49] ibid [168].
[50] ibid [108].
[51] ibid [146].

retroactive pay (*Alliance*). Justice Abella for the majority in *Alliance*, found a breach of women's equality rights and conducted a section 1 justification-stage analysis. She explained that when accounting for the purpose of the law, the analysis must not focus on the overall purpose of the equal pay reforms but on the objective of the infringing provision, as this is the measure that needs to be justified.[52] When the purpose analysis bleeds into the equality-stage, it is a corrupted version of the justification analysis.

The blinkered emphasis on the ameliorative objective also blinds the court to the inconvenient truth that a legitimate purpose does not prevent the law or policy from in effect perpetuating inequality against women.[53] This is true even when the law seeks to achieve women's equality. And what is missing from the equality-stage, in each of these judgments, was a careful assessment of the impact of workplace policies and equal pay laws on women. In *Wal-Mart*, Justice Scalia presumed good faith on the business by virtue of it having a formal policy on women's equality and this good faith was unquestionably taken to align with women's experience of working at Wal-Mart. The equal pay laws in *Alliance* and *Centrale* tolerated women's continued economic disadvantage, the undervaluation of work performed by women and power imbalances between employers and women.[54] Yet these negative impacts on women were deflected by the dissent by referring back to the law's good purposes and the benevolence of the state in seeking to correct pay inequality.[55] And much like Justice Scalia in *Wal-Mart*, if any negative impacts perpetuated gender disadvantage against women, these were permissible imperfections in a statutory scheme that sought to undo stubborn nodes of women's inequality.[56] The impact of the job-sharing and pension scheme in *Fraser* were written off as the result of private decision made within the home or as the necessary latitude given to the state to incremental address 'a deeply ingrained, complex and persistent social phenomenon'.[57] The dissent exhibited no awareness that women's choice to move to part-time work to balance caring responsibilities was connected to gender norms and structures.[58] Women's legal right to equality became stuck in a cul-de-sac, where the effects of the law exacerbate women's inequality but the law is upheld as the state or employer's purposes were benevolent.[59]

In all of these decisions in marriage and work, justification concepts and criteria were used at the equality-stage to minimise the severity of women's

[52] *Alliance* (n 39) [46].

[53] *Quebec v A* (n 10) [333], [421]; *Nguyen* (n 31) 87; Martin (n 2) 311.

[54] *Centrale* (n 44) [34]; *Alliance* (n 39) [38].

[55] *Alliance* (n 39) [64]; *Centrale* (n 44) [65], [67].

[56] *Alliance* (n 39) [84], [111]; *Centrale* (n 44) [144].

[57] *Fraser* (n 40) [207], [215]; Sonia Lawrence, 'Choice, Equality and Tales of Racial Discrimination: Reading the Supreme Court on Section 15' (2006) 33 *Supreme Court Law Review* (2d) 116.

[58] *Fraser* (n 40) [91].

[59] Oddly, in *Alliance* (n 39) [76] Justices Cote, Brown and Rowe were alert to the fact that a law that has an ameliorative purpose can have discriminatory effects in the context of s 15(2), the affirmative action provisions of the Charter, but fail to bring this insight into women's s 15(1) equality claims.

inequality to the point where no breach of the right was found. The implication is that equality law becomes a search for salutary purpose. The concept of equality becomes meaningless as the ameliorative aims of the law are the start and end point of the assessment. The logical end point of reducing the equality-stage to a pseudo-justification inquiry becomes that a violation of women's equality could only be found if there was a non-ameliorative purpose. Invariably the state or the employer can identify a purpose that is commendable. Diluting equality with the aims of the law dooms the claim from the start.

B. Women's Inequality is Rational

Untangling the role that rationality plays at the equality-stage is not an easy feat. For long periods of time, equality was conceptualised exclusively in terms of rationality. The belief that women lacked rationality had been the basis for legal subordination and early feminists argued that women were equally as rational as men.[60] Extending to women an equal right to be treated as rational, however, was unable to undo power hierarchies, gendered prejudices, exclusion or patriarchal structures. Feminist legal scholars argued that rationality should be scrapped from the conceptualisation of the right to equality.[61] Rationality, however, remains pivotal to the justification-stage. Many jurisdictions employ it as a standard of review for the limitation analysis, a breach of women's equality is justified if the justification claims are rational. It also plays a role in the second limb of proportionality, the measure that limits women's equality must be rationally connected to the legitimate competing aim. In practice, equality, justification, and rationality are often melded together and treated as synonymous.[62] It can be difficult, particularly in jurisdictions like India or the US that do not have a fully developed equality-stage, to categorise what the work rationality is doing at the equality-stage and what it is doing at the justification-stage. This subsection argues that rationality is being used to determine whether an inequality exists and much like when legitimate purpose seeps into the equality-stage, rationality when used in this manner conceals inequalities against women.

i. Concealing Gendered Assumptions in the Rationality of the Labour Market

Prohibiting women from working at night 'does not embody a principle of discrimination on sex' but was deemed rational by the Indian Supreme Court as it was 'calculated to save women from the hazards of working during night in

[60] Sandra Fredman, *Women and the Law* (Oxford University Press, 1997) ch 1.

[61] ibid; Catharine MacKinnon, 'Toward a Renewed Equal Rights Amendment: Now More Than Ever' (2014) 37 *Harvard Journal of Law and Gender* 569.

[62] *EP Royappa v State of Tamil Nadu* 1974 AIR 555; Martin (n 2); Reaume (n 2).

factories' and to protect their role of providing love and care for their children.[63] The law's purported logic camouflaged essentialist stereotypes on women as mothers, as well as operating to exclude women from economic opportunities and public life. It was rationality that was used to explicate why there was no breach of Article 14 of the Indian Constitution which guaranteed to women equality before the law and equal protection of the law. This decision was overturned in *Anuj Garg v Hotel Association of India* where the prohibition on night work was held to violate the equality guarantee in the Indian Constitution.[64]

Rationality played a similar role in the dissenting judgment in *Fraser*. Along with emphasising the ameliorative aims of flexible working, the dissent also held there was no breach of the right to equality because restricting women in job-sharing roles from buying back pension credits was rational.[65] As mentioned above, the equality analytical framework under section 15 of the Charter required the dissent to assess whether the buy-back restriction widened gendered disadvantage not whether it had a basis in logic. Women in job-sharing roles worked less than 40 hours a week and barring them from buying pension credits as if they had worked full-time was, according to the dissent, not irrational or arbitrary. Justices Brown and Rowe held that it was simply following the logic of work for compensation and could not be in breach of women's section 15 right to equality in the Charter. They concluded that 'prorating compensation, including benefits, according to work is not arbitrary or discriminatory'.[66]

However, the logic of work for compensation did not capture the gender power dynamics of childcare responsibilities nor how the design of workplace compensation and benefits, including pensions, were structured around not having childcare responsibilities. As MacKinnon observed, asking if the law was rational was 'asking the wrong question' as rationality accepted gendered 'schemas and routines and habits and biases that have been ingrained for centuries'.[67] And in the case of *Fraser*, it shielded from judicial scrutiny normalised, everyday workplace practices that trap women into never-ending cycles of inequality. The dissenting judgment, by focusing on whether it was rational to exclude job-sharers from the buy-back scheme, ignored how pension design economically punished women later in life. Justice Abella, for the majority in *Fraser*, called out this bleeding of justification into the equality-stage. She expressed concern that 'the perpetuation of disadvantage … does not become less serious … simply because it is relevant'.[68]

[63] *Leela v State of Kerala* (2003) 6 SCC 611 [15], [19].
[64] *Anuj Garg v Hotel Association of India* (2008) 3 SCC 1.
[65] *Fraser* (n 40) [198].
[66] ibid.
[67] MacKinnon (n 61) 570–72.
[68] *Fraser* (n 40) [79]; Jonette Watson Hamilton and Jennifer Koshan, '*Kahkewistahaw First Nation v Taypotat*: An Arbitrary Approach to Discrimination' (2016) 76 *The Supreme Court Law Review* 243, 259.

ii. The Gendered Illogic of Biology

The most prominent use of rationality diluting inequality against women was from *Nguyen v Immigration and Naturalization Service (INS)*.[69] Unmarried fathers and unmarried mothers who had children outside of the US were subjected to different criteria when passing their citizenship to their children. An unmarried mother only had to meet a residency requirement while an unmarried father must legitimate the child; provide a declaration of paternity under oath; or a court order of paternity. This difference was challenged under the Fourteenth Amendment of the US Constitution. Premised on the rationality of biological differences, the US Supreme Court held the different naturalisation rules did not violate the Constitution. Rationality, however, operated to cloak assumptions in immigration law that essentialised women as nurturing mothers.

Identifying how the US Supreme Court employed rationality when adjudicating claims of sex inequality, requires pausing to investigate the Equal Protection Clause in the Fourteenth Amendment. It holds that no state shall 'deny a person within its jurisdiction the equal protection of the laws'. Unlike the Canadian or South African Constitution, there is no justification clause in the US Constitution outlining when it is permissible to limit women's equality. The Court has eschewed developing a fully-fledged equality analysis and instead has interpreted the Equal Protection Clause more akin to a justification framework. When analysing women's claim for equality, the Court first examined if law treated men and women differently. It then proceeded to assess whether the state had 'important governmental objectives' to pursue that difference and whether 'the discriminatory means employed … are substantially related to the achievement of those objectives'.[70] This framework was designed to test whether the classification was rationally connected to achieving the state's objective. Yet, rationality is also being used to develop a more substantive concept of equality that teases out the irrationality of gendered stereotypes,[71] and yet in other cases the Court uses rationality to deny that these stereotypes exist.

Nguyen v INS, a case on gender differences in naturalisation criteria, is an example where the majority of the US Supreme Court drew on the reasonableness of men and women's role in biological reproduction to avoid confronting the gendered stereotypes embedded in that criteria. Men and women, the Court held, were not 'similarly situated with regard to the proof of biological parenthood'.[72] A woman could easily identify her child through the act of giving

[69] *Nguyen* (n 31).
[70] *United States v Virginia* 518 US 515__(1996).
[71] Julie Nice, 'The Gendered Jurisprudence of the Fourteenth Amendment' in Robin West and Cynthia Grant Bowman (eds), *Research Handbook on Feminist Jurisprudence* (Edward Elgar, 2019); Neil Siegel and Reva Siegal, 'Pregnancy and Sex Role Stereotyping from *Struck* to *Carhart*' (2009) 70(4) *Ohio State Law Journal* 1096; Cary Franklin, 'The Anti-Stereotyping Principle in Constitutional Sex Discrimination Law' (2010) 85 *New York University Law Review* 83.
[72] *Nguyen* (n 31) 63.

birth and childbirth created a unique 'opportunity for a meaningful parent-child bond' between the woman and the child.[73] A man would not inherently know whether he was the father of the child and Justice Kennedy opined it was not 'always clear that even the mother will be sure of the father's identity'.[74] There was a risk of unwed fathers inadvertently passing their US citizenship to a child with whom they do not have a blood relationship and the difference in naturalisation criteria was logically in place to mitigate that risk. Justice Kennedy used rationality to reject the argument that the different criteria were premised on gendered stereotypes as legal differences do

> … not result from some stereotype [as there] was nothing irrational or improper in the recognition that at the moment of birth … the mother's knowledge of the child and the fact of parenthood have been established in a way not guaranteed in the case of the unwed father.[75]

Justice O'Connor in dissent came to the opposite conclusion, marking out how rationality was employed to downplay women's inequality in citizenship. While there might be a logic to biological difference, the naturalisation laws were riddled with gendered assumptions on responsibility for children. The law essentialised women as nurturing mothers who immediately bear full caring responsibility and automatically form unique bonds with their children. Digging into the history of how immigration law treated children born out of marriage, the less onerous requirements for women was 'paradigmatic of a historic regime that left women with responsibility, and freed men from responsibility for nonmarital children'.[76] The difference stemmed from the law's desire to relieve men from the consequences of sex and protect them 'from unwanted burdens of childcare and support for their nonmarital offspring'.[77] Women and men have different roles in the biological process of reproduction, but the rationality of this fact did not scrub out the discriminatory gender stereotype in the naturalisation rules.[78]

C. It is Necessary for Women to be Unequal

In some jurisdictions, women's equality can only be justifiably limited when it is necessary to advance the state's competing legitimate purpose. Broadly speaking, at the justification-stage, courts must evaluate whether there are other measures that could achieve the same purpose without breaching women's equality and if such other measures exist, the breach of women's equality could not be

[73] ibid 70.
[74] ibid 65.
[75] ibid 68.
[76] ibid 92.
[77] Laura Weinrib, 'Protecting Sex: Sexual Disincentives and Sex-Based Discrimination in *Nguyen v INS*' (2003) 12 *Columbia Journal of Gender and the Law* 222, 234.
[78] This decision was partially overturned in *Sessions v Morales-Santana* 582 US___(2017).

justified. The use of necessity as an analytical tool is, however, not confined to the justification-stage. Necessity, similar to legitimate purpose and rationality, bleeds into adjudicating whether there has been a violation of women's equality rights, and this perverts the equality-stage. This happens in two ways. First, rather than exploring alternatives that do not impede women's rights, the courts explore the necessity of treating women unequally to preserve other norms and institutions. To prevent traditional systems from unravelling, it is necessary to hold that there has been no breach of the right to equality. Second, if the court does explore alternative measures at the equality-stage, it assesses measures that mitigate or cushion the inequality against women and then uses these mitigating alternatives as proof that there is no inequality. These differing uses of necessity at the equality-stage and how it hides the women's inequality, particularly structural gendered inequality, are explored below.

i. The Necessity of Ignoring Gendered Structures at Work

There are two decisions from the US and Canadian Supreme Court where necessity was drawn upon to analyse whether an inequality against women existed. First, UPS had a policy that relieved employees from lifting heavy objects for a range of work and non-work-related injuries, but there was no specific policy for relieving pregnant women, who for health reasons connected to their pregnancy, could no longer safely perform this type of work.[79] In *Young v UPS*, Young argued at the US Supreme Court that failing to accommodate pregnant women's health needs breached the Pregnancy Discrimination Act (PDA). Second, as mentioned above, the Royal Canadian Mounted Police prohibited women who transitioned to flexible work from buying back pension credits and in *Fraser v Canada*, a group of women argued the pension restriction was discrimination against women. In each of these cases, a robust equality-stage would interrogate how gendered assumptions on living patterns were embedded in the design of employment policies. Workplace accommodations were built around gendered norms that presumed that any limitation on the ability to work would stem from injuries or some other externality, and not from pregnancy. Similarly, the design of pension systems was built around working patterns that were uninterrupted by pregnancy and caring responsibilities. Yet in *Young* and the dissenting opinion in *Fraser*, the equality-stage was misdirected from grappling with these gendered recognition and structural harms. Instead, these judgments centred on the necessity of keeping in place traditional workplace laws and policies, ignoring how these policies punished women from deviating from male norms.

Justice Scalia in the US, and Justices Brown and Rowe in Canada were concerned that women's demands for equality undermined established structures and used the concept of necessity to argue that these structures must be

[79] *Young v UPS* 575 US___(2015).

preserved and as such there was no breach of women's rights. In *Young*, the US Supreme Court had to resolve ambiguities within the PDA and Title VII of the Civil Rights Act. The PDA amended Title VII to clarify that pregnancy discrimination was discrimination on the basis of sex and was prohibited under the Civil Rights Act, unless the employer could provide a bona fide occupational qualification for its treatment of pregnant women. Under the law, pregnant women were to be treated the same as other employees in their ability to work or not work. This is a very formalistic approach to pregnancy as the law is premised on the sameness–difference paradigm. The PDA, however, did not clarify the scope of comparison for assessing whether pregnant women were similar or different from other employees.[80] Could women compare themselves to any employee who received accommodation at work or only to employees who perform a similar employment role? Formal equality gives no tools to resolve these competing comparators, and the Court filled this emptiness with justification. It drew on business necessity, a recognised component of the bona fide occupational qualification justification,[81] to limit the recognition of women's inequality at work.

Justice Breyer for the majority explained that allowing a wide comparison between pregnant women and any other employees would 'grant pregnant workers a "most-favored-nation" status'.[82] If the employer accommodated an employee who was in a hazardous job, who was older or who had worked for that employer for a long period of time, a pregnant women would be able to demand the same accommodation. It was necessary to restrict the scope of the PDA so as to prevent this from happening and to protect employment hierarchies. According to the majority, women would have to demonstrate that they were not accommodated when the employer accommodated others who were similarly unable to work, and the employer would then have to refute why it imposed this burden on women. This decision was criticised as it still tied pregnancy to other forms of workplace injuries or impediments.[83] Women must still fit their experience of pregnancy within pre-existing structures so as to protect employment hierarchies. Justice Scalia, in dissent, also painted a vivid picture of the necessity of placing bounds on the PDA. He warned that

> if Boeing offered chauffeurs to injured directors, it would have to offer chauffeurs to pregnant mechanics. And if Disney paid pensions to workers who can no longer work because of old age, it would have to pay pensions to workers who can no longer work because of childbirth.[84]

[80] Reva Siegel, 'Pregnancy as a Normal Condition of Employment: Comparative and Role-Based Accounts of Discrimination' (2018) 59 *William and Mary Law Review* 971, 975.

[81] *Griggs v Duke* 401 US 424 (1971); ibid 982, 994.

[82] *Young* (n 79) 13 (majority opinion of Justice Breyer).

[83] Jennifer Bennet Shinall, 'The Pregnancy Penalty' (2018) 103 *Minnesota Law Review* 749, 775; Nicole Porter, 'Accommodating Pregnancy Five Years After *Young v UPS*: Where We Are and Where We Should Go' (2020) 14 *St Louis Journal of Health Law and Policy* 73.

[84] Young (n 79) 2 (dissenting opinion of Justice Scalia).

The workplace would be topsy-turvy if a pregnant female mechanic could claim the same accommodations as the injured male CEO. To prevent pregnant women from getting special accommodation at work, Justice Scalia would only have extended the pre-existing categories of workplace accommodation at UPS to pregnant women. In both the majority and dissenting opinions in *Young*, the analysis was focused on the value of preserving workplace structures and the necessity of ensuring the equality-stage did not permit women to 'bootstrap' unwarranted accommodation at work. To protect the status quo, it was necessary to place restrictions on the PDA and these restrictions hid the extent that pregnancy continues to be perceived as a legal anomaly or deviation.

The dissenting judgment of Justices Brown and Rowe in *Fraser* used necessity in a similar manner at the equality-stage. Women in the job-sharing programme who could not buy back pension credits argued that they were treated differently on the basis of sex as it was virtually only women who shifted to job-sharing to manage their caring responsibilities and only women were prohibited from buying back pension credits.[85] Men, or employees who, like men, worked full-time and without interruption, were not disadvantaged when they retired. The dissent conducted a formalistic analysis comparing women on job-sharing programmes with workers not job-sharing, rather than assessing, as required under the Canadian Supreme Court doctrine, whether the restriction disadvantaged women. Further, it also used this comparison to hold that these women were seeking to up-end wage labour capitalism. Women were 'seeking to obtain *full-time* pension benefit … [when] they have worked part-time hours'.[86] How could women who worked less than full-time hours be able to demand a full-time pension? Since employment is predicated on an exchange of work for compensation, allowing women who job-share to buy back full-time pension credits would smash that fundamental tenet. There was no inequality in prorating 'benefits according to hours worked'.[87] Women job-sharers were different than non-job-sharers and this difference was explained via the necessity of preserving wage labour. It was the synergy between formal equality and justification that underpinned the dissent's conclusion in *Fraser* that there was no breach of section 15 of the Charter. Under a section 1 *Oakes* justification analysis, the necessity-limb would have directed the analysis towards assessing whether the buy-back restriction minimally impaired women's equality rights. But when necessity bleeds into the equality-stage, Justices Brown and Young inverted the concept, exploring how women's equality negatively impacted on employment structures and failed to ask any questions on gender and the architecture of pensions. Similar to the US Supreme Court in *Young*, Justices Brown and Rowe observed that the claimants in *Fraser* were 'asking to be put in a better

[85] *Fraser* (n 40) [185].
[86] ibid [160].
[87] ibid [198], [204], [205].

position than everyone else'.[88] Women's claims that the pension system failed to account for childcare responsibilities was distorted, using necessity, to become a claim for benefits that 'no other employee is entitled to'.[89] Asking for a pension system that reflects gendered realities or accommodation at work while pregnant, was not a claim for equality but a claim for an unfair advantage. This use of necessity not only made it more difficult for women to have their equality rights recognised in court, but it implicitly demonised women's equality.

The judgments in *Young* and *Fraser* exemplify how justification concepts can drive the equality-stage into a wrong turn. The analysis was not focused on what the law means for women's lives. In the case of *Young*, she was placed on unpaid leave without pay and lost her employment-based medical benefits.[90] There was no evaluation of how workplace policies can be a tool for gendered exclusion nor any assessment on how the laws devalues reproductive care.[91] The starting point was in figuring out how women's claims destabilised taken-for-granted workplace truths and how preserving those norms and structures dictated the necessity of either limiting the equality analysis or rejecting the claim. This was an inverted understanding of necessity. At the justification-stage, necessity explores whether there are other options to achieve the legitimate aim that do not entail violating women's equality. But as argued through *Young* and *Fraser*, when necessity seeped into the equality-stage it assessed whether limits on women's rights were required to protect other norms and institutions. Underneath these judgments, however, was a darker workplace truth, the continued socioeconomic and cultural disadvantage of women was the necessary price to maintain the status quo.

ii. The Unnecessary Sting of Inequality in Marriage

Necessity can also be inverted at the equality-stage by identifying measures that mitigate the negative impact of the law or policy on women. This draws upon the minimally impairing aspect of the necessity limb. Finding a breach of women's equality rights is not necessary as there are a range of measures that women can avail themselves of to protect their interests. The existence of other measures directs the equality-stage away from the gravity and severity of women's inequality and exposes the harm of a truncated justification analysis conducted under the rubric of the equality-stage.

This use of necessity was most prominent in the Canadian Supreme Court's decisions on de facto intimate partner unions. In *Walsh*, Justice Bastarache

[88] ibid [160].
[89] ibid.
[90] Porter (n 83).
[91] Ruth Rubio-Marin, *Global Gender Constitutionalism and Women's Citizenship* (Cambridge University Press, 2022); Sandra Fredman, 'Care as a Constitutional Issue' (2024) 22(3) *International Journal of Constitutional Law* 741.

explained that the alternative legal mechanisms for non-marital relationships 'supports the conclusion that the extension of the [Matrimonial Property Act] to married persons … is not discriminatory'.[92] These arguments were repeated by Justice LeBel in *Quebec v A*. He held that the existence of other legal protections for intimate partner relationships 'does not indicate that prejudice is being expressed or perpetuated' or that any 'hierarchy of worth is established between different types of couples'.[93] These other measures included entering a domestic contract pursuant to other pieces of legislation, applying to the court for an order of maintenance or support or pursuing a claim for a constructive trust. The existence of other remedies meant, according to Justices Bastarache and LeBel, that there was no violation of the equality rights in the Charter. Necessity was warped when it bleeds into the equality-stage. Rather than asking, as would be required under the *Oakes* proportionality justification framework, whether women's rights were minimally impaired or more broadly exploring other ways to protect individual choice that did not violate equality rights, the Court was investigating whether there were ways for individuals to minimise the sting of inequality. Moreover, Bastarache and Justices LeBel did not consider the viability of these alternative mechanisms as would be required under a fully-fledged *Oakes* assessment. The dissenting judgment of Justice L'Heureux-Dube in *Walsh* and Justice Abella in *Quebec v A*, however, did assess the effectiveness of these other legal remedies. Both observed that there were complex, uncertain, costly, not well-known mechanisms that were plagued with evidentiary and doctrinal difficulties.[94] The ability of these alternatives to protect women's economic interests on relationship breakdown were an illusion. Unjust enrichment has a long history of failing to fully account and properly value women's work within the home.[95] Confining necessity to the justification-stage and removing it from the equality-stage would protect against alternative measures being used to mask the gendered impact of excluding de facto intimate partner unions from marital property regimes.

D. All in the Gender Imbalance

Some jurisdictions, like Canada or the UK, conduct a final balancing assessment, exploring whether the harms to women's equality are justifiably outweighed by the strengths of the competing objective. Balancing does not play a significant role at the equality-stage. The one exception was the dissenting opinion in the equal pay cases from the Supreme Court of Canada. In *Alliance*, Quebec had

[92] *Walsh* (n 9) [62].
[93] *Quebec v A* (n 10) [266].
[94] ibid [365]–[370]; *Walsh* (n 10) [164]–[169].
[95] *Walsh* (n 10) [167]; Simone Degeling and Mehere San Roque, 'Unjust Enrichment: A Feminist Critique of Enrichment' (2014) 36 *Sydney Law Review* 69.

reformed the statutory equal pay laws. In the hope of spurring greater compliance, the statute compelled employers to conduct an equal pay audit every five years but did not require the employer to retroactively pay women for any time periods of unequal pay between the five-year audits. When assessing whether the limits on back pay were a breach of the section 15 equality rights, the dissenting opinion of Justices Brown, Rowe and Côté weighed up policy considerations against finding any breach. They were worried that if the right to equality required back pay between the periodic statutory equal pay audits, this would 'constitutionally entrench pay equity'.[96] This in turn, they warned, would have a chilling effect. Legislatures would be hesitant to pursue statutory reforms as courts could morph these reforms into constitutional obligations.[97] Finding a violation of women's equal rights would stifle legislative innovation and experimentation. Women must accept lesser pay at work so the state will continue to redress other social justice issues. Notably absent from this covert balancing exercise was calculating the harm of unequal pay. Balancing at the justification-stage would demand weighing these potential negative ripple consequences for legislative innovation against the actual harm of continued legal permission to pay women unequally. Balancing at the equality-stage was tipped as it only assessed the impacts on the state. Chapter five argues this imbalance in balancing is often repeated. This, it is argued, can be redressed through enriching the justification-stage with a relational and contextual approach anchored in women's equality. At the equality-stage, imbalanced balancing can be redressed through shifting the analytical focus away from defences of the impugned law and towards the effects and impacts of the law on women's lives.

III. PROTECTING JUSTIFICATION BY IGNORING INEQUALITY AGAINST WOMEN

Along with directly drawing on justification concepts to assess whether the law perpetuates women's inequality, the equality-stage is also indirectly shaped by justification. It is possible to trace how the equality assessment is conducted in the shadow of the justification-stage. The requirement to justify results in the equality-stage being surreptitiously used to skew the limitation analysis in favour of the state. For example, in *Young v UPS*, the majority of the Court held that cost was not a permissible reason for refusing to accommodate pregnant women at work.[98] Costs cannot be used to justify pregnancy discrimination. Dinner argued that the absence of a cost-based justification has resulted in lower courts narrowly construing the comparison between pregnant woman and other employees. This protects employers from being burdened but has also resulted

[96] *Alliance* (n 39) [84].
[97] ibid [85].
[98] *Young* (n 79) 21 (majority opinion of Justice Breyer).

in holding that firing pregnant women was not discriminatory.[99] Fredman has argued that threshold issues with respect to the scope comparator in equal pay cases in the UK have been exploited to avoid the exposing glare of the limitation analysis that would question whether there was material factors that may justify unequal pay between men and women.[100]

Rackley, writing on the Feminist Judgment Project, observed that judges can retell and reshape the facts 'to reinforce their decision on points of law'.[101] In the cases analysed below, the courts do find a breach of women's equality rights but there is a reshaping and retelling of the inequality against women that either ignores the wrongs of inequality or the gender dimensions of women's claims. Critiquing this glossing over is not merely nitpicking as the thin equality analysis is used to reinforce the court's conclusion that it is justified to pursue that inequality. By camouflaging the depth, seriousness and gendered-ness of women's inequality at the equality-stage, the courts amplify the legitimacy, rationality, necessity and benefits to be gained from pursuing the competing objective. Reaume made a similar observation in the Canadian context, noting that if courts do not have robust understanding of the wrongs of inequality it will ease the *Oakes* section 1 limitation burden as 'it will be easy for the government to persuade the court that some other objective was more important'.[102] This chapter argues that there are patterns to this glossing over, the suffering of inequality and its gendered nature are repeatedly ignored, that more firmly pin-down how justification warps the equality-stage.

A. Ignoring the Hardship of Women's Inequality

Courts routinely minimise women's experience of inequality. The US Supreme Court in *Wal-Mart*, assessed above, glossed over workplace sexism. The UK Supreme Court in a recent equal pay case collapsed the analysis into a technocratic exercise on comparators rather than a more substantive assessment on gender job segregation and women's unequal pay.[103] The Indian Supreme Court ignored how triple talaq, instantaneous divorce, discriminated against Muslim women.[104] There is a plethora of intersecting reasons to explain this

[99] Deborah Dinner, 'The Cost of Reproduction: History and the Legal Construction of Sex Equality' (2011) 46 *Harvard Civil Rights Civil Liberties Law Review* 415; Siegel (n 80) 983–89.

[100] Sandra Fredman, 'Inching Forward: Preliminary Victory for Equal Value at Tesco and Asda' (2022) 51(1) *Industrial Law Journal* 166.

[101] Erika Rackley, 'The Art and Craft of Writing Judgments: Notes on the Feminist Judgments Project' in Rosemary Hunter, Clare McGlynn and Erika Rackley (eds) *Feminist Judgments: From Theory to Practice* (Hart Publishing, 2010) 46.

[102] Reaume (n 2) 728.

[103] *Asda Stores Ltd v Brierley and Others* [2021] UKSC 10.

[104] *Shayara Bano v Union of India* (2017) 9 SCC 1; Vrinda Narain, 'Reconciling Constitutional Law, Gender Equality and Religious Difference: Lessons from *Shayara Bano*, India's Triple Talaq Decision' in *The Asian Yearbook of Human Rights and Humanitarian Law* (Brill, 2021).

minimisation including legal-political culture, doctrinal pathways, litigation strategies and political movements and counter-movements. Another chronically overlooked reason is justification. Ignoring women's arguments on the burdens of inequality eases the justification burdens as there is only a thin understanding of the inequality to bring into relation with the limitation claims and no real context on women's lives to test the veracity of these claims.

i. Inflating the Justification by Minimising the Harms of Restricting Social Benefits

This occurred in a series of decisions in the UK Supreme Court on women's inequality in benefits. After the 2008 financial crisis, the state slashed the benefits system. Despite a range of entitlements, the benefits any one person could claim were capped at a certain amount. The cap could be lifted if individuals performed a certain amount of work in the paid labour force. The child-tax credit, a means-tested benefit to assist parents with the subsistence needs of children, was limited to two children. The cap, work conditionalities and the two-child limit impacted women more than men. Women, particularly lone mothers, challenged that these reforms were indirectly discrimination in violation of Article 14 of the European Convention of Human Rights (ECHR) by interfering with the peaceful enjoyment of their property (Article 1 of Protocol 1 of the ECHR) and the right to private life (Article 8 of the ECHR) as domesticated under the Human Rights Act. This was a two-step analysis where the UK Supreme Court examined whether there is differential treatment and then considered whether that differential treatment could be justified. As the women's claims were for indirect discrimination, the UK Supreme Court was meant to assess the prejudicial effects of neutral policy on them.[105] This evaluation should, in theory, have explored in a highly contextual manner, the wide-ranging impacts of the neutral benefit reforms on the lives of women. Yet in *SG v Secretary of Work and Pensions*[106] and *SC v Secretary of Work and Pensions*,[107] the UK Supreme Court only gave a cursorily nod to how the reforms impacted women, and this directly connected to the Court's conclusion that these reforms were justifiable incursions on women's equality.

Justification indirectly truncated the equality-stage in *SG v Secretary of Work and Pensions*, the case which challenged the benefits cap. Lord Reed's equality analysis began with an extensive focus on the legislative history and rationale for the cap, spanning 42 paragraphs. In contrast, assessing whether the cap was indirectly discriminatory against women only took three paragraphs. And one of those paragraphs was to observe that the state conceded the cap was discriminatory and another to dismiss the argument that women who experience

[105] *DH v Czech Republic* (2008) 47 EHRR 3.
[106] *SG v Secretary of Work and Pensions* [2015] UKSC 16.
[107] *SC v Secretary of Work and Pensions* [2021] UKSC 26.

domestic violence were indirectly discriminated against. The inequality of the cap was simply described as 'inevitable' and 'inexorable' as more women than men received high levels of benefits from the state.[108] Women's experiences of living under the benefit cap were dismissed as analytically irrelevant. Lord Reed held that 'the court is concerned … with the question whether the legislation … unlawfully discriminates between men and women, rather than the hardship which might result from the cap in the cases of those most severely affected'.[109] This divorced the harms of inequality from the legal right to equality. This was counterintuitive for an indirect discrimination analysis was meant to account for the impacts of the law. The effects and the hardship of the cap should have been used as a diagnostic tool to bring to the fore gendered inequalities perpetuated by the cap, including stigmas against women living in poverty as work-shy and the gendered norms and structures of the labour market that channel women with children into low-paid, low-valued and precarious work.[110] The inattention to the burdens of inequality was repeated in *SC v Secretary for Work and Pensions* which upheld the two-child limit as justifiable discrimination against women. Lord Reed accepted that limiting the child tax credit to two children affected women more than men in contradiction to Article 14 in conjunction with Article 1 of Protocol 1 of the ECHR.[111] At the outset of the judgment, there was a brief biographical description of the claimants and Lord Reed observed that one of the claimants was unable to afford birthday parties at commercial venues for her children.[112] Beyond equating the inequality of the two-child limit to frivolity, there was no further analysis at the equality-stage. Why or how the law disproportionately and negatively impacted women was judicially ignored.

The failure to unearth gendered hardships – the disadvantage, prejudice, marginalisation and oppression – within the benefit cap and two-child limit not only marked a disturbing development in equality law it also revealed how a thin equality analysis can be instrumentalised to strengthen the state's limitation arguments at the justification-stage. At the time of deciding *SG*, the majority of the UK Supreme Court utilised, at the justification-stage, the 'manifestly without reasonable foundation' test. The state only had to establish that the benefits cap had a basis in rationality. The appropriateness of this standard in the context of women's inequality is critiqued in chapter four. At the equality-stage, the UK Supreme Court deemed the inequality as inevitable, and an inevitably is inherently easier to justify as there was no rational way the state could avoid a supposed inevitable inequality on women.[113] Lord Reed extensively echoed and lauded the state's multi-fold purposes of the cap: curtailing welfare dependency;

[108] *SG* (n 106) [61], [76], [96].
[109] ibid [76].
[110] Meghan Campbell, 'The Austerity of Lone Motherhood: Discrimination Law and Benefit Reform' (2021) 41(4) *OJLS* 1197.
[111] *SC* (n 107) [46].
[112] ibid [12].
[113] *SG* (n 106) [96].

incentivising work in the paid labour force; and reducing public spending.[114] Without excavating the harms of the cap and how these harms violate the right to equality, there were no counterarguments from the equality-stage to put in relation to or in context to query whether these limitation claims were in fact reasonable. An equality analysis that was more than three paragraphs would have radically challenged the reasonableness of the state's limitation arguments. A robust substantive equality analysis would have unearthed how the benefit restrictions perpetuated stereotypes on gendered welfare dependency and the gender barriers in the labour market that make it extremely difficult for women to escape poverty through paid work.[115] This would have destabilised the logic of the justification for the cap. It was not rational to limit women's equality on a belief that it will spur them into paid work when the equality-stage would uncover that this belief was stigmatic and not supported by the empirical evidence. In disregarding the hardship of inequality, the majority of the UK Supreme Court used the equality-stage to reinforce the state's core justification arguments.

In *SC*, the absence of a detailed assessment of the suffering imposed by the two-child limit weighed the analysis heavily in favour of the state at the justification-stage. In this case, due to doctrinal shifts at the European Court of Human Rights, the UK Supreme Court applied the proportionality justification framework rather than the manifestly without reasonable foundation standard of review.[116] In *SC*, the state claimed the two-child limit was a proportionate measure to restrain public spending and to incentivise greater reflection on financial readiness to have children which, in contrast to the scant equality analysis, the Court canvassed these limitation arguments in careful detail.[117] The crux of the justification was a fair balance. Was imposing income poverty on women in breach of their equality rights balanced against the need to promote fiscal restraint and personal responsibility for the care of children? Answering this question would require a robust equality-stage that fully grappled with the hardships of inequality. Yet due to the paucity of the Court's equality-stage, on one side of the scale, there was only a superficial assessment of the equality impacts on women. On the other side, there was the detailed consideration of the value of reducing public expenditure and the importance of ensuring taxpayers were not subsidising the childcare responsibilities of women in poverty. The Court ensured that the scales of the fair balancing exercise were tipped to the state by gliding over the equality-stage.

[114] ibid [67]–[77].

[115] Campbell (n 110); Virginia Mantouvalou, 'Welfare-to-Work, Structural Injustice and Human Rights' (2020) 83(5) *MLR* 929.

[116] *JD and A v UK* Apps no 32949/17 and 34614/17 (ECtHR, 24 October 2019).

[117] *SC* (n 107) [2]–[10], [13]–[21], [186]–[197].

B. Stripping Out Gender

Courts will also ignore the gendered nature of inequality, and this too eases the justification burden. Courts remove sex and gender from the equality-stage, focusing on other identity characteristics, such as geography. Given the prominence of gender power relations as an explanatory factor for women's inequality it is perplexing to ignore this at the equality-stage, but it also matters to the justification-stage. It reshapes the inquiry at the justification-stage in a way that presupposes the competing law meets the required threshold to permissibly limit women's equality.

i. Erasing Gender from Sexual and Reproductive Health

The lack of a gendered equality analysis explained why the UK Supreme Court held it was justifiable to put limits on women's sexual and reproductive health.[118] Prior to 2019, the criminal prohibition on abortion forced Northern Irish women to travel to England. However, the state did not fund abortion services for Northern Irish women when seeking abortions in England. A and B argued this was discrimination in relation to private life violating Article 14 of the ECHR in conjunction with Article 8. The majority of the UK Supreme Court agreed but held that the infringement was justified to protect the constitutional architecture of the UK. The strengths of the state's limitation arguments, that not providing funding to Northern Irish women was required to protect devolution, were bolstered by ignoring the gendered harms at the equality-stage.

The Court in *A and B v Secretary of State for Health* framed the inequality purely in geographic terms. Lord Wilson explained the differential treatment as the state was treating 'women usually resident in England different from women who, although UK citizens, were usually resident in Northern Ireland'.[119] The fulcrum of the inequality was residency within different parts of the UK and the gender dimensions of abortion restrictions were ignored. An equality-stage that was sensitive to gender would acknowledge the stigmas that women had to navigate in Northern Ireland and England, the dangers in trying to access an illegal abortion, the stress and anxiety of having to travel to obtain a legal abortion, and the physical and mental health impacts from the lack of post-abortion care when returning to Northern Ireland.[120] These inequalities were exacerbated for women in poverty, women who become pregnant from the result of sexual

[118] *A and B v Secretary of State for Health* [2017] UKSC 41.

[119] ibid [31].

[120] UN Committee on the Elimination of All Forms of Discrimination Against Women, 'Inquiry Concerning the UK of Great Britain and Northern Ireland under article 8 of OP-CEDAW' (2018) CEDAW/C/OP.8/GBR/1.

violence and women whose pregnancies involve a fatal fetal abnormality.[121] The criminalisation of abortion in Northern Ireland combined with the funding prohibition in England deprived women of 'privacy, self-determination and autonomy of decision, offending women's equal status'.[122] These gendered equality harms to Northern Irish women, however, were invisibilised in *A and B*.

In ignoring the gendered nature of the inequality at the equality-stage, the UK Supreme Court tipped the justification-stage in favour of the state. The Court employed the traditional four-part proportionality review. Examining whether the funding prohibition had a legitimate aim; whether it was rationally connected to that aim; whether a less intrusive measure could have been used; and where the prohibition struck a fair balance between the women of Norther Ireland and the interests of the community. The purpose in excluding Northern Irish women from accessing funding for abortion when in England was to protect the devolved health system. The power to enact certain laws and policies was devolved from Westminster to legislative bodies in Wales, Scotland and Northern Ireland. Geographic differences are inherent in devolution and a cornerstone of the UK constitution. The Court accepted that the funding prohibition met this test and was justified, its application of the criteria is explored further in chapter five. The equality-stage determined the answer to the limitation analysis. By framing the inequality as based exclusively on geography, the equality-stage pulled in tandem with the justification for limiting that equality, protecting a constitutional structure that permits geographic differences. Unsurprisingly, a geographic inequality did not outweigh devolution, a geographic power-sharing agreement. Bringing a full accounting of the gendered nature of the prohibition in relation to the state's limitation claim would have shifted the analytical question. Rather than asking whether geographic differences were permissible to protect devolution the question becomes whether it is fair to require Northern Irish women to bear harm to their sexual and reproductive health to protect devolution? The justification-stage would no longer focus on fairness between Northern Ireland and England but whether it is fair for Northern Irish women to shoulder the intimate, grave and potentially long-ranging costs to protect the UK's constitutional system. By stripping gender out of the equality-stage, by diluting the complexity of inequality against women, the UK Supreme Court used the equality-stage to tilt the justification-stage towards upholding the prohibition.

IV. CONCLUSION

Justification dilutes the equality-stage resulting in a façade of an equality analysis. When courts draw on limitation concepts, tests or criteria to evaluate whether

[121] ibid.
[122] ibid [59].

the law is in breach of the constitutional guarantee of equality, the analysis becomes a defence of the law or policy. Limitation reasoning is simply unable to unearth and understand why a law breaches equality rights as it cannot evaluate whether the law demeans, stigmatises, marginalises, oppresses or disadvantages women. The seeping of justification into the equality-stage permits judges to ignore the hardships and suffering the law imposes on women's lives. This in turn tilts the analysis towards finding no breach of equality rights regardless of the gravity of the inequality or the weakness of the justification arguments. The equality-stage can also be shaped to defeat women's claims at the justification-stage and how the judicial re-telling of women's inequality can camouflage its depth and seriousness. This glossing over serves a purpose at the justification-stage as it eases limitation burdens. The next chapter explores what tools are available to protect the equality-stage from being warped by justification.

3

The Protective Function of Substantive Equality

I. INTRODUCTION

IT IS IMPERATIVE to maintain a strong boundary between equality and justification when adjudicating whether there is a violation of women's right to equality. This argument is salient not only for jurisdictions with a clearly demarcated equality-stage and justification-stage but also for jurisdictions that blur these stages. This is because when justification doctrines bleed into assessing equality wrongs, courts struggle to account for the gravity and severity of the impact of the impugned law on women and repeatedly fail to grapple with the gendered nature of that impact. This results in courts giving limited constitutional weight to women's equality regardless of the marginal benefits of the competing objective or the magnitude of the gendered harms perpetuated by that law. How can the integrity of the equality-stage be protected? There are a range of measures that could be taken. Building on the doctrinal mapping in chapter two, which identified a correlation between the bleeding of justification into the equality-stage with formal equality, this chapter argues that substantive equality can best protect the equality-stage from this bleeding.

Substantive equality has revolutionised equality law. It arose from a frustration with formal equality which conceptualised equality exclusively in terms of consistency. Women were either similarly or different than men and if women were categorised as different it was constitutionally permissible to treat women differently, and invariably, worse. Formal equality has many flaws. It erases women's antecedent disadvantage, fails to identify when similar or differential treatment is required, ignores the differential impacts of similar treatment, fails to grapple with women's intersectional identities and is a mask for norms and structures built around men's experiences. Substantive equality infuses equality with normative aims and values, although there are strong debates in theory and in practice on what those normative value(s) should be. As canvassed in chapter one, some courts will hold there has been a breach of women's equality rights when the measure in question widens disadvantage, while others, for example, will test whether the measure perpetuates gendered stereotypes. Substantive equality has brought a profound change to the equality-stage, but what it means for the relationship between the equality-stage and justification-stage has not been the subject of serious attention. This chapter makes two claims on how substantive equality can protect both the equality-stage and the justification-stage.

First, substantive equality provides a complete set of analytical tools when determining if there is a breach of the right to equality such that there is no need to borrow any from the justification-stage. Substantive equality blocks the equality-stage from being warped by limitation criteria and prevents the harms of inequality against women from being pushed out to the margins. Using substantive equality as an analytical frame means that when assessing if the alleged inequality breaches constitutional rights courts do not need to assess the legitimacy of the competing law, its rationality or necessity or whether there is a fair balance between equality rights and the competing objective. Instead, courts must focus on determining whether there is a substantive breach of women's equality, and only after on whether such a breach can be justified.

Arguing that substantive equality operates as a bulwark against justification concepts infecting the equality-stage should not be read as arguing for a universal concept of substantive equality. In the jurisdictions studied in this monograph, there are overlapping yet still distinct approaches to substantive equality. Protecting justification form bleeding into the equality-stage does not require a specific model of substantive equality to be adopted. All that is required is that the court explore the substantive wrongs, however defined or understood in that jurisdiction, rather than use the equality-stage to covertly defend the choice to prioritise other objectives or values. When a substantive equality framework is adopted, courts are not pulled into evaluating whether the law is justified at the equality-stage but are focused on whether it perpetuates or re-entrenches gendered equality harms.

Second, to protect against limitation concepts creating barriers at the equality-stage and to set up a fair justification assessment, substantive equality must be robustly utilised and applied. This is needed first and foremost so that women's lives are accurately reflected in the jurisprudence, but it also ensures that the equality-stage operates as a necessary ballast against claims that it should be permissible to restrict women's rights. Without comprehensively identifying the inequalities perpetuated by the law, there is a lack of clarity on what harms need to be justified and there is a paucity of counterarguments to test the strengths of the limitation arguments. As argued in chapter two, skirting over the gendered equality harms in the prohibition on accessing social benefits at the equality-stage, concealed the gendered stereotypes embedded in the state's justification claims. This chapter explores how a robust and comprehensive substantive equality analysis can provide the foundational knowledge on the extent of the burdens the law imposes on women and how this knowledge can positively shape the justification-stage. How this knowledge can be utilised to guide and enrich the justification-stage is further developed in Part II of this book. Although it is not inherent that a fully developed substantive equality analysis will reveal a breach of the right to equality, if the analysis does identify a breach, the robustness protects against the justification arguments being accepted at face-value.

This chapter concludes by taking a step back and considering the theoretical and practical implications flowing from the findings and the arguments made across chapters two and three. On the theoretical side, there are arguments that rights are of minimal significance in comparison to justification, as it is at the justification-stage where the contours of rights are established.[1] Yet in the context of women's equality, it is perilous to diminish the importance of the equality-stage. It can result in inequality against women being erased and could jeopardise the fairness of the justification-stage. Women's equality rights matter to justification. The limitation analysis must know the costs women are being asked to bear before deciding if those costs are worth it. On the practical side, in some jurisdictions there are a range of barriers to adopting the arguments in this chapter and chapter two. A clearer understanding of the protective function of substantive equality will hopefully provide further impetus for needed doctrinal developments.

II. JUSTIFICATION MUST NOT APPLY

When justification concepts are deployed at the equality-stage this twists the analysis, making it significantly more challenging for women to successfully argue that their rights have been infringed. This dilution correlates with employing a formalistic and abstract model of equality. Adopting a substantive model protects the equality-stage from becoming a covert assessment of the rationales for pursuing the law. Substantive equality operates as a bulwark against justification and protects the equality-stage from being diluted. Across the United Kingdom (UK), India, the United States (US), Canada and South Africa, courts have developed unique understandings of substantive equality. These differences are irrelevant to the protective function substantive equality can serve. All that is required is moving away from the sameness–difference paradigm and then it can be determined whether there is a breach of women's equality rights without reference to justification criteria. To analyse how substantive equality protects the equality-stage from the hazards of justification concepts, this section does not assess whether a specific understanding of substantive equality is used. Instead, it examines how courts employ the hallmarks of substantive equality reasoning, attention to histories, social realities, gendered norms, institutions, contexts and impacts[2] – to argue that it offers a complete analytical toolkit

[1] Mattias Kumm, 'The Idea of Socratic Contestation and the Right to Justification: The Point of Rights-Based Proportionality Review' (2010) 4(2) *Law and Ethics of Human Rights* 141; Kai Möller, 'The Right to Justification and the Culture of Justification' in Neha Jain and Mila Versteeg (eds), *The Oxford Handbook of Comparative Human Rights Law* (Oxford University Press, 2025).

[2] Simone Cusack and Lisa Pusey, 'CEDAW and the Rights to Equality and Non-Discrimination' (2013) 14 *Melbourne Journal of International Law* 54, 64; Colleen Sheppard, *Inclusive Equality* (McGill-Queen's University Press, 2010) ch 3.

such that there is no need for courts to reach across to the justification-stage to borrow concepts to determine whether there is a breach of equality rights.

Notably, removing justification out of the equality-stage shifts the outcome of the claim. When the focal point of the equality-stage is the substantive gender harms and no weight is given to justification, the courts tend to find a violation of the right to equality. Whereas when courts adopt a formalistic approach, using justification concepts as the analytic touchstone for whether an inequality exists, it is more likely, as argued in chapter two, that the courts will not find a breach of the right to equality. This is not to hold that it is impossible for women's inequality to be justifiably limited, but prior to the justification exercise, there needs to be a full understanding of what needs to be justified: the inequality against women.

A. Equality in Family Life

i. The Unfairness of Marriage Laws

Marriage and inheritance laws continue to reflect patriarchal understandings of women's role within the family and within public life. Women in certain forms of intimate partnerships have been excluded from the protection of marriage laws. This can have devastating economic consequences for these women and entrench gendered stereotypes. Yet, as argued in chapter two, the Canadian Supreme Court in *Nova Scotia (Attorney General) v Walsh*[3] and *Quebec v A*[4] and the South African Constitutional Court in *Volks v Robinson*[5] used the equality-stage to defend the decision to protect marriage. A core justification concept, the legitimacy of the law was used in these judgments to hold that since the exclusion of de facto intimate partner unions aimed to protect autonomy there was no inequality. By latching onto limitation rationales at the equality-stage, these courts failed to grasp how these marriage laws have been used to buttress gender hierarchies, and in the context of South Africa, also racial and religious subordination. A series of more recent decisions from the South African Constitutional Court and dissenting judgments from the Canadian Supreme Court have shifted the equality-stage away from a stealth justification of the status quo in the family. Using substantive equality, these judgments zero in on the impact of marriage laws on women's lives.

Turning first to South Africa, marriage, inheritance and family life laws were and continue to be deeply enmeshed with colonialism and apartheid domination.[6] According inferior legal status to family life between non-married

[3] *Nova Scotia (Attorney General) v Walsh* [2002] 4 SCR 325.

[4] *Quebec v A* [2013] 1 SCR 61.

[5] *Volks v Robinson* [2005] ZACC 2.

[6] Elsje Bonthuys, 'Pluralist Marriage Laws in a Former Colonial System: Cultural Authenticity or Hybridisation?' (2020) 34 *International Journal of Law, Policy, and the Family* 84.

persons, African persons, Muslims and Hindus was part of the state's apparatus to maintain racial, religious and gender systems of supremacy. Under the democratic constitution, Muslim women, women in de facto intimate partner unions and women living and married under customary law argued that their exclusion from personal status laws breached the right to equality.[7] With the exception of *Volks*, discussed in chapter two, these claims have all been upheld by the Court. Unpacking how the Court sealed off the equality-stage from justification in these cases, requires an understanding of South African constitutional equality law.

At first glance, the substantive equality framework in South Africa appears primed to permit justification to seep into the equality-stage. Section 9(3) prohibits unfair discrimination and discrimination based on sex or gender is presumptively unfair.[8] While the South African Constitutional Court is unequivocal that equality in section 9 of the Constitution is substantive and that a core constitutional goal is to achieve 'substantive equality between men and women',[9] in assessing unfairness, however, there appears to be a borrowing of concepts from the justification-stage. Unfairness can be demonstrated by assessing, inter alia, the purpose of the law.[10] This can be weaponised as per Justice Ngcobo in *Volks*. Married and non-married people were different and since the purpose of this difference was to enhance autonomous choices there was no unfairness and no breach of the equality rights in the Constitution.[11] This was a covert justification assessment that examined the legitimacy of the state's aims. But adopting a substantive equality framework would radically shift how this factor should be used at the equality-stage. Under section 9(3), along with investigating the nature of the discriminating law, the Court must also look at the past patterns of disadvantage, the position of the complaint in society and the dignity impacts and it has repeatedly stressed that the thrust of the section 9(3) analysis is the impact of the law.[12] At the equality-stage, the purpose of the law analysis should be directed towards understanding the impacts of the law on women. What does the purpose reveal about gendered power relations, the history of oppression, material conditions, as well as different forms of vulnerability, stigmatisation,

[7] *Daniels v Campbell* [2004] ZACC 14; *Bhe v Khayelitsha* [2004] ZACC 17l; *Shilbuna v Shilbuna* [2008] ZACC 9; *Gumede v President of the Republic of South Africa* [2008] ZACC 23; *Hassam v Jacobs* [2009] ZACC 19; *Mayelane v Ngwenyama* [2013] ZACC 14; *Ramuhovhi v President of the Republic of South Africa* [2017] ZACC 41; *Moosa v Minister of Justice and Correctional Services* [2018] ZACC 19; *Bwanya v Master of the High Court* [2021] ZACC 51; *Women's Legal Centre Trust v President of the Republic of South Africa* [2022] ZACC 23.

[8] Catherine Albertyn and Beth Goldblatt, 'Equality' in Stu Woolman and Michael Bishop (eds), *Constitutional Law of South Africa*, 2nd edn (Juta, 2013).

[9] *Daniels* (n 7) [22].

[10] *Harksen v Lane* [1997] SACC 12 [50]; Pierre de Vos, *South African Constitutional Law in Context*, 2nd edn (Oxford University Press, 2022) 505.

[11] *Volks* (n 5) [88].

[12] *KG v Minister of Home Affairs; EB v ER* [2023] ZACC 32 [130].

social exclusion, stereotyping and violence.[13] This is different to how purpose is used at justification, as it is not an examination of the properness or legitimacy of the law's aim. It is a contextual and sociolegal analysis, key methods for any substantive equality analysis, that seeks to use the nature of the discriminating law to illuminate its impact on women's lives. A purpose analysis that is inherently connected to substantive equality protects the equality-stage from being diluted by justification reasoning. The marriage equality decisions from the South African Constitutional Court illuminate this argument.

These cases firmly rejected that a simple examination of the worthiness of the law's objective was analytically relevant to assessing whether the measure perpetuates unfair discrimination against women. Justice Tlaletsi in *Women's Legal Centre Trust v President of the Republic of South Africa* commented that assessing whether the Marriage Act, which excluded Muslim marriages from legal protection, enhanced autonomy in family life did not answer whether the law unfairly discriminated against women.[14] In *Bwanya v Master of the High Court*,[15] which overturned *Volks* and included permanent life partnerships in the Maintenance of Surviving Spouses Act, the South African Constitutional Court did not assess the legitimacy of the exclusion of these unions at the equality-stage. Justice Madlanga dismissed the analytical relevance of justification-like arguments at the equality-stage, observing that 'whether parties to permanent life partnerships choose not to marry is the wrong question to ask'.[16] In a similar vein, when assessing a prohibition that applied to civil marriages conducted after November 1984 which prevented courts from ordering an equitable distribution of property upon divorce, Justice Rogers soundly rejected examining the worthiness of the purpose in imposing the time limits. Although the primary reason for the prohibition at stake in *KG v Minister of Home Affairs*[17] was to protect individual choice with respect to marriage and property, he concluded that this reason 'was not necessarily sufficient to render discrimination on the basis of gender fair … the lawmaker's emphasis on choice cannot be decisive in the fairness enquiry'.[18] In all these cases, the South African Constitutional Court refused to conduct a limitation-like analysis at the equality-stage and did not draw a straight line between the purported objective of the law and the fairness of the discrimination.

However, the Court in these cases did not ignore the doctrinal requirement under section 9(3) to consider the nature of the discriminating law, but utilised it to deepen and strengthen the substantive equality analysis, thereby drawing on substantive equality to protect against justification. In *Women's Legal Centre*

[13] Albertyn and Goldblatt (n 8) 77–78.
[14] *Women's Legal Centre Trust* (n 7) [56].
[15] *Bwanya* (n 7).
[16] ibid [68].
[17] *KG* (n 12).
[18] ibid [131].

Trust and *Bwanya*, the Court examined the historical context of the legislation, noting that the non-recognition of customary and Muslim marriages was 'the result of racism'[19] and that the exclusion of de facto intimate partner unions stemmed from dominant conservative religious ideologies.[20] In *Women's Legal Centre Trust*, Justice Tlaletsi observed that Muslim marriages were perceived as immoral and not according 'with so-called "civilised" religious practices'.[21] This animus and 'deep-rooted prejudice ... ethnocentric bias and arrogance' towards Muslim marriages explained the law's silence.[22] Understanding the historical context of the law sharpened the impact analysis as it directed the Court to investigate the material and social impacts of this codified revulsion and suspicion. Due to patriarchal social practices, family property was owned and controlled by men. Women, who bore the responsibility for childcare, found it more challenging 'to receive income and acquire property'.[23] In 'a society dominated by men' women were forced to rely 'on the financial strength of men'[24] and must accept men's decisions on the status of their relationships. Muslim women and women in de facto intimate partner unions would bear the socioeconomic burdens of the non-recognition of their relationships. Their lack of control over family assets coupled with the lack of legal protection meant that at relationship breakdown these women would face 'significant and material disadvantage'[25] that could result in potential 'dependence and ... homelessness'.[26] It was these factors in tandem – legislative animus towards certain unions and the legal indifference to the socioeconomic precarity of women in these unions – that lead the Court in both *Women's Legal Centre Trust* and *Bwanya* to hold the exclusion was demeaning and in breach of the commitment to substantive equality.

There was a similar substantive equality approach to the purpose in *KG*. With respect to the temporal limit on equitable divorce orders, the Court did not examine the purpose of excluding marriages after 1984, but the underlying motivations that animated bringing in the remedial provision. This also required a historical and sociolegal understanding of how marital property laws functioned, which is different than assessing the legitimacy of the law as would be done at the limitation stage.[27] The substantive equality analysis identified how in the past marriages that were community out property (broadly understood as the parties being financially independent of each other and no joint ownership of marital property) did not have an accrual regime and that the remedial order provision sought to provide economic relief upon divorce for

[19] *Bwanya* (n 7) [58], [194]; *Women's Legal Centre Trust* (n 7) [43].
[20] *Volks* (n 5) [188].
[21] *Women's Legal Centre Trust* (n 7) [43].
[22] *Daniels* (n 7) [74].
[23] ibid [22].
[24] *Bwanya* (n 7) [62]–[63].
[25] *Hassam* (n 7) [33].
[26] *Daniels* (n 7) [22].
[27] *KG* (n 12) [103].

these types of marriages. Capturing the nature of this law assisted in crystallising the impact analysis, required under the substantive equality framework, as it directed the Court towards assessing the economic impact of the exclusion on marriages conducted after 1984. Despite shifts in gender norms and roles, the evidence indicated that women continued to 'enter into marriage poorer and more dependent than man and therefore have less bargaining power' and due to persistent gendered constraints in the labour market, the burden of childcare and risks of violence within marriage, women remained in economically weaker positions.[28] Again, it was the combination of a contextual understanding of the law and the contemporary realities of women's lives that resulted in Justice Rogers concluding that withholding relief despite a gendered need for the judicial remedy was unfair and in breach of section 9.[29]

This use of purpose was similar to the dissenting opinion of Justice O'Connor in *Nguyen v Immigration and Naturalization Services (INS)* as discussed in chapter two.[30] She examined the sociocultural norms that motivated the gendered history of citizenship laws to conclude that different naturalisation laws between mothers and fathers was a continuation of gender cultural attitudes that assigned the primary care of children to women. In both *Nguyen* and *KG*, a substantive equality investigation into the context of legislative purpose was used to better understand gendered impacts, structures, assumptions and norms.

In all of the marriage equality cases, the South African Constitutional Court did not seek to assess the legitimacy of the law's purpose or use that legitimacy to explicate whether there was a breach of women's equality. Instead, it linked the purpose of the law to substantive equality, undertaking a contextual analysis, that unpacked the historical sociocultural norms at stake in the law. It then connected these norms to the impact on women to provide a complete analysis as to whether there was a breach of section 9 of the Constitution that was disconnected from the limitation analysis.

ii. The Indignity and Disadvantage of Marriage Laws

The South African Constitutional Court, using a substantive equality analysis, assessed women's claim for equality without reference to justification. The dissenting opinions in the marriage equality cases in the Canadian Supreme Court also analysed the exclusion of de facto intimate partner unions using a substantive model of equality without drawing on the limitation framework under section 1 of the Canadian Charter. In doing so, the dissents deviated from the majority judgments in *Walsh* and *Quebec v A*, which relied heavily on the purported ameliorative aims of excluding these unions from marital property

[28] ibid [122]–[123].
[29] ibid [130]–[143].
[30] *Nguyen v Immigration and Naturalization Services (INS)* 533 US 53 (2001).

regimes to hold there was no breach of section 15 of the Charter. The dissenting Canadian judgments adopted a different substantive equality framework than the South African Constitutional Court, employing dignity (*Walsh*) and disadvantage (*Quebec v A*). But similar to the South African Constitutional Court, the dissenting opinions did not resort to justification concepts. To protect the equality-stage from being infiltrated by justification it is not required to adopt a specific model of substantive equality, rather what is needed is to use substantive equality, with whatever normative underpinning given by the court, to explore the history, context, social realities and impact of the law on women.

In *Walsh*, Justice L'Heureux-Dubé did not use the equality-stage to assess the legitimacy or pressing and substantive objective underpinning the exclusion.[31] In this case de facto intimate partner unions were excluded from the Nova Scotia Matrimonial Property Act (MPA). The doctrinal framework for section 15 at the time equated substantive equality with dignity, and the dignity analysis required considering whether the MPA had an ameliorative purpose. Unlike the majority decision which myopically latched on the legitimacy of the exclusion in protecting autonomy, Justice L'Heureux-Dubé reframed the purpose of the MPA, holding its objective was protecting against economic precarity upon relationship breakdown. The fact that the state claimed its decision to exclusively protect marriage was designed to protect the individual choice to marry or not to marry had no analytical weight for Justice L'Heureux-Dubé at the equality-stage. She took a more substantive approach, exploring the historical context of marital property laws, concluding these laws were in place to recognise the legally and culturally undervalued gendered labour performed in the home.[32] Similar to Justice Rogers in *KG*, she adopted a substantive approach to the purpose analysis, refusing to adopt limitation-like reasoning at the equality-stage. Also, in alignment with *KG*, she then used this equality-driven purpose assessment to sharpen her substantive equality analysis. Besides ameliorative purpose, the equality framework at the time also required considering the nature of the interest affected. It was against the backdrop of the invisibility of women's labour, that Justice L'Heureux-Dube assessed the impact of the exclusion. While women in married and de facto unions were similarly at risk of poverty at relationship breakdown, the law ignored the economic risks for women in de facto unions.[33] From this Justice L'Heureux-Dubé determined that the exclusion from marital property law perpetuated that belief that individuals in de facto union were 'less worthy of respect and consideration'.[34]

A decade later in *Quebec v A*, the Canadian Supreme Court again had to consider the exclusion of non-registered de facto unions from marital

[31] *Walsh* (n 3).
[32] ibid [105]–[117].
[33] ibid [107], [108], [116]–[120].
[34] ibid [118].

property regimes.[35] At this point, the Canadian Supreme Court had moved away from dignity as the touchstone for determining a breach of the right to equality. Section 15 claims were adjudicated by examining whether the law disadvantaged women, with disadvantage being understood broadly.[36] The state's purpose in excluding these unions did not answer the question as to whether the exclusion widened disadvantage. Despite this, Justice LeBel in the leading judgment, utilised the salutary purpose of the law, protecting choice, to conclude it did not perpetuate disadvantage. The faults in this reasoning were analysed in depth in chapter two. Justice Abella in dissent chastised the majority in *Quebec v A* for permitting justification concepts to creep into the equality-stage. She warned that 'an emphasis at this stage on whether the … exclusion was well motivated or reasonable is inconsistent with [a] substantive equality approach … since it redirects the analysis from the *impact* of the distinction ….to the legislatures *intent* or *purpose*'.[37] She clarified that 'the assessment of the legislative purpose is an important part of a Charter analysis, but it is conducted under section 1, the justification section.[38] The equality-stage should not become a surreptitious justification evaluation.

Justice Abella explained that the equality-stage should be a 'flexible and contextual inquiry into whether a distinction has the effect of perpetuating arbitrary disadvantage'.[39] Although there is no requirement under the disadvantage framework to examine the purpose of the law, she placed marital property laws in context so as to better understand the substantive impacts of the exclusion. Her dissent began by reviewing 'the reasons motivating the development of the modern approach to spousal support'.[40] The law in Quebec had evolved to redress gendered economic vulnerability at relationship breakdown.[41] Justice Abella held 'this is the history that animates [the] s 15 inquiry'.[42] It directed the equality-stage towards assessing the current economic impacts of excluded non-registered de facto unions from the Quebec Civil Code. She traced the gender power relations in marriage and the economic consequences of relationship breakdown. De facto unions, Justice Abella observed, have a high degree of financial interdependence and upon breakdown, due to the gender division of labour in the home, 'a disproportionate number of women … experienced poverty'.[43] The economic and social disadvantage of women in de facto unions perpetuated by the non-recognition of these relationships amounted to disadvantage, Justice Abella concluded, which infringed the right to equality. Drawing on

[35] *Quebec* (n 4).
[36] ibid [331].
[37] ibid [333].
[38] ibid.
[39] ibid [331].
[40] ibid [292].
[41] ibid [293]–[318].
[42] ibid [319].
[43] ibid [300], [308], [313].

her analysis of the purpose of marital property laws, she held 'the disadvantage this exclusion perpetuates is a historic one, it continues to deny de facto spouses economic remedies … considered indispensable for the protection of married … spouses'.[44] A limitation-like analysis of the purpose of these laws was not used to analyse whether there was a breach of section 15. Justice Abella did not assess the legitimacy of the exclusion at the equality-stage but used purpose in alignment with substantive equality, drawing on the sociolegal contextual history of marriage laws to better understand the gendered socioeconomic impacts of the exclusion.

B. Equality in Pay, Promotion and Pensions

Women's inequality in the workplace is routinely minimised using justification doctrines at the equality-stage. As argued in chapter two, legislation which tolerated women's unequal pay have been held not to breach the right to equality as the state had an ameliorative purpose (dissenting in *Quebec v Alliance du personnel professional et technique de la santé at des services sociaux*).[45] Or commendable high-level policies guaranteeing women's equality at work were accepted by courts as accurately describing the on-the-ground situation and used to deny women's claims to equality despite the multitude of evidence of gender bias in pay and promotion (*Wal-Mart v Dukes*[46]). The logic or necessity of the basic tenets of employment structures, such as wage labour, were used to conclude that workplace policies do not constitutionally violate women's equality when they fail to account for women's role in reproduction (dissenting opinions in *Young v UPS* and *Fraser v Canada*[47]). The fear that protecting women's equality at work will have a chilling effect, causing legislative bodies to think twice before embarking on any social justice initiatives, has also been the basis for concluding, that on balance, there was no infringement of equality rights (dissenting in *Alliance*). The legitimacy of the state's aims, the rationality or necessity of the law and the calculation of costs-benefits in pursuing the state's aims, are elements of a justification assessment. Yet these elements were used time and again to erase the severity and gravity of women's inequality at work to the point where there was no legal recognition of that inequality.

Employing substantive equality when assessing alleged inequalities at work, isolates justification from the equality-stage and prevents it from distorting the analysis. Several majority and dissenting judgments in the US, India and Canada have adjudicated women's claims for equality at work in this substantive manner.

[44] ibid [349].

[45] *Quebec v Alliance du personnel professional et technique de la santé at des services sociaux* [2018] 1 SCR 464.

[46] *Wal-Mart v Dukes* 564 US 338 (2011).

[47] *Young v UPS* 575 US___(2015); *Fraser v Canada (Attorney General)* (2020) SCC 28 64.

They explore the history of marginalising women within formal employment structures, contemporary cultural attitudes on women's role in care and how this impacts labour force participation. This prevents the equality-stage from being distracted by whether the employment law or policy is a permissible limit and directs the analysis to whether there has been a breach of women's equality rights. While these courts apply different analytical tests for substantive equality, with some courts focusing in on gender stereotypes at work and others on institutional employment structures, uniting these judgments is a shunning of justification concepts at the equality-stage.

i. Gender Stereotypes at Work

Wal-Mart's pay and promotion decisions were delegated to local managers. The discretion was broad as there were no formal criteria to guide decision-making. Women filed a class action against Wal-Mart claiming that this neutral policy perpetuated the gender pay gap and job segregation in breach of Title VII, which prohibited sex discrimination at work. For the class action to be certified, the US Supreme Court had to be satisfied that there was commonality in discrimination at work. This required the Court to conduct a prima facie equality-like analysis to determine if the proposed class had a common experience of inequality such that it could be certified. The majority opinion of Justice Scalia in *Wal-Mart*, however, used justification concepts, particularly the ameliorative aim of Wal-Mart's internal policies, to erase the common experience of discrimination at work. He held that there was no significant proof of discrimination as 'Wal-Mart's announced policy forbids sex discrimination' and it 'imposes penalties for denials of equal employment opportunity'.[48] As argued in chapter two, the salutary purpose of the umbrella, high-level policy, prohibiting sex discrimination, played a pivotal role in concluding that there was no evidence that the specific policy, granting discretion to local managers, resulted in a common experience of gender bias in pay and promotion. Justice Ginsburg, in dissent, however, did not get diverted by justification concepts when evaluating whether there was a common experience of discrimination against women at work. While the US Supreme Court has yet to develop a robust understanding of substantive equality,[49] Justice Ginsberg in dissent in *Wal-Mart* implicitly adopted a substantive approach as she explored the impact of the unfettered discretion.

The quantitative data revealed that women earned less than man, even when they performed the same jobs and women were concentrated into hourly waged labour.[50] A regression analysis demonstrated that the gender pay gap

[48] *Wal-Mart* (n 46) 353.

[49] Cary Franklin, 'The Anti-Stereotyping Principle in Constitutional Sex Discrimination Law' (2009) 85 (83) *New York University Law Review* 83, 152.

[50] *Wal-Mart* (n 46) 369–72.

and job segregation were not happenstance but could only be explained by discrimination.[51] The qualitative evidence also revealed how managerial discretion was infected with gender bias. The claimants marshalled over 100 incidents of managers making 'explicit sex-based comments or admit[ing] paying women less because they believed men deserved more money'.[52] The commonality of discrimination assessment in Justice Ginsburg's dissent did not accept at face-value that employment policies that prohibited discrimination against women matched the reality of working at Wal-Mart. A workplace policy with a good purpose did not prevent the breach of women's equality rights in practice. She traced how the specific policy operated in practice and in doing so was able to identify the powerful role that gender stereotypes played. Arguments on whether the grant of discretion could be justified would only be relevant when the litigation moved squarely to adjudicate the Title VII claim. At the preliminary class action certification stage, justifications for the unfettered grant of discretion were irrelevant and worked to dilute the harms of that policy. Justice Ginsberg correctly ignored them in her dissent in *Wal-Mart*. By shifting the assessment away from the employer's aim, Justice Ginsberg was able to identify how gendered prejudice, stereotypes and negative cultural attitudes perverted the operation of the grant of discretion.

ii. Systemic Oppression at Work

It is not only negative cultural attitudes towards women that perpetuates their inequality at work. Employment structures, such as promotion criteria and pension entitlements, are designed around the needs and interests of men. Traditionally, women have either found ways to adhere to these structures or borne the burdens of non-conformity. Women are now turning to the courts to argue that employment institutions are perpetuating systemic oppression in violation of their right to be equal. When justification concepts or doctrines seep into assessing whether promotion criteria or pension entitlements infringe equality rights this can re-enforce the normalcy of highly gendered systems. A substantive equality analysis, on the other hand, can accurately diagnosis whether the design of institutions marginalises, stigmatises, and impoverishes women. Leading judgments from the Indian and Canadian Supreme Court used substantive equality to ring-fence the equality-stage from analysing whether the employment structures are legitimate, rational, necessary or on balance worth limiting women's equality.

For decades, women had been banned from obtaining permanent commissions in the Indian army and this ban was struck down by the Indian Supreme

[51] ibid 372.

[52] Deborah Thompson Eisenberg, '*Wal-Mart Stores v Dukes*: Lessons for the Legal Quest for Equal Pay' (2012) 46 *New England Law Review* 229, 233.

Court as unconstitutional.[53] Women on short service commissions could then apply for permanent commissions. However, the exact same promotion criteria that were used for men when they applied in their 20s and 30 was now being used for women, who because of the long-standing promotion prohibition, were now applying for promotion in their 50s and 60s. Women on short service commissions argued that the failure to modify promotion standards in light of the long history of excluding women from permanent commissions was indirectly discriminatory and in breach of Articles 14 and 15 of the Indian Constitution. *Lieutenant Colonel Nitisha v Union of India* is an intriguing case for exploring how substantive equality protects against the justification-stage bleeding into the equality-stage as it is a landmark decision where the Indian Supreme Court began to develop a more discrete equality-stage.[54]

Traditionally, the Indian Supreme Court has eschewed delving into and articulating why a law or policy violates the right to equality; instead, it has examined the rationality of the state's choices, a concept endemic to the justification-stage. Article 14 guarantees equal benefit and protection of the law to all people and Article 15 holds the state shall not discriminate on the grounds of religion, race, case, sex or place of birth. There is no specific provision in the Constitution permitting the state to limit rights. Articles 14 and 15 evolved into, what has been described as, the reasonable classification and the non-arbitrary tests.[55] The courts have traditionally explored whether there was 'intelligible differentia' for treating women differently and whether there was a rational basis to conclude that drawing those differences would achieve the objective of the law.[56] The right to equality under the Indian Constitution centred on the state's reasons and defences for the law and equality was devoid of any real meaning.[57]

This justification-centred approach to equality would be inadequate to analyse whether the promotion criteria in *Nitisha* was a breach of Articles 14 and 15. The promotion policy required women to have positive performance reviews and meet physical fitness standards. Demanding positive performance reviews for promotion was not irrational or arbitrary, nor was meeting physical fitness requirements un-intelligible. The promotion structure was designed to ensure highly qualified staff were in prestigious positions of authority. Failing to substantively assess the gendered impact of the identical application of promotion criteria and only focusing on the desirability of that criteria would erase how employment hierarchies can marginalise women, particularly older women. Without a dedicated equality assessment and only relying on justification-like

[53] *Secretary Ministry of Defense v Babita Puniya* (2020) 7 SCC 469.

[54] *Lieutenant Colonel Nitisha v Union of India* 2021 SCC OnLine SC 261.

[55] Shreya Atrey, 'Feminist Constitutionalism: Mapping a Discourse in Contestation' (2022) *International Journal of Constitutional Law*.

[56] Tarunabh Khaitan, 'Equality: Legislative Review Under Article 14' in Sujit Choudry and others (eds), *The Oxford Handbook of the Indian Constitution* (Oxford University Press, 2016) 701.

[57] Atrey (n 55); Lalit Panda, 'Rationality By Any Other Name: Common Principles for an Evolving Equality Code' (2023) 10 *Indian Journal of Constitutional Law* 200.

reasoning, the nature and extent of structural oppression would remain hidden. Moreover, the assessment must be rooted in women's substantive equality. If the Court had adopted a formalistic approach, there is a risk, as argued in chapter two, that this would have collapsed into a covert justification assessment and the equality-stage would still be a defence of the promotion criteria.

Justice Chandrachud, for the unanimous Court in *Nitisha*, however, avoided these pitfalls and evolved a more discrete equality-stage under Articles 14 and 15. This was grounded in substantive equality and was devoid of justification concepts or doctrines. He emphasised that the guarantee of equality in the Indian Constitution was substantive. The Court held that there was a breach of the equality provisions in the Constitution if the law or policy, even a neutral policy like promotion criteria, disadvantaged women. Justice Chandrachud adopted the disadvantage framework originated by Justice Abella in *Fraser v Canada*, discussed below. The Indian Supreme Court adopted an expansive understanding of disadvantage that included economic, social, psychological, physical, political, and historical disadvantage.[58] Notably the purpose of the law, its rationality or necessity were absent from the definition of substantive equality. Justice Chandrachud interrogated how the consistent application of promotion criteria disadvantaged women without reference to any justification for the continued use of those criteria.

The various promotion requirements were complex but two are worth zoning in on for the purposes of this chapter. Positive annual confidential reports during the fifth and tenth year of service were required to be submitted when applying for a permanent commission. Women struggled to produce positive reports in their promotion application. Due to the ban that had only recently been lifted on women holding permanent commissions, their annual confidential reports were filled out in a casual and lackadaisical manner. Women were disincentivised from participating in career progression opportunities as prior to the ban lifting they could never progress beyond a short service commission. The army refused to modify the promotion criteria to, for example, take account of women's achievements beyond the fifth and tenth year of service. Justice Chandrachud concluded that the formulaic application of the pre-existing criteria froze 'an unjust status quo' and blocked women who had served with distinction from promotion.[59] Women, who due to the prohibition, were applying later in life for a promotion, also had to meet medical-fitness standards designed for men who applied for promotion typically when they would be between 25 to 30 years old. Justice Chandrachud held that 'a retrospective application of the supposedly uniform standards' caused 'serious hardship' for women.[60] The legitimacy, rationality, necessity, or value of the promotion criteria was beside the point

[58] *Nitisha* (n 54) citing *Fraser* (n 47) [66], [77].
[59] ibid [44], [66].
[60] ibid [105], [112].

for the Indian Supreme Court when determining whether those criteria violated women's equality. A discrete substantive equality assessment that zoned in on the 'systemic impact of the prolonged denial of permanent commissions to women' revealed how the purported logic and desirability of the criteria operated to lock women out of career development and progression.[61] The Indian Supreme Court was only able to wrestle with the structural discrimination against women by conducting a substantive equality analysis that focused not on the reasons why the army has promotion criteria but the impact of these criteria on women.

The Canadian Supreme Court also considered systemic oppression at work, specifically the design of pension systems and in *Fraser v Canada*, Justice Abella examined this claim using substantive equality without any reference to the *Oakes* justification test.[62] The Royal Canadian Mounted Police (RCMP) introduced job-sharing to allow employees to balance work-life commitments. The vast majority of employees who took advantage of the job-sharing scheme were women with childcare responsibilities. While the programme permitted women to remain connected to the workforce, it negatively impacted their pension entitlements. There was a buy-back scheme, where employees who had gone on different forms of leave could buy back pension credits, but this scheme was not open to job-sharers. Using substantive equality, Justice Abella found there was a breach of the Charter. By employing a disadvantage framework, she was able to identify how the pension scheme exacerbated women's economic and social oppression. Substantive equality protected the equality-stage from being distorted by justification and in doing so brought to the fore structural violations of section 15 of the Charter.

Akin to the Indian and South African Constitutional Court, to understand whether there was a breach of the right, Justice Abella in *Fraser* looked at how the restriction on the buy-back scheme interacted with the legal and social forces that shaped women's lives. The decision to move to part-time work and the negative pension consequences that move entailed was a function of women's traditional caregiving role. Women continued to be the providers of care and were

> forced to manage family care without impinging on their work obligations. Their strategies – euphemistically labelled "choices" – often include part-time and precarious forms of work that typically come with lower wages, fewer benefits, fewer promotional opportunities and minimal or no retirement pensions.[63]

Gender divisions within the private sphere meant the restriction on buying back pension credits for job-sharers disproportionately disadvantaged women because they were women. The scheme economically penalised women at the

[61] ibid [78].
[62] *Fraser* (n 47).
[63] ibid [104] citing Elizabeth Shilton 'Family Status Discrimination: "Disruption and Great Mischief" or "Bridge Over the Work-Family Divide"' (2018) 14 *Journal of Law and Equality* 33, 35.

end of their careers for not fitting within a male model of continuous full-time employment. This was in breach of women's constitutional right to equality.

The majority judgment in *Fraser* was centred on the impact of the law on women not on the RCMP's reasons for limiting the buy-back scheme. Justice Abella explained that 'the perpetuation of disadvantage … does not become less serious … simply because it is relevant to a legitimate state objective'.[64] A good purpose does not expunge a negative impact. The logic or necessity of restricting the buy-back scheme was also held to be irrelevant to the assessment of whether the scheme disadvantaged women in contravention of their constitutional rights to substantive equality.[65] While there may be sound reasons for limiting pension buy-backs and those may even justify limiting women's equality, analysing justification claims at the equality-stage would be misplaced. The primary question at the section 15 step was whether the restriction on the pension buy-back scheme disproportionately disadvantaged women. The purpose of job-sharing and the logic or necessity of the buy-back did not assist in answering that question. A substantive equality assessment was the best tool to assess whether there had been a breach of constitutional law as it aimed to answer why the law might be unequal. And in the case of *Fraser*, it was able to understand how the institutional infrastructure has been built around gendered assumptions on 'how the world works'. It was only after it had been established that there was a breach of the constitutional right, that the scheme placed real harms on women, was it possible to investigate whether it could be justified under section 1 of the Charter.

iii. Equality in Property

Decisions on women's equal right to property, outside of the intimate partner relationship, are rare. A case from South Africa regarding gender and land tenure thus stands out. Even more so because it acts as a stark reminder on why and how limitation concepts should be confined to the justification stage.

The South African Government sought to redress the historic systemic deprivation of property rights for Black persons through The Upgrading of Land Tenure Rights Act (ULTRA). The Act automatically converted rights in property, such as deed or grants, to ownership rights. ULTRA had praiseworthy aims as it sought to narrow racial inequalities. In *Rahube v Rahube*, Justice Goliath recognised ULTRA was 'part of a scheme … to redress injustice of the colonial and apartheid regime'.[66] Yet despite the obvious value in this legislation, Matshabelle Mary Rahube argued that ULTRA violated the equality rights guaranteed in the South African Constitution.

[64] ibid [79].
[65] ibid [80].
[66] *Rahube v Rahube* [2018] ZACC 42 [23], [26], [38].

If the simple formula, equating a law with a salutary purpose with a law that is equal, was used the equality-stage would have concealed the gendered and racist impact of ULTRA. African women under apartheid were not able to hold tenuous forms of land rights and the upgrade system which converted these types of rights to property ownership operated 'in favour of the male head of the family'.[67] The ameliorative purpose of ULTRA failed to account for how African women were systematically disadvantaged by apartheid laws. The implementation and operation of ULTRA compounded African women's oppression by continuing to exclude them from property ownership. The bleeding of justification into the equality analysis would result in the Court holding that a commendable law did not violate women's equality notwithstanding the exclusion of African women from holding property.

The South African Constitutional Court, however, did not turn the equality-stage into a defence of ULTRA but assessed whether it breached African women's substantive equality rights. It did this by taking full account of historical disadvantage and contemporary impacts. It traced the legislative history of apartheid era laws that systematically oppressed African women, much like how it placed marital property laws in their broader context in *Women's Legal Centre Trust*, *Bwanya* and *KG*. The Court then built upon this knowledge to observe that by failing to account for how African women were disenfranchised and made subservient to male relatives under apartheid, these remedial measures further compounded the economic and sociocultural inequality of African women. Without attention to the 'historic omnipresence of patriarchy', the implementation of a remedial law was unfair discrimination in violation of section 9(3) of the Constitution.[68] Only by conducting a substantive equality analysis that was attuned to history and context could the Court grapple with the wrongness of ULTRA and any justification of the Act could only come after determining the gravity and extent of the harm the law imposed on African women. In this case, the South African Constitutional Court summarily concluded the inequality was not justified.

Substantive equality prevents justification concepts from masking the gravity and severity of women's inequality when courts consider whether the right to equality has been breached. Investigating the inequality on a substantive basis directs the court away from considering whether the law or policy has a salutary purpose, is logical, necessary or on balance worth it. There is no requirement to adopt a specific model of substantive equality to insulate the equality-stage from justification. Courts can develop and evolve a conception of substantive equality that reflects an array of factors unique to that jurisdiction. While there are strong criticisms on each of these models of substantive equality, pointing out that these courts have failed to fully use substantive equality to its

[67] ibid [43].
[68] ibid [74].

transformative endpoint,[69] even an imperfect conception of substantive equality can protect the equality-stage from being corroded by justification. The key is to apply the substantive analytical framework in a manner that is highly attuned to the history of gendered oppression, contemporary social attitudes, norms, systems and structures and the impact of the law on women's everyday lives.

III. ROBUSTNESS REQUIRED

Although there is no obligation to adopt a specific model of substantive equality for it to act as a bulwark against justification concepts and doctrines from seeping into the equality-stage, there is however one requirement. The substantive equality analysis must be a thorough interrogation of the alleged inequality against women. It is not sufficient to merely conclude that there has been a breach of the right, there needs to be a searching investigation into why the law violated women's equality. It can be tempting to gloss over inequalities and jump to the justification-stage, particularly when the state concedes that the law violates women's rights. In one of the UK benefit reform cases, the state agreed that the law was discriminatory against women.[70] The UK Supreme Court accepted this but did not conduct a robust equality analysis. As argued in chapter two, that by skipping over assessing why the reforms breached women's rights, the case was tipped in favour of justifying the reforms. In contrast, the South African Constitutional Court when faced with a similar situation, where the state conceded the inequality, still conducted a searching equality analysis. This is because it held that 'this Court must satisfy itself that the [laws] are indeed inconsistent with the Constitution … despite the respondents' concession, it remains necessary for the Court to analyse all the issues …'[71] This is required so that powerful institutions meaningfully listen to women and reflect their concerns. But a robust equality-stage also positively impacts the justification-stage. It is a ballast to weigh against the state's claims that the strength of the law is worth violating women's rights and as developed in Part II of the book, it provides the necessary foundation for equality to both guide the calibration of the justification-stage and to enrich the application of justification criteria. There must be a comprehensive diagnosis of the inequalities so there can be an accurate assessment of the burdens the state is asking women to shoulder. Substantive equality offers the best analytical framework to excavate the depth and severity of the alleged inequality as it is designed to grapple with the

[69] See, eg, Jennifer Koshan and Jonnette Watson Hamilton, 'Women's Charter Equality at the Supreme Court of Canada: Surprising Losses or Anticipated Failures' in Howard Kislowicz and others (eds), *Canada's Surprising Constitution* (UBC Press, 2024); Gauri Pillai, 'The Continuing Constitutional Conversation: Locating Nitisha' (2022) 22(1) *International Journal of Discrimination and the Law* 87.

[70] *SG v Secretary of State for Work and Pensions* [2015] UKSC 16 [61].

[71] *Mahlangu v Minister of Labour* [2020] ZACC 24 [29].

contexts, realities and impacts of the impugned measure. The requirement for a robust equality-stage does not preclude the possibility of justifying women's inequality, it simply ensures a precise and transparent calculation of the permissibility of limiting rights.

A. Listening to Domestic Workers

A good example of a robust substantive equality analysis that positively shaped the justification-stage comes from a decision from the South African Constitutional Court. In *Mahlangu v Minister of Labour*,[72] the Court had to determine whether the exclusion of domestic workers from a legislative workplace injury compensation scheme was a violation of the right to equality. In concluding that there was a breach, the Court explored the material impact of the exclusion on the individual plaintiff and other domestic workers, the historical and contemporary working conditions for domestic workers, social attitudes towards domestic work and how the exclusion was a product of racism, sexism and classism. This level of engagement with the overlapping inequalities against domestic workers ensured that the judgment listened and responded to the voices of domestic workers.[73] This was of vital importance, particularly as the experiences of domestic workers have long been invisible.[74] This in-depth engagement with women's inequality was also a pre-requisite for the justification assessment. It exposed the harm domestic workers were expected to bear and clarified the nature of the arguments and evidence that the state would have to provide to justify placing these burdens on women. In the case of *Mahlangu*, the rich substantive equality analysis clarified the constitutional impossibility of justifying the exclusion of domestic workers from workplace injury compensation schemes.

The equality-stage can only act as a ballast for the justification-stage when the judgment adopts a substantive analytical framework and applies that framework in a rigorous manner. In *Mahlangu*, the Court assessed if the exclusion of domestic workers from the Compensation for Occupational Injuries and Diseases Act (COIDA) was unfair discrimination in breach of section 9(3) of the South African Constitution. Justice Victor, for the majority decision, adopted a substantive frame. She held that the Court must pay attention to 'the nature and context of the individual or group at issue, their history, as well as the social and legal history of society's treatment of that group'.[75] Notably, the overall legitimate purpose of COIDA, an easily accessible fund to provide compensation for the employed injured at work, did not play any role in determining

[72] ibid.
[73] ibid [195].
[74] ibid [186].
[75] ibid [95].

that the exclusion of domestic workers was unfair. The equality-stage eschewed against exploring any defence of the exclusion. Instead, Justice Victor focused on investigating the gendered, racist and classist historical and contemporary marginalisation of domestic workers. It was through this detailed substantive inquiry that she was able to understand whether the exclusion from COIDA was in breach of section 9(3).

There were three substantive equality layers the Court investigated and each layer was investigated with a high degree of specificity. Taken together, these layers pinpoint what the state must argue to meet its justification obligations under section 36, the rights limitation clause of the South African Constitution. First, attention was paid to the circumstances of the individual claimant and the impact of COIDA on her and her family. This was not just to play on sympathies, but in relation to the justification-stage, starkly laid out the quality and strength of limitation arguments needed to justify these harms. Ms Mahlangu was employed as a domestic worker for 22 years. While in the course of her job, she drowned in the employer's pool. Her daughter, who was dependent on the income Ms Mahlangu made from domestic work, was informed that she could not get compensation under COIDA. Her claim was denied because unlike virtually all other forms of work, domestic work was not protected under the law. Ms Mahlangu's daughter had to suffer the loss of her mother, who died in the course of her employment duties, without any financial compensation. There were significant material consequences for Ms Mahlangu's family, and for any other domestic workers who were injured or died at work. The individual circumstances of Ms Mahlangu vividly highlighted the real and tragic consequences of excluding domestic workers from protection and clarified that the most compelling arguments would be needed to justify these harms.[76]

Second, the substantive equality analysis was broadened to explore the realities of domestic work. The opening paragraph of Justice Victor's decision centred on the value of domestic workers to South Africa, describing domestic workers as 'unsung heroines'.[77] The labour of domestic workers has enabled other members of society 'to propose and pursue their careers … knowing that [their], children, family members and households' were cared for, loved, and supported.[78] Performing this work, however, came at an immense cost for domestic workers. Working hours were long and domestic workers were denied a meaningful social life and often devoted more time caring for their employer's children than their own. They took on this hard and tiring work due to financial straits and the low wages for domestic work left them 'shackled by poverty' and unable to provide for the needs of themselves and their families.[79] As Justice

[76] ibid [103].
[77] ibid [1].
[78] ibid.
[79] ibid [104].

Victor concluded, 'despite these herculean efforts, domestic work as a profession is undervalued and unrecognised'.[80]

Third, the majority judgment of Justice Victor and concurring judgment of Justice Mhlantla explored the historical and sociocultural context and understanding of the harms of excluding domestic workers from workplace protections. This led these judgments to identify the synergy of racism, gender inequality against women and class stratification that underpinned the state's decision not to include domestic workers in COIDA. The exclusion was not benign or accidental but a product of both antagonism and ignorance of Black women. This stands in contrast to the judgments from the UK Supreme Court, argued in chapter two, that ignored the role of gender in *A and B v Secretary of State for Health* when assessing whether a funding prohibition on abortion was discriminatory.[81] Domestic workers in South Africa were and are predominantly Black women. Under colonialism and apartheid, Black women were at the lowest point on the social hierarchy and legally in the position of perpetual minors. Apartheid labour control laws and the cultural perceptions of Black women as the 'despised race' forcibly channelled them into work that was low paid, low in status and precarious, such as domestic labour.[82] The racism permeating domestic work in South Africa intersected with gender inequality against women. Domestic work was and continues to be conceptualised as a women's natural labour of love devoid of any economic value.[83] Justice Mhlantla observed that washing, cleaning, cooking and childcaring were not seen as psychologically challenging, physical strenuous or as socially productive as work traditionally assigned to men.[84] It was not perceived as work which was worth being protected in legislation. The exclusion from COIDA, which predominantly impacted Black women, was thus a manifestation of social and legal racism, sexism and classism. The majority of the Court held this was unfair discrimination in violation of section 9(3).

The rich and textured substantive equality analysis in *Mahlangu* operated as a ballast at the justification-stage. It marked out the severe nature of the equality rights violation that needed to be justified and Justice Victor noted that 'the limitation of rights … is quite egregious and far-reaching'.[85] Implicit in this observation is that the state would need extremely compelling arguments to justify excluding domestic workers from COIDA, a scheme that protects virtually every other form of work in South Africa. By mapping how privilege, power, vulnerability, oppression, social position and structural dynamics impacted domestic workers, the Court was able to persuasively demonstrate the

[80] ibid [2].
[81] *A and B v Secretary of State for Health* [2017] UKSC 41.
[82] ibid [110].
[83] ibid [189].
[84] ibid.
[85] *Mahlangu* (n 71) [116].

ludicrousness of the state asking Black women to continue to bear the economic and status harms of being excluded from COIDA. Although the state conceded that there was no legitimate purpose that could justify the exclusion and already had plans in place to amend COIDA, thoroughly engaging with the substantive inequalities at stake clarified the implausibility of ever being able to limit the workplace compensation scheme rights of domestic workers.[86]

Not every case will be as clear-cut as *Mahlangu*, where the state conceded the inequality and accepted that the inequality cannot be justified, but there are still insights to be drawn from this case. The equality-stage, via a detailed substantive equality analysis that genuinely interrogates all aspects of the claim, can set out the parameters of the state's limitation rationale. Grasping the gravity and severity of the harm is a prerequisite for accurately assessing if the strength of competing public policy objectives is worth the suffering placed on women.

IV. THE HOPE OF EQUALITY FOR JUSTIFICATION

This investigation, across chapters two and three, into the relationship between equality and justification when assessing whether there has been a breach of women's equality rights, reveals the normative importance of an asymmetric relationship. Justification should be irrelevant and absent from the equality-stage and equality is of prime importance to this stage and as the remainder of the book argues, equality matters deeply to the justification-stage. This has both theoretical and practical implications for the adjudication of women's claims to equality and this section concludes by considering these implications.

A. Women's Equality Rights Matter to Justification

Theorists have repeatedly attempted to untangle the rights-limitation matrix and have proposed different theories on the optimal relationship between rights and the justification of rights. The challenges of limiting rights and the importance of justification to the outcomes of claims has led some prominent theorists to argue that rights themselves are not of much consequence and the main function of rights is to trigger justification. Kumm argued that

> a rights-holding does not have very much in virtue of his having a right … the fact that a rights holder has a prima facie right does not imply that he holds a position that gives him any kind of priority over countervailing considerations of policy. An infringement of the scope of the right merely serves as a trigger to initiate an assessment of whether the infringement is justified.[87]

[86] ibid [118].
[87] Kumm (n 1) 150.

The analytical heavy lifting is exclusively with justification and 'little is decided by acknowledging that a measure infringes a right'.[88] Möller observes that the 'focus is not on the objects of human and constitutional rights – freedom of speech, freedom of religion, life, property etc. Rather it is on justification'.[89] Kumm and Möller both appear to go so far as to collapse any distinction between rights and holds that all rights can be captured under the umbrella of a meta-right to justification via the proportionality framework.[90] Mathews and Stone Sweet make a similar claim, noting that 'a right gives … an entitlement to have her claim evaluated under the proportionality framework, and nothing more'.[91] The right that matters is the right to justification. Correspondingly, rights, such as right to equality, should be interpreted broadly as it is the work of justification that places boundaries on the nature, breadth and scope of rights. By implication, under this framing of the rights-limitation matrix, the blending of equality and justification at the justification-stage is unproblematic as equality is only a prompt for the more crucial investigation into whether the measure in question is defendable under justification criteria. Similarly, only cursorily assessing whether women's equality rights have been breached would not be unwarranted as the crux of the case is decided at the justification-stage. While judges rarely openly engage or defend a choice of theoretical frames when adjudicating women's claim to equality, the power of these claims, that only justification matters, are evident, as argued in chapter two, as judicial reasoning repeatedly elide articulating the wrongness of equality and focusing on the justifications for the law.

Conceptualising rights as triggers to justification has been critiqued from multiple angles including that it fails to give due moral and political weight to the conception of rights.[92] The arguments in this chapter and the previous reveal another problem with giving no weight to ascertaining why the law is a breach of women's right to equality and points to a new way of thinking about the rights-limitation matrix. Merging equality and justification reasoning into the equality-stage or skipping over the nuance and complexity of the violation of the right hides the severity of women's inequality. It can do so to such an extent that no violation of the right is found despite overwhelming evidence that women are being disadvantaged, stigmatised, excluded and oppressed. Or if a breach is found, there is no clarity on the harms that need to be justified which ultimately operates to inflate the strengths of limitation claims. Ignoring

[88] ibid.

[89] Möller (n 1).

[90] Kumm (n 1) 168; Kai Möller, *The Global Model of Constitutional Rights* (Oxford University Press, 2012) 87, 208.

[91] Jud Mathews and Alec Stone Sweet, 'All Things in Proportion? American Rights Review and the Problem of Balancing' (2011) 60 *Emory Law Journal* 797, 809.

[92] Gregorie Weber, 'On the Loss of Rights' in Grant Huscroft, Bradley Miller and Gregoire Weber (eds), *Proportionality and the Rule of Law: Rights, Justification, Reasoning* (Cambridge University Press, 2014).

equality and centering justification affects outcomes and ultimately operates to stymie women's equality rights. Equality rights matter, it is not a stage to merge or skip over, and a substantive concept of equality offers the best tools to protect the integrity of the equality-stage. It gives courts an analytical framework to explicitly articulate with a high degree of sophistication the harms of inequality without the need to resort to borrowing justification concepts. Equality is not a mere pit stop on the route to the justification-stage, it matters.

B. Practical Challenges to Equality Mattering

The arguments in chapters two and three are normatively prescriptive. In jurisdictions that have demarcated equality-stage and justification-stage and a strong and repeated commitment to substantive equality, these arguments have strong salience. But not all courts reason through claims to women's equality in this manner. Some jurisdictions forgo a dedicated assessment of why the measure violates women's equality and not all courts have explicitly or consistently adopted a substantive equality approach. Notwithstanding the doctrinal differences across different apex courts, the claim that equality matters prior to undertaking any assessment of the measure's justification remains relevant and can be a springboard for evolving judicial reasoning on women's equality.

Women's constitutional and legal right to equality is never frozen or static. What it means to be equal continually pushes against theoretical and doctrinal boundaries. This dynamism can include advancing arguments for a focused, robust substantive equality analysis prior to any assessment of the permissibility of any limits to women's equality. There is a long-track record of evolving equality law through women's claims. For example, the promotion criteria that disadvantaged older women prompted the Indian Supreme Court in *Nitisha* to develop a conception of indirect discrimination under the Indian Constitution. There are also glimmers of these arguments taking root in dissenting opinions in the *Nguyen* and *Wal-Mart* cases from the US Supreme Court, where judgments have carefully examined the stereotypes that underpin the law.

At the same time, it is important to acknowledge that the opportunities for evolving women's equality rights can be contingent and fragile. There may be long periods of time when arguing that limitation concepts should be confined to the justification-stage and that a robust substantive equality analysis is required is not only foolhardy but risks rolling back women's rights. These challenges require creative advocacy to ensure that arguments, in some form or another, on the equality harms of the law are put before the courts. It also requires hope. Constitutional recognition and protection of women's equality has been a constant struggle and 'current challenges are not insurmountable … defeats are not final'.[93] Innovative and dynamic strategies on how to navigate challenging

[93] Meghan Campbell, 'Does the UDHR Matter to Women's Equality?' (2024) *European Human Rights Law Review*.

legal circumstances are required but the importance of constitutionally securing women's equality demands constant advocacy and hope for a transformative gendered world.

V. CONCLUSION

Substantive equality protects the equality-stage from the hazards of justification. It forces the court to ask whether the law, policy or programme contributes to women's economic disadvantage, retrenches stigma, stereotypes or negative cultural attitudes, fails to account for women's needs, interests or traditional roles and excludes women from participating in all aspects of life. Substantive equality protects the equality-stage from being drawn into questioning whether the law is legitimate, rational, necessary or balanced and focuses the analysis on the effects and impacts of the law on women's lives. Substantive equality acts as a bulwark against justification rationale hiding the gravity and severity when assessing whether women's equality rights have been infringed. There is no requirement that courts adopt a specific model of substantive equality. What matters is that courts apply the hallmarks of substantive equality reasoning – close attention to the contextual reality of women's lives, lives that have been shaped by strong patriarchal forces, and how the law impacts on women. Substantive equality must be applied robustly as grappling with the nature of women's inequality cannot be glossed over. Skipping over women's substantive inequality can dangerously inflate the strength of justification claims. The integrity of the justification-stage hinges on an in-depth substantive equality analysis at the equality-stage that marks out precisely what harms and wrongs need to be justified. In the context of women's equality, adjudication should not be collapsed into an overarching right to justification. Equality is of the utmost importance.

Part II

The Justification-Stage

4

Guiding the Calibration of Justification with Equality

I. INTRODUCTION

BEFORE EVALUATING WHETHER women's equality should be constitutionally limited, courts must decide how closely it will assess limitation arguments. If the state argues it must impose income poverty on women to incentivise labour force participation, should the court accept this argument, or should it interrogate its veracity? Or if the state claims that excluding women from certain roles in the military is necessary to protect operational effectiveness should the court take this argument at face-value, or should it demand strongly persuasive evidence that this argument is true? These questions are almost never explicitly dealt with by the courts. Yet calibrating the intensity of the standard of review at the justification-stage dramatically shapes the outcome of women's claims for equality. A light-touch standard of review correlates with courts permitting women's equality rights to be justifiably limited, whereas an intense standard tracks with courts refusing to limit women's equality. There is an extensive amount of theorising on the standard of review. But most of it was developed in the context of human rights writ large, not within the specific context of women's equality. This matters. Many of the doctrines that underpin the calibration exercise do not ring true for women's constitutional right to equality and when these doctrines are used in practice, they are misapplied to insulate decisions to pursue measures that burden women's equality from any degree of scrutiny. This chapter makes the case that women's equality can guide the calibration of the justification-stage. The severity of women's inequality in tandem with the fundamental importance of women's legal right to equality requires courts to *always* undertake a high intensity, searching assessment when deciding whether breaches of women's equality rights can be justified.

Calibrating the intensity of review at the justification-stage is never an easy task. This exercise is deeply enmeshed in long-standing debates on the legitimacy of courts evolving human rights. Harmoniously fulfilling women's equality and achieving a myriad of other policy objectives is difficult and how to achieve that difficult harmony is primarily the task of democratically elected bodies. To protect the hard choices legislatures or executives make, so the argument goes, unelected courts should not second-guess those decisions. Calibrating a minimal intensity of review at the justification-stage is the court's way to defer and respect the decisions made by these bodies.[1] Democratically elected bodies, however, are not perfect and can fail to give due weight to the rights of minority groups, like women.[2] A searching standard of review prevents majoritarian political processes from too easily infringing women's equality rights. Courts must navigate these conflicting imperatives. Adding a further layer of complexity to the calibration exercise, courts must also determine the depth of the standard of review when legislative bodies choose to prioritise women's equality over other aims such as religious pluralism or federalism. In the United States (US), judges from the Supreme Court are ratcheting up the standard of review when assessing these types of claims and searching scrutiny is being utilised to hold it is unconstitutional to take measures to enhance women's equality.[3] Calibrating the justification-stage reveals deep divergences on judicial understandings on the normative weight of women's equality in the constitutional ordering and the role of courts in protecting that equality.

There are overlapping approaches to navigating these calibration challenges but many of these theories and doctrines sit jaggedly with the realities of women's inequality. Although there are nuances, broadly speaking, pinpointing the standard of review requires weighing up a range of well-established factors.[4] These factors seek to balance the need to rigorously protect human rights against the desire to protect the integrity of constitutional decision-making that is fractured across executive, legislative and judicial bodies. There are overlooked and unresolved opposition points in the factors with respect to women's equality. Many of the factors designed to protect constitutional legitimacy automatically condemn women's claim to a light-touch application of justification frameworks. This is because women are routinely bringing to court allegations that law has been used in controversial areas of life to construct their socioeconomic inequality. This lowering of the standard of review, however, is in tension with the recognition that the gendered oppression of women is a serious constitutional wrong. Many courts are currently traversing this dissonance by overamplifying and even distorting calibration factors to protect the choice to downgrade the importance of women's equality from any degree of scrutiny. The theory, doctrine and practice of calibration points towards the need for a new understanding of calibrating the justification-stage, one that gives primacy to the seriousness of women's equality.

Section II of this chapter argues that calibration orthodoxy is embedded with assumptions that do not correspond with the realities and experiences

[1] See Alison Young, 'In Defence of Due Deference' (2009) 72(4) *MLR* 554; Jeff King, 'Institutional Approaches to Judicial Restraint' (2008) 28(3) *OJLS* 409 for an explanation of these arguments.

[2] Rosalind Dixon, 'The Core Case for Weak-Form Judicial Review' (2017) 38(2) *Cardozo Law Review* 2193.

[3] *Burwell v Hobby Lobby* 573 US 682 (2014).

[4] Aileen Kavanagh, *The Collaborative Constitution* (Cambridge University Press, 2023) 278.

of patriarchy, nor with the constitutional weight assigned to women's equality. Section III exposes how the current dominant approaches to the standard of review are being utilised by courts to misrepresent the breach of women's equality rights and to overamplify trepidations that a searching justification assessment would pose a serious threat to institutional boundaries. Sections IV and V seek to correct these mistakes. Section IV proposes that the distinctiveness to women's inequality – its lack of respect for traditional conceptual boundaries, its unbounded nature – combined with the central importance of achieving women's equality in the constitution is a powerful and overriding calibration factor. This means when assessing the constitutionality of limits on women's equality rights courts must calibrate the justification-stage to the highest degree of scrutiny. Section V reflects how this can work in practice and marks out how, in assigning significant weight to women's equality when calibrating the standard of review, courts are not overstepping institutional boundaries but are protecting women's equality from being eroded by justification arguments that lack merit.

II. JAGGED PIECES: CALIBRATING JUSTIFICATION AND WOMEN'S EQUALITY

There are large and unyielding debates on the proper methodology for calibrating the degree of scrutiny the courts should employ when assessing limitations on human rights.[5] Much of these debates are in the context of the United Kingdom (UK), as there was a deep consternation in having courts involved in defining and evolving human rights when the European Convention on Human Rights was domesticated via the Human Rights Act 1998. Women's equality is largely absent from this theorising. There are (un)spoken beliefs on the value of human rights, the nature of human rights violations, the role of courts and where accountability for violations should lie that ring hollow with women's experiences of inequality. Yet these beliefs are foundational for calibrating the justification-stage and are being drawn upon to immunise decisions to burden women's equality rights from judicial scrutiny. This section canvasses prominent theories and doctrines that inform calibrating the justification-stage, teasing out where they sit awkwardly with women's constitutional right to equality. Women's equality is not so much hanging in the balance at the justification-stage but because of the weaknesses in the leading approaches to calibration, it is tipped towards always permitting limitation of these rights.

[5] Cora Chan, *Deference in Human Rights Adjudication* (Oxford University Press 2024) ch 1 for a good snapshot of these debates.

A. Nothing Special about Women's Equality

The calibration crucible, ascertaining the precise intensity of review, is animated by fears of overstepping judicial institutional boundaries and the desire for judicial guarding of constitutional rights. There is no universality to calibrating the justification-stage. A non-weighted approach, however, has become 'a common juridical tool' and is dominant in the discourse on calibrating the standard of review.[6] Under this methodology, a catalogue of factors is examined, some factors pull towards an intense standard of review while other factors push towards a lower standard. In each case, courts must decide how to resolve tensions between these push-and-pull factors to arrive at a degree of scrutiny for the justification-stage. All factors are equivalent. Kavanagh, in her recent study on the role of different actors in the constitution, argues that none of the factors 'are conclusive or determinative' or have a 'pre-ordained weight'.[7] This echoes an optimisation approach to the entire justification-stage. As canvassed in chapter one, Alexy holds that rights are not shields, trumps or firewalls demanding special consideration but are optimisation principles.[8] The justification-stage should be directed towards investigating how to optimise rights and competing public interests 'to the greatest extent possible given the legal and factual possibilities'.[9] Similar to optimising, women's equality is given no specific weight at the outset when calibrating the limitation analysis. In the abstract, it is of the same value and importance as other common calibration factors, such as legislative debates or indications that executive or legislative bodies intend to undertake some future action. Women's equality, and its normative significance, is merely one factor of many that goes into the calibration crucible. Advocates argue that leaving the weight of factors open avoids the straitjacket of rigid formulas and the blackhole of unrestrained judicial decision-making.[10] A non-weighted approach means calibration can be attuned to background contexts and there is space for courts to be responsive to the unique factual-legal matrix of the claim.

The desire for flexibility through drawing an equivalence between calibrating factors is in dissonance with the constitutional importance assigned to women's equality. Equality rights in general, and women's equality in particular, stand-out in the canon of rights protected in constitutional instruments. For millenniums it was believed to be either natural or religiously ordained that women were inferior and subordinate to men. Law was a powerful instrument

[6] Chan (n 5) 151; Kavanagh (n 4) ch 9.

[7] Kavanagh (n 4) 279; Murray Hunt, 'Sovereignty's Blight: Why Contemporary Public Law Needs a Doctrine of "Due Deference"' in Nicholas Bamforth and Peter Leyland (eds), *Public Law in a Multi-Layered Constitution* (Hart Publishing, 2003) 353.

[8] Robert Alexy, *A Theory of Constitutional Rights* (Oxford University Press, 2002) 47.

[9] ibid.

[10] Kavanagh (n 4); Jeff King, *Judging Social Rights* (Cambridge University Press, 2012) ch 5.

to further these beliefs.[11] The statute books are littered with examples of laws that cemented women's inequality such as prohibitions on the right to vote and to work, legal exemptions of marital rape, the criminalisation of abortion, limitations on the right to contract and own property, protective legislation on working conditions and legally mandated unequal pay.[12] Patriarchal beliefs also manifested in law's silence as the lack of legal acknowledgement of differing forms of intimate relations, care and household work, violence and sexual harassment reflect ideological beliefs that excluded women from the legal framework. Law, in the words of MacKinnon, has been the story of institutionalised male power over women.[13] Countless women have through diligent, creative, disruptive and innovative activism demanded constitutional reform to include guarantees of women's equality.[14] Similarly, Carter in her study on the history of Black resistance in the US analyses how equality for Black men and women was not bestowed by the privileged but was powerfully and radically demanded and fought for.[15] Historical memory is important in calibrating the justification-stage. Calibration must respect the historical oppression of women, the political and legal struggle to achieve equality and treat contemporaneous violations of women's equality rights seriously.

The inclusion of women's equality in the constitutional structure of the state was a recognition of the power of law to subjugate women and an entrenched commitment to end that oppression. The constitutional recognition of the full worth and humanity of women represents 'the human capacity to act, to innovate, to break the causal chain of process and launch something unprecedented'.[16] Justice Chandrachud, in the Indian Supreme Court, explained that the drafters of the Indian Constitution wanted to

> transform Indian society by remedying centuries of discrimination against Dalits, women and the marginalised. They sought to provide them a voice by creating a culture of rights. Above all, placing those who were denuded of their human rights before the Advent of the Constitution whether in the veneer of caste, patriarchy or

[11] *Bradwell v State* 83 US 130, 141-12 (1873).

[12] Sandra Fredman, *Woman and the Law* (Oxford University Press, 1997) ch 2; UN Working Group on Discrimination Against Women and Girls, 'Country Report: Afghanistan' (2023) A/HRC/53/21; World Bank, 'Women, Business and the Law' (2023), available at https://wbl.worldbank.org/en/reports.

[13] Catherine MacKinnon, 'Toward Feminist Jurisprudence' in Patricia Smith (ed), *Feminist Jurisprudence* (Oxford University Press, 1993); Robin West, 'Feminism, Critical Social Theory and Law' (1989) *University of Chicago Legal Forum* 59.

[14] Fredman (n 12); Jill Hasday, 'Women's Exclusion from the Constitutional Canon' (2013) *University of Illinois Law Review* 1715; Geetanjali Gangoli, *Indian Feminism: Law, Patriarchies and Violence in India* (Routledge, 2007); Shireen Hassim, *ANC Women's League: Sex, Gender and Politics* (Ohio University Press, 2015); Mary Eberts, 'The Fight for Substantive Equality: Women's Activism and Section 15 of the Canadian Charter of Rights and Freedoms' (2015–16) 37(1) *Atlantis* 99.

[15] Kellie Carter Jackson, *We Refuse: A Forceful History of Black Resistance* (Basic Books, 2024).

[16] Hanna Pitkin, 'Idea of a Constitution' (1987) 37 *Legal Education* 167.

> otherwise, were to be placed in control of their own destinies by the assurance of equal protection of the law.[17]

In *Bhe v Khayelitsha*, the South African Constitutional Court came to a similar conclusion, Justice Langa explained that the right to equality is one of

> the most valuable rights in any open and democratic state. [It] assume[s] special importance in South Africa because of our past history of inequality and hurtful discrimination on grounds that include race and gender.[18]

Enshrining equality rights within a constitution is meant to break with that past and transform the future. Equality, not only for women but for other disadvantage groups, is not just a right but a constitutional value that permeates and infuses the entire constitution.[19] Women's constitutional equality stands as an entrenched landmark, signalling that legal power hierarchies based on the superiority of men and the inferiority of women must end. It is unique in seeking to reverse deeply entrenched political, legal, social, cultural and economic legacies of seeing women as lesser human beings. This rings out not only in the South African and Indian courts but also in judicial decisions from the US, Canada and UK.[20] Although it is imperfectly realised, there is little debate on the normative significance of women's equality. Reducing women's equality to one factor of many when calibrating the justification-stage is jarringly inconsistent with constitutional histories, guarantees, values, morals and ideologies that rarify women's equality. On a theoretical level, calibration methodologies should mirror rather than undercut the weight constitutions place with respect to women's equality. And as argued below, on a practical level, there is a line of jurisprudence, stretching across jurisdictions, that weaponises the non-weighted approach to not only ignore but also denigrate women's equality rights when pinpointing the degree of scrutiny at the justification-stage.

B. Misunderstandings and Artificial Boundaries

Examining more closely common factors that inform the calibration exercise also reveals a series of disjuncture points between determining the standard of review and women's equality which are exploited, as argued below in Section III, in judgments to uncritically accept the need to limit women's equality rights. These fracture points between calibration orthodoxy and women's equality

[17] *Indian Young Lawyers Association v State of Kerala* (2019) 11 SCC 1 Part A (concurring opinion of Justice Chandrachud).

[18] *Bhe v Khayelitsha* [2004] ZACC 17 [71].

[19] Sandra Fredman, *Discrimination Law*, 3rd edn (Clarendon, 2023) ch 1.

[20] *Frontiero v Richardson* 411 US 677 (1973); *US v Virginia* 518 US 515 (1996) 531–36; *Symes v Canada* [1883] 4 SCR 695 (dissenting opinion of Justice L'Heureux-Dube); *Fraser v Canada* [2020] SCC 28 [136]; *Asda v Brierley* [2021] UKSC 10 [11].

point to the need for new methodologies for determining the standard of review at the justification-stage.

Although there is no universal canon on factors that need to be considered when pinpointing the degree of scrutiny, there are overlapping taxonomies.[21] Drawing on Kavanagh's work on constitutional actors, when determining whether a searching or minimal standard of review should be deployed at the justification-stage, inter alia, there are two umbrella categories of factors: (i) rights and (ii) democratic legitimacy.[22] Under the *rights* rubric, courts must weigh the nature of the right and the severity of its breach. In relation to *democratic legitimacy*, courts should reflect on which body is appropriate within the separation of powers to be making the decision to deprioritise women's equality. This can involve looking at several factors including, most important for the purposes of this chapter, the subject-matter. This push factor is designed to make sure the calibration exercise is able to express respect, leeway and deference to executive and legislative decision-making. Not all theorising on calibrating the standard of review would use these categories or factors, some may even reject the salience of a specific factor or argue that other factors are more determinative, but the two factors, nature of the right as well as the subject-matter are prominent in the jurisprudence and thus give a helpful way of thinking through the ill-fit between calibration and women's equality.

i. Rights

Turning first to the rights category, the argument goes that the greater the significance of the right or the more serious the breach, the justification-stage should be calibrated towards vigilance.[23] The intensity of review can shift depending on quality of the rights violation.[24] This, however, assumes that rights violations can be neatly categorised as either serious or non-serious. Women's equality does not fit this paradigm. Patriarchy is a totalising force that touches upon every aspect of life. It is a system of political, legal, economic, social and cultural norms, institutions, relations and practices that is marked by its depth, pervasiveness and interconnectedness.[25] Seemingly inconsequential aspects operate to bolster more insidious elements of women's inequality. The drudgery of housework or punishing beauty standards are not minor. They reflect deeply entrenched gendered norms which in turn are connected to women's legal

[21] Kavanagh (n 4) 287–88; Chan (n 5) chs 2 and 6.

[22] Kavanagh (n 4) 287–88; Chan (n 5) chs 2 and 6.

[23] Mark Elliott, 'From Bifurcation to Calibration' in Hanna Wilberg and Mark Elliott (eds), *The Scope and Intensity of Substantive Review* (Hart Publishing, 2015).

[24] Julian Rivers, 'Proportionality and Variable Intensity of Review' (2006) 65(1) *Cambridge Law Journal* 174.

[25] Sylvia Walby, *Theorising Patriarchy* (John Wiley and Sons, 1990) ch 1.

subjugation and should be taken as a serious aspect of oppression.[26] The seemingly meaningless decision on which parent is responsible for the school-run is emblematic of grave gender inequalities against women as childcare obligations are connected to laws on division of property and pension entitlements. Or the inability to afford a child's birthday party when receiving social benefits is not frivolous but raises crucial questions on whether the state values women's caring roles and the social inclusion of lone mothers in poverty. The famous slogan 'the personal is political' pushed against attempts to segment women's lives between the personal, private and unimportant and the political, public and serious. US feminists argued back that this splicing was artificial and did not coincide with the experience of inequality as 'personal problems [were] political problems'.[27] This is because women's inequality is a polycentric web. Everyday norms and expectations on dress, attitude, daily chores are inherently linked, inter alia, to women's legal denigration, political exclusion, extreme forms of violence and continued economic oppression. Attempting to argue that there is a less severe breach of women's equality is simply wrong. Arguments that downplay the severity of the infringements of women's equality so as to push the court to a light-touch standard of review at the justification-stage misunderstand how women's inequality is a highly interconnected reinforcing web of norms, practices, standards, policies, regulations and law.

ii. Democratic Legitimacy

There are a range of arguments centred around the democratic illegitimacy of courts intensely reviewing decisions to pursue other aims at the expense of human rights. The illegitimacy of courts revolves around the democratic credentials and the relevant expertise of different bodies of the state.[28] Political matters, such as controversial social or economic policy, are felt to be within the institutional realm of executive and legislative decision-making and courts should employ a minimal standard of review when assessing justifications in these areas of life.[29] Executive and legislative bodies have greater institutional competence to make these decisions and in comparison to courts, stronger democratic credentials and inclusive decision-making processes to make hard choices between competing priorities. Courts should respect these choices through a low degree of scrutiny. Justice Scalia warned that a searching justification analysis, in the context of pregnancy discrimination in the US, was a 'flabby … invitation to judicial arbitrariness and policy-driven decision making. [G]rading of Congress's homework is a task we are ill suited

[26] Carol Hanisch, 'The Personal is Political' (January 2006), available at https://webhome.cs.uvic.ca/~mserra/AttachedFiles/PersonalPolitical.pdf.

[27] ibid.

[28] Chan (n 5) 32; Kavanagh (n 4) 278.

[29] Kavanagh (n 4) 278.

to perform and ill advised to undertake'.[30] These calibrating factors that are aimed at protecting institutional boundaries, however, have dangerous implications for women's constitutional equality.

First, it assumes that there is an easy division between legal decisions, which should attract a higher degree of scrutiny and political decision, which should attract a lower one. Many have pointed out that this distinction is untenable.[31] West argued that law is 'both a product of politics and itself a political force'.[32] Law and politics are not separate spheres but interact and mutually reinforce the other. There has also been an extensive reaching of law into politics. Barak accurately summarises the interconnection:

> The law is everywhere ... there is no limit to the law's reach ... there are no areas of human life that are external to law ... Even the most political activities – such as making peace or war – are examined by legal standards ... Indeed, an issue's nature as 'political' – that is, the fact that its resolution involves political implication – does not negate the fact that it is under law's control.[33]

Women's equality is a prime example of straddling the law-politics divide. Patriarchy itself is political but, at the same time, law has a prominent role in maintaining patriarchy.[34] For example, political beliefs on women's role in marriage have manifested in laws which criminalise adultery.[35] Women's legal right to equality is also connected to broader political movements, as rights to vote were linked to controversial political debates on whether the civic participation was contingent on owning property and marriage equality rights were entangled with the politics of colonialism.[36] As Betty Friedan explained, women's equality is 'messy, paradoxical, impossible to pin down, every changing [and] complex'.[37] Women's equality is enmeshed within both law and politics, so trying to untangle which strands or threads are law and which are political for the purposes of calibrating the justification-stage is conceptually incoherent.

The conceptual wooliness of this calibration factor also belies a normative darkness. Attempts to categorise women's equality as political or legal is symptomatic of ideological beliefs that push women out of the constitutional frame. For example, categorising women's caring roles within the political domain reflects traditional assumptions on who and what is of constitutional importance. Gender-based violence and sexual and reproductive health are similarly branded as political issues rather than of as the upmost constitutional

[30] *Coleman v Court of Appeals of Maryland* 566 US_(2012) (Concurring Opinion of Justice Scalia).

[31] King (n 10) 123–24.

[32] West (n 13).

[33] Aaron Barak, 'On Judging' in Martin Scheinin, Helle Kruke and Marina Aksenova (eds), *Judges as Guardians of Constitutionalism and Human Rights* (Edward Elgar, 2016) 42.

[34] Carole Pateman, *The Sexual Contract* (Stanford University Press, 1988); Fredman (n 12).

[35] *Joseph Shine v Union of India* [2018] 11 SCR 765.

[36] Fredman (n 12) Chapter 2.

[37] Marlene LeGates, *In Their Time: A History of Feminism in Western Society* (Routledge, 2001).

significance. In *Dobbs*, the US Supreme Court kicked abortion rights out of the highest legal instrument in the land, holding that the determination of access to abortion was exclusively and solely a matter for political actors.[38] This position reflects gendered beliefs.[39] Framing issues like sexual and reproductive health or care as exempt from constitutional norms and standards means decisions on, for example abortion access, are only accountable against the whims and vagrancies of political majorities. Decisions like *Dobbs* prompted one Canadian feminist legal scholar, Donna Greschner, to pose the question on whether 'constitutions could be for women too?'[40] Constitutional invocations of subjecthood, such as 'we the people' should more accurately, as Hasday argues, be framed as 'we the men'.[41] The exclusion of women and aspects of life that are of central concern to millions of women's lives ultimately operates to cement their gendered second-class status. Characterising breaches of women's inequality as too political for searching scrutiny at the justification-stage is a continuation of a constitutional lineage that conceptualises women's traditional roles as insignificant and invisible to constitutional norms, values and rules.

Second, when the subject-matter of the claim is marked as divisive, contentious or controversial, courts should tread lightly when assessing how executive and legislative bodies have chosen to legally resolve political, economic or sociocultural tension points. These bodies, it is argued, are better equipped and designed to be inclusive of differing perspectives and arrive at innovative compromises and solutions.[42] Their decisions on matters that spark disagreement should be respected through minimal scrutiny at the justification-stage. This aspect of subject-matter also appears to automatically trigger a lower standard of review for assessing claims that it is permissible to limit women's equality. This is because every element of women's equality can be branded as transgressive. Achieving women's equality requires challenging the 'way things have been done', dismantling orthodox positions, and breaking through sacrosanct conceptual barriers. Rubio-Marin observes it 'cannot be contained, in terms of domains, and should instead inspire a transformative agenda'.[43] This transformation is routinely labelled controversial and destabilising. At almost every step, achieving women's equality has been painted as radical, even measures

[38] *Dobbs v Jackson Women's Health Organization* (2022) 597 US 215, 44.

[39] Jaclyn Neo, 'Constitutionalisng Care: How Can We Expand Our Constitutional Imaginary After COVID-19?' (2022) *International Journal of Constitutional Law* 1307; Sandra Fredman, 'Care as a Constitutional Value' (2024) 22(3) *International Journal of Constitutional Law* 741; Ruth Rubio-Marin, *Global Gender Constitutionalism and Women's Citizenship* (Cambridge University Press, 2022) ch 1.

[40] Donna Greschner, 'Can Constitutions Be for Women Too?' in Dawn Currie and B MacLean (eds), *The Administration of Justice* (University of Saskatchewan Social Research Unit, 1986).

[41] Jill Hasday, *We the Men: How Forgetting Women's Struggles for Equality Perpetuates Inequality* (Oxford University Press, 2025).

[42] Kavanagh (n 4) ch 9; Jeremy Waldon, 'The Core Case Against Judicial Review' (2006) 115 *The Yale Law Journal* 1346.

[43] Rubio-Marin (n 39).

that today are, largely, perceived as uncontroversial. Feminists arguing for political equality in France were imprisoned and accused of trying to overthrow the Government.[44] Women's suffrage in the nineteenth century was dismissed in a report by the Constitutional Convention in New York as

> public sentiment does not demand and would not sustain … an innovation so revolutionary and sweeping … so openly at war with a distribution of duties and functions between the sexes as venerable and pervading as government itself and involving transformation so radical in social and domestic life.[45]

In the modern era, women's equality is still deemed as radical and revolutionary as evident by the shocking levels of violence against women human rights defenders.[46] The Indian Government recently framed arguments for women's equality in marriage, through the removal of the criminal law exemption of marital rape, as a 'serious disturbance on the institution of marriage'.[47] Women's equality queries foundational assumptions and by its very nature is a radical demand.[48] Elizabeth Cady Stanton, a leading figure in the nineteenth century feminist movement in the US, explained, 'If there is any revolutionary claim … it is that of women … it revolutionizes society, it revolutionizes religion; it revolutionizes the Constitution and laws.'[49]

This calibration factor then from the outset appears to demand that women's claims to equality be subject to lower standards of review. This in turn can permit infringements of women's rights regardless of how flimsy the arguments that such infringement is justified and at a deeper level contributes to a constitutional status quo that continues to frame women's equality as aberrant.

Taking the push and pull factors together, orthodox approaches to calibration operate to create justification hierarchies for women's equality. The orthodox view entails that when women's claims to equality are solidly within the legal realm and safe or socially accepted, then a searching standard should be employed, and cogent, compelling arguments with highly probative evidence are needed to justify limiting women's equality. On this view, however, when women's claims stray from the legal towards the political and are divisive or contentious a lower standard can be used, and equality rights can be constitutionally limited

[44] LeGates (n 37) 190.

[45] ibid 223, citing 'New York Constitutional Convention' in Elizabeth Cady Stanton and others (eds), *History of Women Suffrage 1861–1876* (reprint Arno and The New York Times, 1969) 285.

[46] UN Working Group on discrimination in law and practice, 'Tackling the Challenges Faced by Women Human Rights Defenders through a Gender Lens', available at www.ohchr.org/en/special-procedures/wg-women-and-girls/tackling-challenges-faced-women-human-rights-defenders-through-gender-lens.

[47] Geeta Pandey and Cherylann Mollan, 'India Government Says Criminalising Marital Rape "Excessively Harsh"' (*BBC Delhi and Mumbia*, 4 October 2024), available at www.bbc.co.uk/news/articles/c80r38yeempo.

[48] Patricia Smith, 'Introduction' in Patricia Smith (ed), *Feminist Jurisprudence* (Oxford University Press, 1993) 10.

[49] Elizabeth Cady Stanton, *Eighty Years and More: Reminiscences 1815–1897* (Schocken, 1971) 319 cited in LeGates (n 37) 11.

on weaker arguments and evidence that is less than strongly persuasive. This methodology belies constitutional aims that seek to transform rather than ossify women's equality and places artificial conceptual boundaries on when women's equality is of constitutional importance and when it is not.

III. CALIBRATING WOMEN'S EQUALITY IN PRACTICE

The dominant approaches to calibrating the justification-stage sits jaggedly with the constitutional importance of women's equality. But the non-weighted methodology is marked by its openness and sensitivity to the context of the claim. This means it could potentially be employed in a manner that smooths out the jagged edges between calibrating the justification-stage and women's constitutional right to equality. Little attention, however, has been paid to systematically assessing how the push-and-pull factors of calibration operate in the practice of courts adjudicating women's claims to equality. The analysis in this section reveals worrying trends. The practice of calibration by courts has not redressed the dissonance but rather overamplified it and arguably weaponised it to protect choices to pursue competing objectives at the expense of women's equality rights from any meaningful limitation investigation. Across the jurisprudence, particularly from the UK, Canada and the US, the pull factors, the severity of women's inequality, is trivialised and downgraded and the push factors, the subject-matter that pertain to that inequality, is morphed and repurposed to lower the standard of review. Instead of seeking to resolve tensions between calibration factors that may pull in opposing directions, courts are constructing a synergy between pull-and-push factors so both types of factors point towards a light-touch justification review. This insulates decisions to erode women's equality from the searching glare of justification criteria and creates significant risk that the justification-stage will give constitutional imprimatur to limitation claims that lack veracity. This pattern can be seen below.

A. Politicising the Law on Social Benefits

Women argued, in a series of cases from the UK Supreme Court, that the design of social benefits exacerbated their income poverty and devalued care work. After the banking crisis of 2008, the UK adopted a policy of austerity. The amount of benefits any one person could claim was capped unless they could work a certain number of hours in the formal labour market. This disproportionately affected lone mothers in poverty as they were more reliant on benefits than any other group and faced a multitude of constraints in finding employment. Similarly, the limit on the child tax credit, a means tested benefit to assist in the raising of children, which was restricted to the first two children, impacted women more as women had greater primary responsibility for the care of children. These policies were challenged as breaching legal equality guarantees in the Human Rights Act. In *SG v Secretary of State for Work and Pensions*,[50] the cap was held to be prima facie discrimination against women and the UK Supreme Court came to a similar conclusion in *SC v Secretary of State for Work and Pensions* with respect to the two-child limit.[51] The next step under the Human Rights Act was the justification-stage. The state argued that the negative impact on women's equality rights was justified to make fiscal savings; to incentivise certain behaviour: paid labour force participation via the cap or the financial readiness to have children via the tax limit; and to ensure benefit fairness by not rewarding non-working people with benefits that exceeded the income of average working people.[52] The Court had to determine whether the assessment of the veracity of the state's claims were owed restraint or whether vigilance was required.

This is not an easy calibration. On one hand, *SG* and *SC* are serious and grave instances of inequality against women. The structure of the reforms system was premised on women in poverty being independent individuals with perfect autonomous control over their lives. The reforms failed to consider the multitude of constraints within and outside of the home that restricted women's agency. There was also no account taken of how imposing income poverty on women pecuniarily punished different living patterns and denigrated care work. The benefit reforms straddled multiple inequalities, the material harms (the imposition of income poverty) and the recognition harms (ignorance of gendered caring roles). On the other hand, the social benefit reforms were broadly within the fiscal policymaking space. Lord Reed observed in *SC* that there were 'a range of factors' in these cases 'which tend to heighten, or lower, the intensity of review … pulling in different directions'.[53] This echoes the dominant approaches canvassed above to calibration. But acknowledging the tension points between calibration factors gives little guidance on how to resolve them. This looseness was harnessed by the UK Supreme Court to insulate the state's choices to financially burden women from being subject to any justification scrutiny.

Factors that would pull towards a more searching justification-stage were either minimised or ignored. As argued in chapter two, the gendered recognition inequalities of the social benefits in *SG* were muted, and the harms were framed exclusively in material terms. The economic inequalities were in turn treated as insignificant. There was no accounting for how the cap and the two-child limit made it virtually impossible for lone mothers to 'adequately … house, feed, clothe and warm themselves and their children'.[54] With respect to the two-child limit in *SC*, the Court reduced the impact of the child-tax credit to the inability

[50] *SG v Secretary of State for Work and Pensions* [2015] UKSC 16 [60]–[61].
[51] *SC v Secretary of State for Work and Pensions* [2021] UKSC 26.
[52] *SG* (n 50) [63]–[66]; *SC* (n 51) [191], [193], [208].
[53] *SC* (n 51) [99].
[54] *SG* (n 50) [180].

of women to afford luxurious birthday parties for their children.[55] When the destitution imposed by the law was acknowledged, the suffering was recognised as 'undoubtedly harsh' but this was written-off as inherent in the reforms.[56] It was not used to require the state to have convincing and compelling reasons for pursuing the cap. Moreover, there was a subtle or implicit demonisation of the rights violation. The Government repeatedly emphasised that the reforms were designed to discourage benefit dependence, channel women into paid work and assist them in making better financial choices.[57] The Court did not challenge this conceptualisation of the reforms. This implicitly rooted the severity of the reforms not in the law of social benefits but in individualised moral failings. This diluted the heft of the pull factor as a searching standard of review would not be mandated for the consequences of the individual choices of undeserving poor women. At no point did the importance of ending patriarchy, sexism, or misogyny overtly factor into how closely the Court should examine the reasons for limiting women's equality. There was only passing reference that ending sex inequality was a priority for the Council of Europe but no recognition of the insidiousness of inequality nor the significance of legally protecting women's equality within the UK.

With respect to the 'push factor', the subject-matter of the claim centred on how gender bias had infected the design of social benefits. This did not require assessing the amount of benefits an individual should be able to claim from the state nor the amount of funds required to be an equal member of the community. It only required examining why in trying to achieve fiscal balance, benefit fairness and incentivising certain behaviours the state chose to ignore women's caring realities. Yet the UK Supreme Court mutated these claims into an abstract political claim on how much financial entitlement the state was required to provide an individual. Lord Reed for the leading judgment in *SG* characterised the benefit cap as reflecting 'a political view as to the nature of a fair and healthy society'[58] and that restricting social benefits was 'a matter of political judgment' between 'the interests of working and non-working households'.[59] Lord Hughes in his concurring opinion in *SG* similarly molded the subject-matter of the claim. He opined that 'the real complaint' is that the state 'reached the wrong value judgment' on whether the income support for those in poverty should be increased.[60] In a similar vein in *SC*, Lord Reed morphed the claim for the gendered design of social benefits to the broader political question on the responsibility for children. He held that the two-child limit raised 'the difficult question' on 'the extent to which it is fair, economically desirable and

[55] *SC* (n 51) [12].
[56] *DA and DS v Secretary of State for Work and Pensions* [2019] UKSC [120].
[57] *SG* (n 50) [17]–[21].
[58] ibid [66].
[59] ibid [69].
[60] ibid [155].

socially acceptable to impose the cost of supporting children whose parents lack the means to do themselves, on other members of society'.[61] Both the benefit cap and the two-child limit were also characterised as a 'question of intense political controversy'.[62] By this retelling, women's claims to equality were a guise for a large-scale political debate on whether burdens should be shouldered individually or communally. There was no recognition that while the benefit cap and two-child limit were broadly connected to economic policies, the true subject-matter of these claims was legal apathy towards women's caring roles.

This subject-matter recasting was not a benign inaccuracy but was used in the calibration exercise to hold that it would be institutionally inappropriate for the Court to scrutinise the state's decision to impose the cap and two-child limit. In *SG*, Lord Reed explained that since the benefit cap involved 'controversial issues of social and economic policy … the determination of those issues is pre-eminently the function of democratically elected institutions. Unless manifestly without reasonable foundation, their assessment should be respected'.[63]

This is more akin to an administrative law standard of review, as opposed to human rights, and has been described as a submissive standard as all that was required was that the decision to burden women via the benefit cap have some loose basis in logic.[64] The Court concluded that the cap did have this reasonable foundation. In *SC*, after framing the claim as exclusively on the amount of financial support women should receive for caring for children, Lord Reed explained that this 'cannot be answered by any process of legal reasoning'.[65] He warned that courts should not 'undermine Parliament … by requiring it … to conform to a judicial model of rationality … that model is not suitable for resolving differences of political opinion'.[66]

Although by *SC* the manifestly without reasonable foundation test had been jettisoned, due to a doctrinal steer from the European Court of Human Rights, the Court applied a light-touch proportionality standard. In a few short paragraphs, Lord Reed concluded that the impact on women was inevitable. Whether this negative inevitability was worth it, he held 'resolves itself into the question as to whether Parliament made the right judgment'[67] and

> since Parliament had decided that the importance of the objective pursued by the [two-child] limit justified its enactment, notwithstanding its greater impact on women. I see no basis on which this court should properly take a different view.[68]

[61] *SC* (n 51) [207].
[62] ibid [208].
[63] *SG* (n 50) [93].
[64] Tim Sayer, 'Manifest Unreasonableness in the UK Supreme Court: A Doctrine Working Itself Pure' (2022) 33(1) *King's Law Journal* 122; Jed Meers, 'Problems with the "Manifestly Without Reasonable Foundation" Test' (2020) 27(1) *Journal of Social Security Law* 12.
[65] *SC* (n 51) [208].
[66] ibid [171].
[67] ibid.
[68] ibid [199].

The non-weighted approach to calibration was in practice being distorted. Factors that should demand vigilance at the justification-stage were blatantly ignored, demonised, trivialised or chalked off as a harm that women must endure. Treating all calibration variables as equivalent from the outset created space for the Court to attach minimal significance to women's equality. Factors that could have potentially pointed to restraint were manipulated to inflate the fears that a forensic limitation assessment would upend democratic decision-making. Women's concerns in *SG* and *SC* that their caring roles were being legally ignored were mutated into political demands for increased monetary benefits. Not only does this bolster traditional constitutional narratives that shun and disparage care,[69] the metamorphosis of the subject-matter overwhelmed the calibration crucible and directed the limitation analysis away from an inquisitive standard of review. A malleable, contextual non-weighted calibration methodology ultimately reinforced artificial boundaries on women's equality and the exclusion of women from the constitutional ordering.

Moreover, there was little understanding that accounting for the relationship between gender and care will be controversial and radical as it requires accounting for work, effort, skill and responsibility that women have been expected to provide without compensation or even acknowledgement. *SG* and *SC* mean that women's equality only warrants a searching standard of review at the justification-stage when it is not within a politically sensitive area. But given how accounting for women's realities can require a radical rethinking of things that have long been taken for granted – assumptions that fiscal deficits are precipitated by overspending on welfare for women in poverty; that care work is not work as it springs from a fount of maternal love; or women not in formal employment are lazy or work shy – this approach condemns from the outset incursions on women's equality to minimal interrogation at the justification-stage.

B. Individualising and Privatising the Gendered Structure of Pensions

The non-weighted approach to calibration was also utilised in *Fraser v Canada* by the dissenting judges to protect decision-making that continued to rarify male working patterns.[70] Although there are differences in the utilisation of the non-weighted approach from *SG* and *SC*, the dissent in *Fraser* similarly directed all calibration factors towards a lower standard of review. Women argued that the negative pension consequences for shifting to part-time flexible work due to caring responsibilities was a violation of the equality rights in the Canadian Charter of Rights and Freedoms. As argued in chapter two, Justices Brown and

[69] Fredman (n 39).
[70] *Fraser v Canada* [2020] 3 SCR 113.

Rowe, in their dissenting judgments, used justification concepts at the equality-stage to shield from judicial view the state's failure to account for gender and care.[71] The dissents did not find an equality violation of the Charter, so there was no explicit consideration of variables that would shape the standard of review for a section 1 limitation analysis. In *obiter*, however, the dissent simultaneously downplayed the serious nature of the violation of women's equality and reshaped the subject-matter to stress the illegitimacy of constitutional review and the need for judicial restraint. Thus, it is part of a pattern of metamorphosising calibration factors.

Much like *SG* and *SC*, the factors that would pull towards a searching standard of review, the gravity of the violation of women's inequality, were given minimal weight. This is because the dissent mis-conceptualised women's inequality, locating it outside of legal structures and within individualised decision-making and behaviours. They explained that there are 'many *private* sources – that is, longstanding phenomena other than government politics – [which] also contribute to women's ongoing systemic disadvantage'.[72] Decisions on whether men or women should be the primary caregivers for children was a 'social phenomenon' of inequality divorced from situations where the 'government itself has created the inequality'.[73] This was a reassertion of the much-maligned public-private divide. Branding women's inequality as private or social was deeply ahistorical. The dissent failed to account for the long history of using legal instruments to confine women to the private sphere and did not acknowledge how that history has spilled over into contemporary sociocultural practices on care. The dissent stressed that the public was now burdened with these potential increased pension costs.[74] This misunderstood the nature of the violation. Women were arguing that it was no longer constitutional to design pensions systems exclusively around traditional male models of working.[75] Moreover, the dissent's arguments assumed that the burden of the costs would only be borne by the public and failed to account for how the economic costs for building systems based on male living patterns would continue to be borne by individual women. The gravity of building structures that economically punish women's caring realities, a factor that would push towards a searching standard of review, was reduced by the dissent to an odd, quirky, private or happenstance social phenomenon and an expensive public cost. This reformulation of the nature of the violation in *Fraser* stands as a warning that this calibration factor can also be wrongly repurposed to lower the degree of scrutiny.

[71] See also Jennifer Koshan and Jonnette Watson Hamilton, '"Clarifications" or "Wholesale Revisions"? The Last Five Years of Equality Jurisprudence at the Supreme Court of Canada' (2023) *Supreme Court Law Review*.

[72] *Fraser* (n 70) [167].

[73] ibid [207].

[74] ibid [228].

[75] Recognising that for many women the decision to scale back hours in the labour market is not an unencumbered choice; ibid [84]–[91], [104].

This misunderstanding of women's inequality, assuming it can be neatly confined between categories like social-legal or public-private, was then drawn upon to morph another calibration factor: the subject-matter of the claim. The dissent characterised the claim as the state incrementally addressing social sources of inequality against women.[76] The state permitted women to retain their jobs while balancing caring responsibilities by shifting to flexible working. Its failure to redress the negative pension consequences for this shift was labelled as incomplete but ultimately incremental ameliorative measures to redress women's disadvantage. They held the state 'must be afforded the latitude to act ... when addressing deeply ingrained complex and persistent social phenomenon such as inequality'.[77] Intensely reviewing the decision to restrict pension credits for women who went on flexible working patterns would require that the Court inappropriately adjudicate whether the state had made a good or bad policy decision.[78] The dissent argued judicial restraint was needed to protect what Parliament and the executive deemed the incremental and 'safer route'.[79] The subject-matter shifted from the constitutionality of the gender design of pensions to the temporality of undoing inequality. This shift was harnessed to frame intense scrutiny as crossing institutional boundaries. Justices Brown and Rowe also stamped the subject-matter as a 'radical measure ... with new financial obligations'.[80] This failed to recognise that undoing women's inequality inherently requires rethinking and dismantling supposed normal systems. In *Fraser*, the dissent used the subject-matter to calibrate the judicial role towards restraint and to protect decisions to pursue women's inequality from interrogation. As argued above, almost every element of women's equality can be twisted into a radical political claim and thus the justification-stage can always be calibrated to shield the decision to burden women from judicial scrutiny. Since the calibration exercise is crucial to the outcomes of claims, the mis-conceptualisation of women's equality can effectively shut women out of legal accountability and consigns the breadth and scope of their equality to the vicissitudes of the political realm.

C. Ignoring the Harms of Pregnancy Discrimination

There are two cases on sexual and reproductive health from the US Supreme Court which further emphasise the malleability of non-weighted approaches to calibrating the justification-stage. In these cases, instead of the state seeking to erode women's rights to pursue other policy goals, its aim was to strengthen

[76] ibid [210], [228].
[77] ibid [207].
[78] ibid [164].
[79] ibid [229].
[80] ibid.

equality. Other individual, groups and actors, including other actors of the state, were seeking to undo these measures and prioritise other objectives. The fact that in these cases it was the federal Government, which has strong democratic credentials, actively seeking to further women's equality would, in theory, minimise concerns on the calibration exercise and democratic illegitimacy. Yet notwithstanding this, these fears were still invoked when calibrating the degree of intensity with which these measures should be reviewed. Under the more traditional paradigm, where the state deprioritises women's equality, a low standard of review is utilised to protect democratic decision-making at the justification-stage. Conversely, when the state seeks to protect women's equality, the judgments hold that democratic legitimacy concerns mandate an uncompromising and impossible standard of review. The malleability of calibration factors, and how they can be similarly deployed even when the paradigm of the case has shifted, reveals the dangers of non-weighted approaches when women's equality is at stake.[81]

In *Nevada Department of Human Resources v Hibbs*,[82] and *Coleman v Court of Appeals of Maryland*,[83] it was the federal Government that sought to strengthen protection against pregnancy discrimination, and it was the departments in the local-level state that sought to undo these measures. Turning to *Hibbs*, to counteract women being discriminated at work due to pregnancy, Congress passed the Family and Medical Leave Act.[84] Arising out of concerns that gendered protections would result in employers continuing to perceive women as more costly to employ,[85] the Act guaranteed women and men up to 12 weeks of unpaid leave from work to care for a serious health condition of oneself, one's spouse, child, or parent. If the employer breached the Family and Medical Leave Act, the individual could bring suit. The question in *Hibbs* was whether this federal statute would apply to a local-level state, like Nevada, when the state was the employer. The Nevada Department of Human Resources objected as they argued allowing women to sue their employer, when their employer was the state, would undermine the federalist structure of the US. To protect the federal structure of the US, Congress is not permitted to pass legislation which infringes on the powers of the local-level state. Section 5 of the Fourteenth Amendment creates an exception. To remedy and deter breaches of the equal protection clause, Congress may enact appropriate legislation that places obligations upon the local-level states. The Nevada Department of Human Resources argued that the Act

[81] A similar pattern emerges when examining the US jurisprudence on affirmative action and race; see *Ricci v DeStefano* 557 US 557 (2009).

[82] *Nevada Department of Human Resources v Hibbs* 584 US 721 (2003).

[83] *Coleman* (n 30).

[84] Samuel Bagenstos, '*Nevada Department of Human Resources v Hibbs*: Universalism and Reproductive Justice' in Melissa Murray, Katherine Shaw and Reva Siegal (eds), *Reproductive Rights and Justice Stories* (Foundation Press, 2019).

[85] Deborah Dinner, 'The Costs of Reproduction: History and the Legal Construction of Sex Equality' (2011) 46 *Harvard Civil Rights-Civil Liberties Law Review* 415.

did not meet the doctrinal requirements of section 5, requirements that directly mirror justification criteria. They claimed that there was neither the evidentiary track record of the local-level state committing pregnancy discrimination nor was the Act a proportional intrusion into the local-state level sphere.[86] The majority rejected this argument but Justice Kennedy in dissent downplayed the seriousness of pregnancy discrimination while he simultaneously morphed the subject-matter of the claim to calibrate the justification assessment to defeat women's claims to equality. Although this is a dissenting opinion, it illuminates the slipperiness of non-weighted approaches to calibration. Moreover, the approach he developed in dissent in *Hibbs*, he utilised when he was in the majority in *Coleman*, analysed below, so it is worth unpacking how the push-and-pull factors were distorted in dissent in *Hibbs*.

How closely should the Court interrogate that it is constitutionally permissible for the federal Government to impede on federalism to protect women's equality? There was no explicit reflection on this question in Justice Kennedy's dissenting opinion, but he implicitly used the well-established calibration factors to defend the decision to apply a searching and penetrative degree of scrutiny to the federal Government's decision. In *Hibbs*, the push-and-pull factors were inverted from *SG*, *SC* and *Fraser* but this was a distinction without a difference as the factors were repurposed in a similar manner and with similar results. Factors that would push to a lower standard of review, such as the seriousness of women's inequality, were completely ignored by Justice Kennedy. There was limited reference or acknowledgment of the seriousness of women's inequality and the harms of pregnancy discrimination, which for many women would equate to being fired for becoming pregnant.[87] Instead he described the Family Medical Leave Act as a 'benefit' or 'entitlement program' implying that redressing pregnancy discrimination was charitable largesse rather than a grave violation of equality rights that required accountability.[88] The pull factors, the subject-matter, was amplified into a question of distributive politics. From the opening sentences of his dissenting opinion, he stressed that *Hibbs* was whether Congress was justified in 'permitting private suits for money damages against the States'.[89] He explicitly stated that 'what is at issue is *only* whether the States can be subjected, without consent, to suits brought by private persons seeking to collect moneys from the state treasury'.[90] The subject-matter of the claim was repackaged from accountability for pregnancy discrimination to women insisting that the treasury be open to them.

[86] *City of Boerne v Flores*___521 US 507 (1997).
[87] Stephanie Bornstein, 'The Politics of Pregnancy Accommodation' (2020) 14 *Harvard Law and Policy Review* 293.
[88] *Hibbs* (n 82) 744, 745, 754, 756.
[89] ibid 744.
[90] ibid 759.

This was a non-weighted approach as Justice Kennedy determined the weight that would be assigned to the calibration factors. He glided over pregnancy discrimination, the heart of the claim, and emphasised the subject-matter not as accountability for employment discrimination but as impact on public finances to ratchet up the standard of review. Justice Kennedy concluded that 'Courts should be more careful to insist on adherence to the analytic requirements' of abrogating local-level state sovereign immunity.[91] Public funds cannot be used to remedy pregnancy discrimination at work on the basis of 'conjecture' and it is insufficient to 'simply not[e] the problem' of gender inequality at work.[92] The standard of review when the state advances women's equality was high. This proved fatal for the dissent and manifested in a lack of deference to Congress' decision-making. The history of state laws that limited women's employment opportunities, witness testimony before Congress and the shortcomings in current state-level caring laws were dismissed as 'too remote' to justify opening up local-state level budgets to accountability for discrimination.[93] The dismissal of detailed and extensive evidence of systemic and severe discrimination against women indicates an impossible standard of review. Much like in *Wal-Mart v Dukes*, as argued in chapter two, evidence of women's inequality was brushed off. The repeated rejection of concrete proof on inequality implies an ideological resistance to constitutionally protecting women's rights. Turning back to calibration, although there was an inversion of push-and-pull factors and the standard of review was ratcheted up, the result was the same as in *SG*, *SC* and *Fraser*. The gravity of women's inequality was muted, the democratic legitimacy of opening up public funds was overemphasised, and the standard of review was calibrated so as to defeat women's claims for constitutional equality.

Justice Kennedy's non-weighted methodology for calibrating the justification of using section 5 of the Fourteenth Amendment was reiterated in *Coleman*, but as mentioned above, this time he was writing in the majority. In *Coleman*, the Family and Medical Leave Act was again challenged as breaching section 5 of the Fourteenth Amendment. The Court of Appeals of Maryland argued it was unconstitutional to allow employees 12 weeks of unpaid leave to care for themselves and to permit them to sue their employers, including the local-level state if that was their employer, if they were not given this leave. Although both men and women need self-care leave, the provision was connected to women's equality. Feminists at the time the Act was passed were worried that signalling out pregnancy leave would continue to legitimatise employers disadvantaging women at work.[94] The majority opinion ignored this context when assessing the justification for intruding on federalism and this failure is examined in chapter five. But with respect to calibrating how intensely the Court would look

[91] ibid 746.
[92] ibid 748, 749.
[93] ibid 749.
[94] *Coleman* (n 30) (dissenting opinion of Justice Ginsburg).

at the federal Government's arguments, Justice Kennedy employed a similar calibration method as he used in *Hibbs*. The push factor of women's equality was treated much like the dissent in *Fraser* as a social harm disconnected from the Constitution. Justice Kennedy explained that 'documented discrimination against women in the general workplace is a persistent, unfortunate reality, and, we must assume, a still prevalent wrong'.[95] It is disturbing that Justice Kennedy would only assume that women's inequality at work was prevalent against the wealth of evidence in Congress, explored in Justice Ginsburg's dissent, on the systemic nature of discrimination at work. The pull factor of the subject-matter was again framed in terms of protecting individual access to public funds.[96] This ratcheted up the standard of review and the Court branded the voluminous evidence on Congress' strategy with respect to the self-care provision as unconvincing. Throughout the judgment, the majority opinion held the Act was only justified if the federal Government's arguments were not based on 'supposition and conjecture', 'abstract generalities', a 'few fleeting references' or 'isolated sentences clipped from floor debates'.[97] According to the majority, the federal Government did not meet this standard and the self-care provision which aimed to prevent women from being discriminated at work for becoming pregnant was struck down as unconstitutional.

Although not all judgments fall into this trap, there is a trend where the practice of non-weighted approaches is riddled with misunderstanding and misconceptions which operate to distort the exercise and wrongly calibrate the justification-stage. Women's inequality is repeatedly downplayed, trivialised, ignored and written off as a social phenomenon divorced from the law. The subject-matter of the claims, which in the cases above all centre on women's caring roles, are repurposed into macro-level debates on distributive politics. The misshapen subject-matter of the claim is then used to hold that it would be institutionally inappropriate to apply a searching standard of review. The practice of calibrating does not overcome the theoretical jaggedness between non-weighted approaches to calibrating the justification-stage and women's equality. Rather, it accelerates them and condemns women's equality to minimal review.

D. The Disingenuousness of Non-Weighted Approaches

Decades ago, MacKinnon warned that 'to the extent that feminist law embodies women's point of view … it will be said that it undermines the legitimacy of the legal system'.[98] This branding is manifesting in the calibration of the

[95] ibid 42.
[96] ibid 41.
[97] ibid 41–42.
[98] MacKinnon (n 13) 618.

justification-stage when assessing limits on women's equality. In the traditional paradigm where the state has breached women's equality, the courts are minimising the severity of women's inequality, a factor that should pull towards a searching standard of review and mischaracterising the subject-matter of the claim so as to push towards a light-touch standard of review to protect the separation of powers. When it is the state seeking to advance women's equality despite the negative impact on other rights and interests, there is a similar pattern: the seriousness of women's inequality is downplayed, and the subject-matter is morphed. The manipulation and arguably disingenuousness use of non-weighted approaches is marked when contrasting *SG*, *SC*, *Fraser*, *Hibbs* and *Coleman* with other high-profile decisions that had similar tension points between calibration factors. In prominent decisions from the UK and US Supreme Court, judges who expressed scepticism on the institutional appropriateness of interrogating decisions to limit women's equality are much more interventionist when applying limitation criteria when assessing limits with respect to other rights. In these cases, the seriousness of the rights breach is fully accounted for and overwhelms the calibration crucible despite the subject-matter of the breach being in relation to fiscal policymaking. While this subsection only examines two prominent cases, this destabilises any idea that calibration factors that seek to protect the constitutional nature of human rights and redress democratic legitimacy concerns are objectively applied. Noting this disjuncture provides further evidence of the malleability, and perhaps emptiness, of non-weighted approaches.

A landmark case on the rule of law from the UK helps illustrate the elusiveness of the non-weighted methodology to calibrating the justification-stage. In *UNISON v Lord Chancellor*, the UK Supreme Court had to determine whether imposing user fees to access employment tribunals was unlawful.[99] Women argued the user fees were indirectly discriminatory, but this claim was rejected.[100] The case was primarily decided based on European Union and common law rights to access justice. There was a similar array of calibrating factors in *UNISON* and *SG* and *SC*. On one hand, this was an incursion on access to justice, but, on the other hand, the user fees were broadly in the field of economic and fiscal policy, as fees were meant to transfer the costs of maintaining a justice system to individual users.[101] The resolution of these tensions in *UNISON* was diametrically different than when the Court resolved push-and-pull factors when women's inequality in social benefits was at stake.

The seriousness of the violation of an individual's access to justice was fully weighed. Lord Reed observed employment tribunals serve individual and social aims by seeking to redress the power imbalance between employers

[99] *UNISON v Lord Chancellor* [2017] UKSC 51.
[100] ibid [133].
[101] ibid [11].

and employees.[102] With respect to the nature of the right, by crunching the numbers, the Court observed that the imposition of user fees would demand that individuals be required 'to sacrifice ... ordinary and reasonable expenditure [as] ... the process of access to one's rights'.[103] Affordable access to accountability mechanisms to resolve individual employment disputes was also elevated as necessary to the lifeblood of democracy. Lord Reed explained that

> without ... access, laws are liable to become a dead letter, the work done by Parliament may be rendered nugatory and the democratic election of Members of Parliament may become a meaningless charade. That is why courts do not merely provide a public service like any other.[104]

As argued above, there was no equivalent understanding of the constitutional importance of ending women's inequality, the grave impact of the reforms on individual women's lives or the expressive harm the reforms had towards women's caring roles. There was a similar differential treatment of the subject-matter factor. In *UNISON*, despite the state repeatedly arguing the fees were in place to ease financial burdens on taxpayers, the subject-matter of the claim was not framed in terms of executive and legislative economic decision-making.[105] Neither did Lord Reed evaluate any political controversary with respect to the fees nor whether in a pluralistic democracy individuals should bear the cost of enforcing their own employment rights. The majority in *UNISON* did not frame the subject-matter of the claim as such but rather stressed the fundamental value of access to justice to the rule of law and constitutional democracy.[106] The characterisation of the core issues in *UNISON* did not activate separation of power concerns and consequentially there were no factors that pushed the Court towards a minimal standard of review at the justification-stage.

Despite the existence of similar calibration tension points between *UNISON* and *SG* and *SC*, the Court in *UNISON* latched onto the seriousness of the breach of rights and used this factor to employ a searching justification standard when assessing the veracity of the state's reasons for undermining access to justice. The Court was there to ensure that user fees were only in place if they could be 'justified as reasonably necessary to meet a legitimate objective'.[107] This was the more searching proportionality standard. Notably, the fiscal aspects of the case did not push the Court towards using the lower manifestly without reasonable foundation test it employed in *SG*. And unlike *SC*, in *UNISON* Lord Reed applied proportionality in a forensic and rigorous manner not accepting the state's claims at face-value but sifting evidence and testing claims against the

[102] ibid [6], [8].
[103] ibid [55].
[104] ibid [68].
[105] ibid [9], 11], [56], [99].
[106] ibid [66]–[72].
[107] ibid [89].

criteria.[108] In taking this searching approach to justification there was no reference made to the sacrosanctity of democracy requiring the Court to accept the budget decisions of the state, claims that were central to the calibration of *SG* and SC. This is not to argue that *UNISON* was wrongly decided or that the Court wrongly calibrated the justification-stage, as the case correctly identified the serious breach of rights, crucially protects equal access to justice and advances a more positive and communitarian understanding of the rule of law.[109] This analysis of *UNISON*, *SG and SC* forms a map on where (and where not) the importance of rights and the fears of democratic illegitimacy arguments feed into the calibration of the justification-stage.

The inconsistency in deploying calibration factors is also evident in the US Supreme Court's jurisprudence on women's affordable access to contraception. This litigation has been protracted, contentious and complex. Under the Affordable Care Act, the employer group health plan must cover preventive health care without cost-sharing to the employee and the Health Resources and Services Administration held that preventive health care included contraception. Hobby Lobby, a closely held corporation, argued that this inclusion was in violation of their religious beliefs which were protected under the Religious Freedom and Restoration Act. Under the Act, the state could not substantially burden religious beliefs unless the state had a compelling interest and the measure was the least restrictive means. This has strong echoes with various limbs of the proportionality justification framework. Although there was no explicit discussion of calibration factors, implicitly the standard of review for determining how compelling and persuasive the state's arguments on the justification for pursuing women's equality over religious freedom was shaped by the well-established push-and-pull factors. This was a difficult calibration as *Hobby Lobby v Burwell* is a case where rights are in conflict.[110] On one side, there is the pull factor, the right to religious freedom and belief which in pluralistic democracies is an important right. On the push side, the state has chosen to prioritise women's equality by ensuring that their health was not compromised by their inability to control their reproductive health.

The calibration exercise in *Hobby Lobby* was highly malleable and lacked fidelity to calibration concerns, expressed by Justice Kennedy in *Hibbs* and *Coleman*. With respect to whether including contraception as preventive health care in an employer group health plan placed a substantial burden on the religious beliefs of closely held corporations, Justice Alito for the majority accepted the claim that it did without subjecting that claim to any real interrogation. The Court employed a light-touch review in assessing the nature of the burden on religious beliefs as it did not interrogate whether the inclusion of contraception

[108] ibid [100].
[109] Michael Ford, 'Employment Tribunal Fees and the Rule of Law: *R (Unison) v Lord Chancellor* in the Supreme Court' (2018) 47(1) *Industrial Law Journal* 1.
[110] *Hobby Lobby v Burwell* 573 US 682 (2014).

in a group health plan was too remote but simply accepted that the corporations believed it would implicate their beliefs.[111] Justice Ginsburg in her dissent repeatedly called out the majority for failing to use a more searching standard to inquire whether the alleged burden was substantial or whether it was too attenuated to meet the standards of the Act.[112]

With respect to the state's compelling interest, the standard of review shifted. When assessing whether the state substantively burdened religion, the Court employed a minimal standard but when assessing whether it was legal for the state to do so it shifted to a searching one. Justice Alito held that the state bears a heavy obligation in defending why it is necessary to burden religion, explaining that this stage of the analysis was 'exceptionally demanding'.[113] There was an implication that the state had not met the compelling interest standard as similar to *Hibbs*, *Coleman*, *SG*, *SC* and *Fraser*, there was a downplaying of the gravity of women's inequality. Justice Alito explained that the state's compelling interests were 'couched in very broad terms, such as promoting "public health" and "gender equality".'[114] The use of scare quotes implied a degree of disbelief or scepticism that contraception was related to women's health and equality. The standard of review was increased to invalidate the strong links between contraception, equality and health. Despite this scepticism, the majority accepted there was a compelling interest in ensuring women had no cost-sharing access to contraception. However, the Court applied this intense standard of review to the least restrictive means and did so in a way that was in conflict with the calibration arguments put forward in *Hibbs* and *Coleman*. Justice Alito queried why the state, which claimed the contraception mandate was designed to further women's equality and public health, did not just use public funds to ensure contraception was affordable and accessible?[115] Couldn't Congress have paid for contraception to avoid burdening religious beliefs? This proposition would have monumental budgetary implications and be politically controversial, as all debates on publicly funded health care are in the US.[116] The Court concluded that protecting religious freedom may require the state 'to expend additional funds to accommodate citizens' religious beliefs'.[117] While the majority opinion ultimately concluded the mandate was not the least restrictive as it felt the state could expand accommodations given to non-profit organisations to closely held corporations,[118] it was not reluctant in *obiter dicta* to tell Congress to spend a significant amount of money. In *Hibbs* and *Coleman*, Justice Kennedy employed

[111] ibid 35–8 (majority opinion of Justice Alito).
[112] ibid 21 (dissenting opinion of Justice Ginsberg).
[113] ibid 40 (majority opinion of Justice Alito).
[114] ibid 39 (majority opinion of Justice Alito).
[115] ibid 41 (majority opinion of Justice Alito).
[116] Frederick Gedicks, 'One Cheer for Hobby Lobby: Improbably Alternatives, Truly Strict Scrutiny and Third-Party Employee Burdens' (2015) *Harvard Journal of Law and Gender* 152, 157–63.
[117] *Hobby Lobby* (n 110) 43 (majority opinion of Justice Alito).
[118] ibid.

a vigilant standard of review so as to protect public funds from being misspent, but in *Hobby Lobby* the Court used a searching standard that disregarded fiscal institutional limits. This was a quintessential example, to borrow from Justice Scalia in *Coleman*, of grading Congress' homework.

The standard of review for the least restrictive means ignored two further democratic legitimacy factors that should have pushed the Court towards a lighter-touch assessment. Congress had specifically rejected including a religious belief accommodation for non-religious organisations, a democratic legitimacy factor that should have pulled the Court towards a more minimal standard of reviewing when assessing the least restrictive means.[119] The democratic branches of the state had evaluated and weighed up the possibility of accommodating, but this was ignored by the majority. Similarly, the repercussions of permitting religious accommodation, the fact that thousands if not millions of women would face a change in their preventative health care and were being told their health came second to a corporation's beliefs did not weigh in the majority's calibration crucible.[120] This is not to be taken as holding that it is constitutionally inappropriate for courts to hold that the fulfilment of rights requires positive duties including through financing policies and programmes. What is required is that the assessment give careful consideration to the degree of scrutiny and skipping over highly relevant calibration factors weakens claims that the state could avoid infringing religious rights through funding contraception. The strength of this claim, that Congress should pay for contraception access, in the context of long and vicious debates on publicly funded health care in the US are explored in chapter five when arguing that courts hollow out justification criteria. For the purposes of this chapter and establishing the high degree of malleability of non-weighted approaches, *UNISON* and *Hobby Lobby* are only two examples, and care should be taken not to extrapolate too far from these decisions. But these cases highlight troubling inconsistencies. Calibration factors were not deployed in a consistent manner. This is concerning as the non-weighted approach doesn't simply allow for flexibility or sensitivity to context but leaves too much space for the calibration exercise to go awry.

IV. WOMEN'S EQUALITY REQUIRES INQUIRING JUDICIAL MINDS

Non-weighted approaches to calibration which dominate the justification-stage create friction points in theory and practice with women's equality. Conceptual misunderstandings of women's inequality along with inaccurate distortions of the subject-matter of the claim have resulted in justification-stages that are wrongly calibrated. This cripples that justification-stage as it is impossible to

[119] ibid 6 (dissenting opinion of Justice Ginsburg).
[120] ibid 2 (dissenting opinion of Justice Ginsburg).

test whether limitation claims meet the rigour of justification criteria. A new calibration methodology is needed when courts are assessing the boundaries of women's equality rights. Calibration is not a blank slate exercise where all calibrating factors are of equal weight, significance and importance. A weighted approach is required.

When restricting women's equality is at stake, the arguments that those restrictions are permissible should always be subject to a high degree of scrutiny. There are two overwhelming pull factors that translate into a searching justification-stage: the severity of women's inequality and the importance of constitutional guarantees of equality.

A. The Severity of Women's Equality

When calibrating the standard of review women's inequality should never be framed as a trivial or non-serious harm. While this point was canvased above, it is worth repeating, as the judicial practice of calibration repeatedly ignores or minimises the harms of sex and gender inequality. There are competing and overlapping theories on the wrongfulness of inequality[121] and different courts utilise different conceptions to explicate the wrong of women's inequality. The aim here is not to develop a theory on the wrong of women's inequality but to argue that the harms are significant, as it is the degree of harm that pulls the intensity of review to the highest standard. The decisions on division of labour within the home is not merely a social phenomenon as these decisions are made in the shadow of the law and have significant legal consequences for women up to the point of economic destitution and homelessness.[122] Women's exclusion from symbolic or ceremonial roles or the pay gaps for women who are high earners are not meaningless or unimportant but convey pernicious attitudes towards the role and value of women. Inequality against women is inherently serious as it expresses beliefs that men are intrinsically more worthy than women.[123] The gravity of all forms of inequality against women should pull the justification-stage towards a searching standard of review. It has been argued that a lower standard of review expresses respect for democratic decision-making.[124] This argument, however, cuts the other way. A searching investigation expresses respect for the acute burdens that women are expected to bear to achieve other competing aims. If women are meant to legally endure economic precarity, patriarchal sociocultural norms that ignore, demean and stigmatise them and

[121] Sophie Moreau, *Faces of Inequality: A Theory of Wrongful Discrimination* (Oxford University Press, 2020); Iyiola Solanke, *Discrimination as Stigma* (Hart Publishing, 2017); Tarun Khaitan, *A Theory of Discrimination Law* (Oxford University Press, 2015).

[122] *Daniels v Campbell* [2004] ZACC 14; *Sithole v Sithole* [2021] ZACC 7; *Women's Legal Centre Trust v President of the Republic of South Africa* [2022] ZACC 23.

[123] Mackinnon (n 13); *Bhe* (n 18) [71].

[124] Chan (n 5) ch 2.

constraints on their agency, it is fitting that the justification-stage respect the magnitude of harms women have endured and continue to endure by applying limitation criteria in a ruthlessly interrogating manner. Women's inequality is a weighted pull factor that demands vigilance against claims it can be further perpetuated.

The load women are being asked to bear is not alleviated or of lesser importance because inequalities seep into areas of life that have not traditionally been conceptualised as legal. Fiscal decisions assume that women do not have childcare duties, immigration rules still conceptualise men as free from responsibility for the care of their own children and criteria for promotion in the army fail to account for women's physiology. Women's inequality is not contained, and laws and policies in all areas of life manifest patriarchal attitudes and structures. The severity of that inequality is not lessened simply because it is in areas of life traditionally protected from judicial scrutiny. Lowering the degree of scrutiny at the justification-stage can dangerously result in courts accepting at face-value claims that breaching women's rights is worth it regardless of the severity of that breach or the flimsiness of limitation claims simply because that inequality occurs within certain realms of life. Patriarchy does not respect subject-matter boundaries, and the calibration exercise should not seek to put artificial constraints on how patriarchy operates. Women's inequality is a constant pull factor for calibrating the justification-stage.

This does not run roughshod over democratic legitimacy concerns that the subject-matter factor seeks to protect. A weighted approach brings much needed nuance and accuracy to the subject-matter factor which in turn rapidly deescalates democratic legitimacy concerns.

Assigning significance to women's inequality shifts the calibration away from broad and even clunky characterisations of the subject-matter from macro-level political debates to the specific inequality issues. Courts are not questioning why the state has not provided greater monetary support or grading policy choices on how best to statutorily protect work-life balance. They are asking why the law has been designed in such a way as to perpetuate inequality against women. The subject-matter is in the inequality and precisely where that inequality occurs is incidental or secondary. Resisting broad and inaccurate characterisations of the subject-matter as a push factor is also a recognition that women's inequality is not contained in the paradigm of serious-trivial or legal-political. Undertaking a searching justification analysis in non-orthodox areas of life is simply another iteration of the radical nature of women's equality. Protecting the legal right to women's equality requires a breakthrough against conceptual boundaries and challenges status quo assumptions on what is or is not amenable to searching judicial review. This is part of the transformative nature of women's equality. Moreover, there is nothing constitutionally inappropriate in asking for a rigorous defence of why inequality is required, be it within criminal law, social benefits or employment. A weighted approach does not demand that courts in the abstract and based purely on their own subjective views decide where constitutional priorities should lie. It does, however, demand that courts assess how the executive and legislative bodies have decided on the constitutional ordering by forensically applying accepted justification criteria. Courts are not overreaching their role in the separation of powers by having inquisitive minds to claims that women's equality should be limited. All that is required is that courts do not accept limitation claims at face-value and that any justification argument be rigorously interrogated for its veracity, strength and persuasiveness against established criteria.

B. Importance of Constitutional Guarantees of Equality

With respect to the second weighted calibration factor, the calibration exercise should echo that women's right to equality is of the utmost constitutional importance. Equality rights serve a central purpose in undoing enduring legacies of gendered disadvantage, stigma, oppression, and exclusion. As a testament to the crucial role of equality rights in the constitutional order, there are arguments and judicial decisions, particularly from the Indian Supreme Court, that the basic structure of the Constitution prohibits amendments that abrogate equality as constitutional value.[125] When considering the prohibition of women of menstrual age entering a religious temple, Justice Chandrachud in the Indian Supreme Court observed the aspirations of equality rights, that the drafters wanted to

> transform Indian society by remedying centuries of discrimination against Dalits, women and the marginalised. They sought to provide them a voice by creating a culture of rights. Above all, placing those who were denuded of their human rights before the Advent of the Constitution whether in the veneer of caste, patriarchy or otherwise, were to be placed in control of their own destinies by the assurance of equal protection of the law.[126]

The importance of achieving women's equality resounds across other jurisdictions. Even jurisdictions like the US, when at the constitutional founding and at key constitutional moments, like the drafting of the Fourteenth Amendment, women's inequality was an (un)spoken assumption.[127] Yet the seriousness of women's inequality, through the mobilisation of thousands of women across decades and centuries, worked its way into the constitutional structure. This is evident not only through the Nineteenth Amendment, women's right to vote, but also through 'pushing the Supreme Court to enforce constitutional protections against sex discrimination after decades in which the Court tolerated, endorsed

[125] Sudhir Krishnaswamy, *Democracy and Constitutionalism in India: A Study of the Basic Structure Doctrine* (Oxford University Press, 2010).

[126] *Indian Young Lawyers Association* (n 17) [2].

[127] Hasday, 'Exclusion from the Canon' (n 14).

and reinforced legalized subordination of women to men'.[128] By protecting the right to equality in constitutions there is, as Nedelsky argues, a communal acceptance on the importance of women's equality and the need to be vigilant against risks to women's equality.[129] The fundamental importance of women's equality is a calibration factor that demands a searching, rigorous, intense or heightened degree of scrutiny at the justification-stage. Allowing other calibration factors to dilute the standard to a light-touch application of justification criteria can permit women's equality to be limited on the basis of ignorance, speculation, conjecture or arguments devoid of logic, rationality and evidence. This grossly undercuts the aims of constitutionalising the right to equality and disrespects the strength of women's equality. Others have argued for a weighed approach to the balancing limb of proportionality as a methodology for respecting the fundamental nature of rights.[130] However, this is insufficient as it confines the respect that rights demand to only one justification criteria. The entire justification exercise including the meta question on how closely to scrutinise limitation claims needs to be in tandem with the value the constitution places on women's equality.

The Indian Supreme Court is instructive as it is using the insidiousness of inequality and the significance of equality rights to calibrate the degree of scrutiny. In *Anuj Garg v Hotel Association*, the Court had to assess whether it was justified to prohibit women working in places that sold alcohol to protect them from workplace violence.[131] The fact-legal matrix of *Anuj Garg* could be manipulated to stress the non-seriousness of the prohibition, only one type of work is being constrained, or the controversy of the claim could have been hyped, changing sociocultural norms, to rationalise a lower standard of review. But the Court did the opposite. It weighed the breach of women's equality seriously as the prohibition struck at women's autonomy and was in breach of that fundamental tenant. This directly translated into the need for a searching justification assessment. Justice Singha held that a 'heightened level of scrutiny is the normative threshold for judicial review in such cases'.[132] He further explained:

> In hard cases, the issue of biological difference between sexes gathers an overtone of societal conditions so much so that the real differences are pronounced by the oppressive cultural norms of the time. This combination of biological and social determinants may find expression in popular legislative mandate. *Such legislations*

[128] ibid 1722; Reva Siegel, 'Gender and the US Constitution: Equal Protection, Privacy and Federalism' in Beverley Baines and Ruth Rubio-Marin (eds), *The Gender of Constitutional Jurisprudence* (Cambridge University Press, 2010).

[129] Jennifer Nedelsky, 'Reconceiving Rights as Relationships' (1993) *Review of Constitutional Studies* 1.

[130] Matthias Klatt and Moritz Meister, 'Proportionality: A Benefit to Human Rights? Remarks on ICON Controversy' (2012) 10(3) *International Journal of Constitutional Law* 687.

[131] *Anuj Garg v Hotel Association* [2007] 12 SCR 991.

[132] ibid [45]; Tarun Khaitan, 'Beyond Reasonableness-A Rigorous Standard of Review for Article 15 Infringement (2008) 50(2) *Journal of the Indian Law Institute* 177.

> *definitely deserve deeper judicial scrutiny*. It is for the court to review that the majoritarian impulses rooted in moralistic tradition do not impinge upon individual autonomy. *This is the backdrop of deeper judicial scrutiny* of such legislations world over (emphasis added).[133]

Rather than trying to splice the degree of inequality or identify its roots in private or social decisions, there was a strong acknowledgement that women's inequality is a helix of biology, social norms and legal practices. There was also a recognition in *Anuj Garg* that women's inequality can seem natural or traditional and that rooting out how normalcy can be a guise for patriarchy required a forensic application of justification criteria. It was a weighted approach as the inequality was serious and so was the need to protect women's autonomy that pulled the degree of scrutiny towards an intense judicial interrogation of the state's reasons for limiting women's rights. The Indian Supreme Court reiterated the weighted calibration methodology in *Hotel Priya v State of Maharashtra* when assessing whether the restriction on the number of men and women performing on stage in bars and restaurants was justified to protect women from exploitation.[134] Justice Bhat held 'it is the *task of judges to scrutinize closely*, whether, if the extent to which the impugned practices, rules or norms are rooted in historical prejudice, gender stereotypes and paternalism. Such attitudes have no place in our society (emphasis added)'.[135] The gendered restriction was socially controversial but notably this did not weigh in the Court's calibration exercise.[136] It was the entwined seriousness of inequality and the need for that inequality to end that pulled the court to a searching standard of reviewing when assessing limitation arguments.

The proposed weighted methodology should be employed when it is other stakeholders, and not the state, seeking to rollback efforts to protect women's equality rights. US feminist legal scholars, like Suk, have worried that an interrogative standard of review will result in the US Supreme Court defeating affirmative action-like measures that seek to advance women's equality.[137] Recent jurisprudence from the Court has used an intense standard of review to gut affirmative action for racial inequality.[138] But reverting to a lower standard of review to protect efforts to advance women's equality through legislation would be a wrong turn.[139] As per the analysis of *Hibbs, Coleman* and *Hobby Lobby*, the impossible standard of review used by the Court was a function of ignoring women's inequality and mutating the subject-matter of the claim. The

[133] ibid [39].
[134] *Hotel Priya v State of Maharashtra* (2022) Civil Appeal No 13764 of 2012.
[135] ibid [48].
[136] ibid.
[137] Julie Suk, 'An Equal Rights Amendment for the Twenty-First Century: Bringing Global Constitutionalism Home' (2017) 28 *Yale Journal of Law and Feminism* 381.
[138] *Students for Fair Admissions v Harvard*___600 US 181 (2023).
[139] Martha Davis, 'Sex-Based Citizenship Classification and the "New Rationality" 89(2) *Albany Law Review* 851.

solution lies not in reverting to a lower standard of review but in bringing suspicion to any argument that women's equality should be rolled back or limited regardless of whether those arguments come from the state or from non-state actors. A weighted approach demands respect for women's equality, and in cases where it is non-state actors arguing for limitations, this requires investigating and not glossing over the state's understanding of how the measure in question advances women's equality. At the same time, it brings an inquiring mind into arguments that women's equality undermines or destabilises other objectives. In *Coleman*, this would translate into respecting the state's argument for how the self-care provision in the Family Leave and Medical Act ring-fences women from pregnancy discrimination and being suspicious of claims that accountability up-ends federalism. Or in *Hobby Lobby*, this would require taking seriously the role contraception plays in women's equality and querying how inclusion of contraception in a group health plan violates the religious beliefs of corporations. More practically, employing a lower standard of review to protect measures to advance women's equality runs the risk of reverting to a lower standard when the state breaches women's equality rights, resulting in women's inequality being justified on the basis of weak arguments.

Calibrating the standard of review is not a blank slate where all calibration factors are in the abstract of similar weight. Equality guides the calibration exercise. The primary calibrating agents at the justification-stage when adjudicating women's claims to equality is the gravity of inequality and the constitutional importance of achieving equality. These weighted factors require an intense standard of review. It is also important to remember that calibration is only the beginning of the justification-stage as it simply directs the court to forensically apply and consider justification criteria. It does not preclude a finding that women's equality cannot be limited. The weighted approach only demands that women's equality rights be limited on the basis of persuasive, compelling, logical and evidence-backed arguments. Placing women's equality beyond limitation is too simplistic and fails to recognise the complexities, contradictions, and complications of modern governance. Moreover, calibrating to an impossible degree of intensity could have negative repercussions as it runs the risk that the equality-stage will operate as a de facto limitation analysis. As argued in chapter two, the spilling over of justification concepts into the equality analysis shields from judicial scrutiny the gravity of women's inequality, makes it significantly more difficult to establish a breach of the right and alleviates the obligation to openly defend the decision to burden women's equality.

V. THE STRENGTHS OF A WEIGHTED APPROACH IN PRACTICE

Pulling the justification-stage to a searching investigation by assigning significant weight to the seriousness of women's inequality and the importance of achieving women's equality has many advantages over non-weighted approaches and addresses the normative objectives that underpin the entire calibration exercise. It ensures that the limitation analysis demonstrates respect for the constitutional imperative of guaranteeing women's equality. It respects that grave gendered disadvantage, stigma, oppression and exclusion occur within all realms of life including areas traditionally thought unamenable to a searching standard of review. And it can correct the mischaracterisation and misunderstandings that riddle the practice of calibration to ensure that a searching standard of review continues to be faithful to the institutional boundaries of the court. This section investigates three decisions which were in subject-matters areas that have long been held to attract a minimal degree of scrutiny: fiscal emergencies, socio-cultural attitudes on sexuality and immigration to mark out how the strengths of a weighted approach to calibration can be harnessed by courts while at the same time respecting the role of courts in the separation of powers.

A. The Crisis of Equal Pay

Women's economic equality was at stake in the management of an unprecedented economic crisis. This, however, did not push the Supreme Court of Canada towards a submissive or deferential standard of review when assessing why the limits on women's equality were required for the fiscal health of the state. It used the weighted approach to simultaneously fully account for the harms of inequality and the limits of courts in navigating an economic collapse. Newfoundland and Labrador agreed to a Pay Equity Agreement with women working in the health care sector. This Agreement laid out a process and methodology for implementing equal pay with full equal pay to be achieved over a four-year period. After the Agreement was signed, and before any part of it had been implemented, the province passed the Public Sector Restraint Act which erased three years of back pay for these women, amounting to close to $24 million dollars. The state's equal pay obligation was statutorily wiped away because the province was experiencing 'a financial crisis unprecedented in the Province's history … to the point where the Province's credit rating in financial markets were seriously at risk'.[140] In *Newfoundland (Treasury Board) v NAPE*, the Supreme Court determined that statutorily removing the equal pay obligation was a violation of women's equality rights.

The lower courts had adopted a non-weighted approach to calibration. The harms of the gender pay gap and the significance of women's equality were not automatic factors pulling the section 1 limitation analysis to an intense standard of review. Much like in *SG* and *SC*, the lower courts in Canada were blinded by the subject-matter. They were concerned that reviewing the state decision would require 'the judiciary to assume the role of final arbitrator of the correctness of

[140] *Newfoundland (Treasury Board) v NAPE* [2004] 3 SCR 381 [7].

policy initiatives within the purview of the political branches of government'.[141] The magnitude of the financial situation and the significant risk of 'burgeoning fiscal deficits'[142] pushed the lower courts to applying the *Oakes* proportionality test in a way that showed 'judicial deference to policy choices adopted by the elected representative to address communal or societal needs'.[143] They held the revocation of the equal pay agreement was a justifiable limit on women's equality.

The Canadian Supreme Court, however, adopted a different calibration methodology, more in-line with the proposed weighted approach. Although *NAPE* was in the realm of the political economy, Justice Binnie for the Court focused the calibration exercise on the seriousness of rights. The opening sentence of the section 1 justification-stage started by anchoring the analysis in women's equality. He explained that 'it should be stated at the outset that legislation aimed at perpetuating pay inequity is a very serious matter'.[144] This framed the entire limitation evaluation around the harms of the unequal pay. Justice Binnie further warned that 'if an individual's Charter right or freedom is violated by the state, it is no answer to say that violation was driven or justified for political reasons'.[145] The subject-matter of the claim, budgetary decisions during a crisis, did not vitiate that serious rights infringements happen within that decision-making space. There was the danger of allowing the subject-matter to overwhelm the calibration crucible, for

> if the 'political branches' are to be the 'final arbitrator' of compliance with the Charter of their 'policy initiatives', it would seem the enactment of the Charter affords no real protection at all to the rightsholders …Charter rights and freedoms … would offer rights without a remedy.[146]

Characterising equal pay as 'too political' would hollow the purpose of constitutionally protecting rights thereby undercutting the central purpose of equality in section 15 of the Charter. A cursory application of the *Oakes* limitation test would render 'superfluous the independent second look imposed on the courts by s1 of the Charter. Deference to the majority view would leave little protection to the minorities'.[147] The court's role at justification was not to rubber-stamp the state's determination through a light-touch review that violating women's equality was worth it, the importance of equality demanded more.

An intense section 1 analysis, however, did not require the Court to weigh in on the best way to manage a fiscal emergency. The weighted approach helped correctly identify the subject-matter of the claim which in turn steered the

[141] ibid [24] citing *Newfoundland (Treasury Board) v NAPE* (2002) 221 DLR (4th) 513 [365].
[142] ibid [26].
[143] ibid [28].
[144] ibid [52].
[145] ibid [81].
[146] ibid [111].
[147] ibid [103].

application of justification criteria in a manner that was sensitive to the difficult choices of the electorate. Within the factual-legal matrix of *NAPE*, the crux at the justification-stage was on whether the revocation of equal pay was minimally impairing. This did not require the Court to overstep its role in the constitutional architecture by conclusively determining the best routes for managing an economic crisis. Using the weighted approach, the Court instead anchored the subject-matter in the alleged inequality. Justice Binnie started this limb of the proportionality analysis by asking 'were the Charter rights of the female hospital workers impaired no more than as reasonably necessary to achieve … fiscal viability?'[148] It was not a freewheeling analysis into competing economic theories but a demand that the state provide persuasive evidence that the state had considered and weighed other financial options. The Court held the state had discharged this burden.[149] It examined the process of how the decision to revoke the equal pay was arrived at and did not seek to impose its own opinion on how competing budget imperatives should be resolved.

NAPE is evidence that a weighted approach does not foreclose limiting rights, but it does mark that any limitation claims must be of the highest quality. This was a controversial decision and has been subject to strong feminist legal critique centering on disputes around whether the evidentiary record proved that the state met the demanding section 1 requirements.[150] The key point, for this chapter, is that calibrating the justification-stage was weighted with women's equality and that the democratic legitimacy concerns were redressed through using equality to accurately articulate the subject-matter of the claim and through a proper application of the *Oakes* test. Courts can and should apply a high degree of scrutiny to burden women in the context of economic and fiscal life. In doing so, they do not overstep their bounds but are properly protecting rights by demanding compelling arguments and evidence for limiting women's equality.

B. The Morality of Sex Work

The criminalisation or legal regulations of sex work is controversial and, even amongst feminists, opinions are split on the relationship between the law, equality and sex work. In *S v Jordan*, the South African Constitutional Court held that the exclusive criminalisation of sex workers was not a breach of section 9 equality rights.[151] Justice Ngcobo in *obiter* for the majority called for judicial restraint as sex work was socially and culturally controversial and decisions

[148] ibid [78].
[149] ibid [90].
[150] Jennifer Koshan, '*Newfoundland (Treasury Board) v NAPE*' (2006) 18(1) *Canadian Journal of Women and the Law* 321.
[151] *S v Jordan* [2002] ZACC 22.

in this realm should be left to the legislature.[152] The dissent, however, found a breach of equality rights as the law only criminalised women who were predominantly sex workers, and alleviated any blameworthiness of the sex purchasers, who were predominantly men. The law reinforced and perpetuated sexual stereotypes that degraded women who sell sex.[153] The dissent did not openly engage in a calibration exercise but there are echoes of the weighted approach. Justice O'Regan and Sachs observed that 'In our constitutional democracy which is committed to gender equality, a criminal prohibition which has the effect of furthering patterns of gender inequality will need powerful justification to meet the [limitation] test'.[154]

The normative significance of women's inequality in conjunction with the perniciousness of a law that entrench deeply embedded sociocultural norms on women's sexuality pulled the dissent towards a demanding standard of review at the justification-stage. This also functioned to bring nuance to the subject-matter calibration factor and to resist it being utilised to lower the standard of review. The subject-matter was not the politically and socially controversial issue on whether commercial sex should be legal. Justice O'Regan and Sachs framed the subject-matter as the decision to only criminalise women.[155] The state could not articulate a legitimate reason for the law and the dissent would have held it to be an unjustified breach of women's equality rights. An intense standard of review that respected women's equality rights ensured institutional responsibility as it did not require the Court to determine the legality of commercial sex, but it did flush out that the criminalisation of sex workers lacked justification.

C. The Biology of Immigration

Lastly, Justice O'Connor's dissent in *Nguyen v Immigration and Naturalization Services (INS)* marked out how a heightened standard is derived from the constitutional guarantee of equality and how intense judicial scrutiny in the sensitive area of citizenship does not require the court to overstep its role.[156] *Nguyen* concerned the requirements for citizenship when children were born outside of the US and outside of marriage. The US Supreme Court had to assess whether the different rules for men and women were consistent with the Equal Protection clause of the Constitution. If the foreign child was born to a mother who was a US citizen, the child was entitled to citizenship if the mother was a citizen at the time of birth and if the mother had previously been in the US for a continuous period of one year. The process was more onerous if the foreign child was

[152] ibid [26], [30].
[153] ibid [63]–[66].
[154] ibid [97].
[155] ibid [95].
[156] *Nguyen v Immigration and Naturalization Services (INS)* 553 US 53__(2001).

born to a father who was a US citizen. The law required there to be evidence of a blood relationship between the child and the father, the father had agreed in writing to financially support the child until the child reached the age of 18 and before the child turns 18 the child must be legitimated, or the father must acknowledge paternity under oath or there must be a court order establishing paternity. It was the final step, the legitimation, acknowledgement or court order that was challenged in *Nguyen*. While it was the men who were burdened by the law, the case had strong implications for women's equality as the thrust of the case was on primary responsibility for the care of children.[157] Under the Fourteenth Amendment, the Court had to determine whether the differential treatment between men and women was justified ascertaining whether the distinction served an important government objective and whether the means were substantially related to the achievement of those objectives.

Seemingly, the US Supreme Court has adopted a weighted approach to calibration as justifications for differential treatment between men and women were meant to automatically be subject to heightened scrutiny.[158] This is not the highest form, as only race-based distinctions are subject to strict or rigid scrutiny, but neither is it the lowest form, as the state cannot justify a sex-based distinction merely on the basis of rationality. There is a high degree of conceptual messiness on these different tiers of scrutiny and how they relate to each other.[159] Justice O'Connor in her dissent in *Nguyen* defended heightened scrutiny as an intense standard of review and her reasoning mirrors the arguments for a weighted approach and how she applied it traverses the imperatives to constitutionally protect equality rights and the separation of powers.

Heightened scrutiny should be pitched towards the high end of intensity. Echoing Justice O'Connor's compatriots in *NAPE, Anuj Garg* and *Jordan*, the pull towards an interrogative standard is rooted in the harmfulness of women's inequality. She observed that there has been a long history of restricting individual opportunity by laws that reflected and reinforced 'fixed notions concerning the roles and abilities of males and females'[160] and, in the specific case of citizenship, the history of sex discrimination warranted judicial circumspection.[161] Although it was not openly articulated as such, the subject-matter, citizenship and immigration, which was extremely politically controversial, did not push the heightened scrutiny towards deference. Rather the long history of gendered nationality and immigration laws raised judicial suspicion, a recognition that women's inequality was embedded into all aspects of law including contentious aspects. Justice O'Connor also implicitly used the normative significance

[157] Albertina Antognini, 'From Citizenship to Custody: Unwed Fathers Abroad at and Home' (2013) 36 *Harvard Journal of Law and Gender* 405.
[158] *Virginia* (n 20).
[159] Suzanne Goldberg, 'Equality Without Tiers' (2004) 77 *South California Law Review* 481.
[160] *Nguyen* (n 156) 74 citing *Mississippi Univ. for Women v Hogan* 458 US 718, 725 (1982).
[161] ibid 91.

of constitutionally protecting women's equality to emphasise the stringency of heightened scrutiny. She explained that any lower standard of review would be wrong as 'fidelity to the Constitution's pledge of equal protection demands more when a facially sex-based classification is at issue'.[162] The weighted approach, manifesting in the US context as heightened scrutiny, was applied in a demanding way. It requires 'exceedingly persuasive justifications' for making distinctions on the basis of sex.[163] This meant the state's justifications for treating mothers and fathers differently must be tenable, genuine, and grounded in reality as opposed to hypothesised or invented.

The dissenting opinion is illuminative of how the weighted approach continues to respect institutional boundaries. In assessing the means-end fit between the distinction drawn between mothers and fathers and the state objective, which in this case was to prove a parent-child relationship, Justice O'Connor did not seek impose her own view on how the parent-child relationship should be proven but queried the rationality of the state's choices. She brought a rigorous inquiring mind demanding that the state explain why given that there needs to be clear and convincing evidence of a blood relationship, what does the requirement for legitimation acknowledge or court order add?[164] And why does the father have to undertake these administrative steps before the child reaches 18 years old, how does that further the aim of proving a relationship?[165] Why do fathers have to prove this relationship differently than mothers? Asking these questions revealed the stereotypes that underpinned the law that assumed women automatically have nurturing relationships with their children and that women, not men, have primary responsibility for children.[166] Heightened scrutiny demanded the Court to be inquisitive, to test out and think through the state's claims. It does not require the Court to adjudicate on whether the naturalisation rules represent a good or bad decision but to ferret out how the state's rationales for the inequality were premised on tenuous logic and gender stereotypes.

VI. CONCLUSION

Equality can guide the calibration of the justification-stage. The magnitude of women's inequality and the fundamental importance of realising the constitutional promise of gender equality is a weighted pull factor requiring arguments that limitation claims must be treated with the upmost suspicion. The analysis must rigorously, forensically and searchingly test whether claims meet the required justification criteria. This proposed guiding function deviates

[162] ibid 83.
[163] ibid 74.
[164] ibid 80.
[165] ibid 85.
[166] ibid 91.

from dominant approaches to calibration and doctrinal trends. Non-weighted approaches might appear attractive as they give courts flexibility to tailor the intensity of review to the specifics of case and provide a framework for balancing tensions between needing to respect institutional boundaries and protect rights. However, the non-weighted approach, which does not assign particular weight to any given factor, but which at the outset treats the catalogue of factors the same, is inconsistent with the significance of women's right to equality. It fails to acknowledge that the law has long been a tool to oppress women and to respect the constitutional struggle to recognise women's full humanity. Digging into the catalogue of factors which push or pull to greater or less intensity, these factors make untenable assumptions. Women's equality cannot be neatly spliced as trivial-serious, legal-political, controversial-non-controversial and thus non-weighted approaches can replicate long-standing conceptual flaws on the nature of inequality against women. Moreover, there is a trend in the practice of calibration to distort and warp calibration factors to exaggerate fears of a searching review and to protect the choice to deprioritise women's right to equality from any meaningful scrutiny. These problems can be redressed via a weighted approach that accords significance to women's equality. Regardless of the seemingly minor nature of the breach of women's equality rights or the apparent controversial or political nature of the breach, courts should approach the justification-stage with an inquiring mind and not accept limitation claims at face-value.

In adopting a weighted approach, the Court is not inappropriately second-guessing executive and legislative decision-making. It is not democratically illegitimate to be cognisant while calibrating on how political actors have historically used law to deprive women of their rights nor to be faithful to the constitutional and communal commitment to gender equality. In practice, guiding the calibration with women's equality can deflate these types of concerns as it points the analysis away from abstract political debates and centres the justification-stage on the legal breach of women's rights. A searching standard does not require courts to supplement their own priorities or preferences with those of the executive and legislative branches, it simply requires that they not give constitutional imprimatur to untested, untried and unexamined limitation claims.

5

Hollowing Justification

I. INTRODUCTION

PART I ESTABLISHED that justification dilutes the equality-stage and argued that justification concepts, doctrines and criteria should be hermetically sealed off from assessing whether there has been a breach of women's equality rights. Part II argues that women's equality is central to the justification-stage. It has established that equality has a guiding function. Specifically, chapter four argued that the seriousness of legally assigning lesser moral worth to women in tandem with the respect demanded by constitutionally protecting women's equality pulls the justification-stage to a searching and probing analysis. This chapter and the next make the case that an intense justification analysis requires a specific methodological approach to the application of limitation criteria. When assessing whether the justificatory burden has been met, courts should employ a relational and contextual approach that uses substantive models of women's equality to test the veracity, accuracy, feasibility and persuasiveness of limitation arguments. The application of justification doctrines must be grounded in the realities of women's inequality and in the constitutional promise of achieving transformative gender equality. This chapter begins to build this argument by exploring how justification actually functions in the practice of adjudicating women's equality, a question that has remained largely unexplored. By identifying how courts are hollowing out the application of justification criteria, it is possible to craft with precision a new methodological approach enriched with women's equality. Crucially this approach can cut through tensions between the laudable aims of the justification-stage and the complications in devising processes for justifying.

Women's equality rights cannot be limited for just any reason. Limitation rationale must meet certain qualitative thresholds. Justification seeks to prevent rights from being limited due to thoughtlessness, hyperbole, inertia or popular ideologies disconnected from realities.[1] Determining whether limitation claims have met this threshold is challenging. For example, when there is a clash

[1] Mattis Kumm, 'Global Constitutionalism, Human Rights and Proportionality: Institutionalizing Socratic Contestation' (2022) 9 *Journal of Constitutional Justice* 193; Mattias Kumm, 'The Idea of Socratic Contestation and the Right to Justification: The Point of Rights-Based Proportionality Review (2010) 4 *Law and Ethics of Human Rights* 140, 160.

between women's equality and federalism, the courts must assess whether there is a rational link between regulating inter-state trade and gender-based violence against women or whether on balance constitutional priority should be given to devolution or to women's equality in sexual and reproductive health. There is scepticism on the feasibility of this task as there is no objective way these incommensurables can be weighed against each other.[2] Any attempts by courts to do so would only reflect individual policy preferences of the judiciary. Yet justification tests, namely proportionality, are trumpeted as providing a methodology that addresses this conundrum. These tests are designed to discipline judicial deliberation through a structured analytical reasoning process which ensures the justification of rights is precise, consistent and logical.[3] Although there remain criticisms that proportionality or any other limitation frameworks remain unable to provide that objectivity, coherency and certainty to the justification-stage.[4] However, many of the claims on the strengths, weaknesses, uses and misuses of proportionality or other tests are not grounded in the empirical realities of the justification-stage. Steiner, Lang and Kremnitzer aptly note that the 'normative literature is geared towards making general claims in support of or against proportionality, it tends to place at its centre either an idealized or deprecated – in any case, abstract, version of the doctrine rather than any specific application.'[5] They go onto to observe that the discourse on proportionality is 'speckled with assumption about how [it] functions'.[6] The theorising on justification is divorced from the messy realities of justification. There is a lack of understanding on how justification doctrines function in the specific context of women's equality and no real knowledge on how concepts are applied. This chapter fills this void and in doing so lays the groundwork for a new methodological approach to the application of justification criteria that moves beyond the all-consuming debates on the utility (or lack thereof) of proportionality.

In combing through the judgments where courts must decide whether it is constitutionally permissible to treat women unequally, it becomes apparent

[2] Timothy Endicott, 'Proportionality and Incommensurability' in Grant Hurscroft, Bradley Miller and Gregoire Webber (eds), *Proportionality and the Rule of Law* (Cambridge University Press, 2014).

[3] Anne Peters, 'A Plea for Proportionality: A Reply to Yun-chien Chang and Xin Dai' (2021) 19(3) *International Journal of Constitutional Law* 1135; Alec Stone Sweet and Jud Mathews, *Proportionality Balancing and Constitutional Governance: A Comparative and Global Approach* (Cambridge University Press, 2019) ch 2.

[4] Stavros Tsakyrakis, 'Proportionality: An Assault on Human Rights?' (2003) 7 *International Journal of Constitutional Law* 468; Stavros Tsakyrakis, 'Proportionality: An Assault on Human Rights? A Rejoinder to Madhav Khosla' (2010) 8(2) *International Journal of Constitutional Law* 307; Iryna Ponomarenko, 'On the Limits of Proportionality' (2019–20) 24(2) *Review of Constitutional Studies* 241.

[5] Talya Steiner, Andrej Lang and Mordechai Kremnitzer, 'Introduction: Analysing Proportionality Comparatively and Empirically' in Mordechai Kremnitzer, Talya Steiner and Andrej Lang (eds), *Proportionality in Action: Comparative and Empirical Perspectives on the Judicial Practice* (Cambridge University Press, 2020) 6.

[6] ibid 3.

that the justification-stage is being hollowed out. The various limbs of differing justification tests are being emptied of content and meaning. There are two strands to the hollowing of the limitation analysis. First, criteria are isolated, decontextualised and misdirected. With respect to isolation and decontextualisation, the justification analysis assesses the limitation argument in isolation from the breach of women's equality rights and decontextualised from broader patterns of women's equality. This operates to artificially inflate the strength and value of the limitation. With respect to misdirection, if the justification test requires assessing a particular feature of the limitation claims, the courts will misdirect the test to examine a completely different and often irrelevant feature. In both scenarios, the justification-stage is steered away from the controversies inherent in determining whether to prioritise women's equality over other objectives. These methodologies present the justification-stage as a simplistic and mechanical analysis that obscures the burden the limitation places on women and the court's value judgment on the priority the constitution should give to women's equality. This elision, however, comes at a cost. Women's inequality is justified, not based on convincing arguments that meet justification criteria, but on dubious, speculative, irrelevant and untested claims.

Second, there is a strand of jurisprudence where courts are not examining limitation rationale in isolation and are paying attention to the relationship between the breach and the justification. However, they have adopted a thin and impoverished relational methodology premised on a misunderstanding of women's equality. In turn, this results in a paradox. Many limitation arguments are themselves premised and built upon gendered stereotypes and assumptions. This is not as surprising as it may initially seem, as argued in chapter four, patriarchy is a totalising force, and it seeps into all aspects of life including justification claims. For example, stereotypes that women are naturally caring towards children and men are inherently promiscuous and irresponsible were used to justify different naturalisation processes for fathers and mothers.[7] Or claims that it is legitimate to impose inequality on women because women in poverty are work-shy and need the threat of income poverty to spur them into the formal job market.[8] Misunderstanding women's equality and then placing that inaccurate version in relation to limitation means courts are unable to grapple with how justification arguments are entwined with gendered misconceptions. This has an almost double-locking effect as gendered conjunctures are used to justify further inequality against women.

Under both hollowing out strands, justification criteria becomes devoid of content. This emptiness may avoid criticism of unbridled reasoning, but the justification loses it central purpose as limitation claims remain untested.

[7] *Nguyen v Immigration and Naturalization Services (INS)* 553 US 53 (2001).
[8] *SG and others v Secretary of State for Work and Pensions* [2015] UKSC 16.

The problem with the justification-stage with respect to women's equality is not so much the utility of different tests. This is a debate that has dominated thinking on the justification-stage. The flaws cut across different frameworks and are rooted in isolating, decontextualising, misdirecting and misunderstanding. The solution lies not in devising new tests or modifying specific limbs of tests. Rather the core function of justification, protecting rights through ensuring limitation arguments are neither flippant nor flimsy, can be achieved by assessing the limitation arguments in *relation* to the specific infringement of women's equality rights and in the broader *context* of women's substantive equality. To reiterate observations made in earlier chapters, this proposal does not preclude constitutionally limiting women's equality, it only requires that any limitations have been searching tested using the proposed methodology. Chapter six develops the relational and contextual approach that is anchored in women's equality while this chapter examines more closely the realities of the justification-stage and diagnoses how the limitation stage is being hollowed out.

II. ASPIRING TO ABSTRACTION

Before investigating how justification functions in the practice of women's equality, this section pauses to canvas the normative aspirations of the limitation analysis and critiques of differing justification frameworks. The justification-stage can be chaotic, contentious and charged. The possibility of limiting rights raises considerable consternation, and it is in working through these anxieties that the aims of the justification-stage become apparent. Courts must assess rival conceptions of the constitutional vision of the state. In doing so, they become vulnerable to a series of allegations including that they lack fidelity to the conception of rights[9] and that they exceed institutional roles.[10] One response to these critiques has been to trumpet justification frameworks, particularly the four-limbed proportionality test (legitimacy, rationality, necessity and balancing), arguing that it provides courts with a persuasive and stable framework to neutrally manage the tensions of the justification-stage.[11] This section argues that justification frameworks aspire to the twin normative goals of rigour and neutrality and then proceeds throughout the remainder of the chapter to argue how these aims have become harnessed to hollow out the limitation analysis. This hollowing impacts the outcome, as it cloaks untested arguments in a shroud of constitutional legitimacy.

[9] Gregoire Webber, 'The Loss of Rights' in Grant Huscroft, Bradley Miller, and Grégoire Webber (eds), *Proportionality and the Rule of Law: Rights, Justification, Reasoning* (Cambridge University Press, 2014) 123; Francisco Urbina, *A Critique of Proportionality and Balancing* (Cambridge University Press, 2017).

[10] Paul Yowell, *Constitutional Rights and Constitutional Design* (Hart Publishing, 2018).

[11] Stone Sweet and Mathews (n 3).

A. Protecting Rights Through Justification

One of the core purposes of the justification-stage is to protect the inviolable character of rights. The mechanics of justification operate to ensure the limitation claims meet qualitative thresholds. It is always possible to proffer a reason, no matter how rickety or insubstantial, to justify infringing on women's equality rights. Women should not be admitted to the upper echelons of the army as the risk to them is too great or there is a lack of privacy in the field.[12] Sign language interpretation cannot be provided to deaf women while giving birth as it is too expensive.[13] If courts merely accept these claims without any interrogation into their veracity, women's equality rights would be compromised to the point of meaninglessness. To protect the special character not only of women's equality rights but all rights, they can only be justifiably limited when claims meet specific criteria.[14] The justification-stage functions as a yardstick to measure the permissibility of limiting women's equality rights. Different jurisdictions employ different yardsticks. The Canadian Supreme Court has consistently applied the traditional four-limb proportionality test which along with balancing requires limitation claims to be legitimate, rational and necessary.[15] The South African Constitution also requires, under section 36, the Constitutional Court to apply a proportionality-like framework to any limitation claim. At times, the United Kingdom (UK) has adopted proportionality whereas at other times it has only checked to ensure that limits to women's equality have a foundation in rationality.[16] The United States (US) and India have not fully embraced proportionality, but there are echoes of different limbs of proportionality when these apex courts assess the strength of claims that women's equality rights should be limited.[17] Regardless of the precise justification criteria used, the aim is to protect rights by ensuring limitation arguments meet the requisite criteria. And as argued in chapter four, women's equality demands that courts apply these criteria in a searching and probing manner.

Using the examples from above helps illustrate how the justification-stage serves this gate-keeping function to protect women's equality. The Indian Supreme Court in *The Secretary, Minister of Defence v Babita Puniya* concluded that the state's justifications for restricting women in the army from being

[12] *The Secretary, Ministry of Defence v Babita Puniya and Others* (2020) 3 SCR 833 [28].

[13] *Eldridge v British Columbia (Attorney General)* [1997] 3 SCR 624.

[14] Matthias Kumm, 'Is the Structure of Human Rights Practice Defensible?' in Vicki Jackson and Mark Tushnet (eds), *Proportionality: New Frontiers, New Challenges* (Cambridge University Press, 2017).

[15] *R v Oakes* [1986] 1 SCR 103; Stu Woolman and Henk Botha, 'Limitation' in Stu Woolman and Michael Bishop (eds), *Constitutional Law of South Africa* (Juta, 2013).

[16] Lewis Graham, 'Has the UK Supreme Court Become More Restrained in Public Law Cases?' (2024) 87(5) *MLR* 1083, 1104.

[17] Vicki Jackson, 'Constitutional Law in an Age of Proportionality' (2015) 124 *Yale Law Journal* 3094; Aparna Chandra, 'Limitation Analysis by the Indian Supreme Court' in Kremnitzer, Steiner and Lang (n 5).

promoted lacked legitimacy as it was based on misconceptions that women were the weaker sex that needed to be protected and that they were unfit for combat roles.[18] The Court observed that the prohibition lacked rationality as there was a well-documented history of women in the Indian army acting courageously in high-risk situations.[19] The Canadian Supreme Court examined the state's claim that it was too expensive to provide sign language interpretation, observing that it both lacked necessity and balance as it only cost 0.0025 of the health budget to ensure deaf women, and all deaf people, were equally able to access health care.[20] These examples are illustrative of the crucial importance the justification-stage can play in protecting rights. Taken at face-value, protecting women from danger and managing finite resources are highly desirable goals. Yet through a searching application of justification criteria the Indian and Canadian Supreme Courts were able to sift out that these limitation claims were based on thoughtlessness, hyperbole, inertia, antagonism, and stereotypes.[21] The Canadian Supreme Court used the justification-stage to expose myths that equality rights were inherently expensive and costly to the public. The Indian Supreme Court was vigilant to guard against inequality against women being used to justify a breach of women's equality rights. *Babita Puniya* is illustrative of the hollowing out of justification via gendered misunderstanding. The ubiquity and normalcy of women's inequality can result in negative gender reasoning infiltrating limitation arguments. An application of justification criteria that is attuned to the relationship between the limitation claims and the precipitating breach of women's equality, as well as the broader context of women's equality can spotlight how restrictions on women's rights are premised on gendered stereotypes. In *Babita Puniya*, the Court was able to point out how the limitation was built upon and perpetuated romantic paternalistic myths. This case is, however, somewhat of an outlier. In decision after decision, as it is argued below, the role of justification in protecting rights is lost in the practice of adjudication.

B. Scepticism on Justification

While justification is designed to serve this gate-functioning role, there is scepticism that it should function in this manner and doubt as to whether this function can be achieved. Understanding the doubts that swirl around the justification-stage provides the basis for identifying how courts seek to redress these suspicions by hollowing out justification criteria.

There are some who argue that any justification to rights trivialises 'the distinctly morality-laden nature of human rights claims' as it permits rights

[18] *Babita Puniya* (n 12) [54], [55].
[19] ibid [54], [56].
[20] *Eldridge* (n 13) [87].
[21] Kumm, 'The Idea of Socratic Contestation' (n 1) 160.

to be too easily sacrificed for the public good.[22] Barak, however, reframes the justification-stage as a measure to guarantee rights. He explained that individuals do not possess rights in isolation from each other but alongside other individuals, groups, as well as 'part of a society with national goals'.[23] Limitations on rights can be necessary 'to maintain the social framework that itself protect human rights'.[24] This is a recognition that in large and diverse communities there are invariably disagreements between individuals, groups and the state and it is naïve to assume that in every set of circumstances rights will trump over other interests. This is an important reminder that the justification-stage is not antithetical to rights being limited and the methodology proposed in the next chapter for using the justification framework does not bar limitations on women's equality rights. Criteria should not presuppose or be designed to produce a specific substantive outcome.[25] Advocates argue that this is one of the strengths of proportionality. Stone Sweet and Mathews explain that proportionality 'is an analytical procedure … but otherwise it is without content'.[26] Proportionality, or any other justification test for that matter, do not presume that limitation arguments will never be successful nor assume that breaches of women's equality rights can never be justified. Justification frameworks should be applied in an even-handed manner.[27] Each side has a fair opportunity to marshal arguments and evidence to convince the court of the (im)possibility of limiting women's equality rights.[28] Fair, however, does not mean the calibration of the justification-stage is a non-weighted balance between women's equality and other factors. This would go against the arguments made in chapter four.

There is deep-seeded doubt on whether justification doctrines, criteria and tests are workable in practice. That in seeking to protect rights by assessing whether limitation claims meet the required cogency and veracity thresholds, courts are in fact imposing their own views. What criteria could objectively determine whether access to abortion should be limited to protect health resources? Or how can justification doctrines decide whether religious tenets should be forced to reform to protect women's equality? There is scepticism that legal standards can be brought to bear to decide these questions. It is impossible for legal doctrine to, in a principled manner, assess the comparative weight of two

[22] Yutaka Aria-Takahasi, 'Proportionality' in Dinah Shelton (ed), *The Oxford Handbook of International Human Rights Law* (Oxford University Press, 2013) 466.

[23] *CA United Mizrahi Bank Ltd v Migdal Cooperative Village* [1995] Israel Supreme Court 49(4) 221, 443 as cited in Aaron Barak, 'A Research Agenda for the Future' in Jackson and Tushnet (n 14) 322.

[24] ibid.

[25] David Beatty, *The Ultimate Rule of Law* (Oxford University Press, 2004) 163.

[26] Stone Sweet and Mathews (n 3) 121.

[27] Robert Bork, *The Tempting of America* (Fee Press, 1990) 151 as cited in Beatty (n 25) 161.

[28] For a contrary view, see Yun-chien Chang and Xin Dai, 'The Limited Usefulness of Proportionality Principle' (2021) 19(3) *International Journal of Constitutional Law* 1110.

normatively desirable but incommensurable values.[29] The justification-stage, so the argument goes, is an exercise in futility. Justice Scalia colourfully described it as 'judging whether a particular line is longer than a particular rock is heavy'.[30] At the justification-stage, law is smokescreen. When courts decide that women's equality should be constitutionally protected regardless of its negative impact on federalism or religious liberty or conversely that women's equality should give way to these other objectives, the determination is not rooted in law but in the personal ideologies and political preferences of the judiciary.[31]

Justification tests, like proportionality, are in place to protect courts from accusations of indulging in 'unrestrained moral reasoning'.[32] The legal doctrine of justification aims towards neutrality and objectivity. Limitation criteria seek to provide a logical system in which to organise conflicting arguments.[33] And they shift the justification-stage away from the court's own view on constitutional priorities and provide a framework for judicially assessing if legislative and executive bodies have considered a range of questions when prioritising other objectives over women's equality. It segments broad questions into technical assessments. Is there another way for the state to protect the religious liberty of corporations while also ensuring women have affordable access to contraception? Is there a rational connection between imposing income poverty on women and nudging women into paid employment in the formal labour market? Tests, like proportionality, distil volatile questions into 'reason and rational argument'.[34] The apotheosis of this is Alexy's weight formula which seeks to discipline the balancing limb of proportionality.

When using proportionality at the justification-stage, the final limb requires balancing the benefit of the competing aim against the harm of the infringement of women's equality. Balancing is where courts are most often accused of imposing 'their own political considerations'.[35] Alexy's weight formula aims to overcome these critiques, as it

> defines the weight of a principle P_i in a concrete case, that is, the concrete weight of P_i relative to a colliding principle P_j ($W_{i,j}$), as the quotient of, first, the product of the intensity of the interference with P_i (I_i) and the abstract weight of P_i (W_i) and the degree of reliability of the empirical assumptions concerning what the measure in question means for the non-realization of P_i (R_i), and, second, the product of the corresponding values with respect to P_j, now related to the realization of P_j.[36]

[29] For a good summary of the problems with judicial balancing, see Stephanie Barclay, 'Constitutional Rights as Protected Reasons' (Forthcoming) *University of Chicago Law Review*.

[30] *Benedix Autolite Corp v Midwesco Enterprises* 486 US 888 (1988) 897 (concurring opinion of Justice Scalia).

[31] For the contours of this argument see Peters (n 3) 3.

[32] Steiner, Lang and Kremnitzer (n 5) 5.

[33] Stone Sweet and Mathews (n 3) 30.

[34] Beatty (n 25) 169.

[35] Johcn von Bernstorff, 'Proportionality Without Balancing' in Liora Lazarus, Christopher McCrudden and Nigel Bowles (eds), *Reasoning Rights: Comparative Judicial Engagement* (Hart Publishing, 2014) 66.

[36] Robert Alexy, 'Constitutional Rights and Proportionality' (2014) 22 *Revus* 51, 54.

Ambiguities, uncertainties and complexities are reduced to quantifiable variables which can be tabulated to arrive at an objective and unchallengeable conclusion. The weight formula is emblematic of the larger ethos of the design and structure of justification frameworks, a desire to provide precision and impartiality to refute claims that rights limitation is a futile and illegitimate exercise.[37]

There continue to be critiques that justification frameworks, like proportionality, are not redressive but further entrench the justification-stage as a subjective political and moral assessment.[38] With respect to proportionality, and particularly the balancing limb, there is no universally accepted moral-mathematical formula where rights and interests can be assigned a 'quantitative common metric'.[39] Judges must assign their own values to women's equality, federalism, and religious pluralism and thus justification doctrines like proportionality do little to negate judicial biases, preferences and ideologies. More fundamentally, attempts to adopt a mechanistic approach risk stripping out the tensions on permitting rights to be limited. Justification is not a technical exercise but a difficult and challenging normative ordering.

The judgments examined below rarely openly articulate these concerns. It is possible, however, to detect how this scepticism operates in the application of justification doctrine and criteria. In aiming to ensure the justification assessment is neutral and objective, the courts isolate, decontextualise, misdirect and misunderstand the various limbs of limitation frameworks. In doing so, they simultaneously empty justification frameworks of meaning and avoid the subjectivity critiques. This hollowing out is not neutral as to outcome but results in courts too readily accepting claims that it is legitimate, rational, necessary and balanced to limit women's equality.

III. ISOLATING, DECONTEXTUALISING AND MISDIRECTING TO AVOID THE GLARE OF JUSTIFICATION

To protect the integrity of the justification-stage from accusations that it is no more than a thinly veiled disguise for judicial subjectivities, courts deploy justification doctrines, concepts and criteria in a manner that aspires to neutrality and objectivity. When assessing claims to limit women's equality, this aspiration becomes hollowed out and there is a failure to utilise the justification-stage to protect women's equality against illogical, fanciful, speculative or unsupported justification claims. As mentioned in the Introduction, there are two strands to this hollowing out. This section investigates the first strand.

In this set of cases, the courts employ two techniques to preserve a façade that the justification-stage is a sterile, technical and objective black-letter assessment. First, the courts examine the limitation claims in an isolated and

[37] Aaron Barak, *Proportionality* (Cambridge University Press, 2012) ch 18.
[38] Tsakyrakis, 'An Assault on Human Rights' (2003) (n 4).
[39] ibid 471; Endicott (n 2).

decontextualised manner. Many justification arguments taken on their face are highly desirable goals in liberal constitutional democracies. Examining the value of religious pluralism and federalist structures in isolation from the breach of women's rights and the broader context of women's equality in the state would only reveal the strength of the justification. This operates to frame the justification-stage as an uncomplicated mathematical application of legal criteria. This squarely avoids confronting the challenges inherent in justification, protecting the court from critiques of judicial subjectivity, but it comes at the expense of a fair justification-stage. As the justification-stage is not simply to ascertain whether the competing aim is in and of itself valuable but whether that aim provides a legitimate, rational, necessary or balanced reason for limiting women's equality rights.

Second, the other technique is to misdirect the application of justification criteria. Each justification criteria directs the court to ask specific questions of the limitation argument. Is it non-arbitrary to prohibit women of menstruating age to enter a religious place of worship? Has a fair balance been struck between the community's needs to protect the devolution settlement and burdening women's equality in sexual and reproductive health? These justification criteria are targeted to explore discrete aspects of the limitation claim. Yet courts are repeatedly misdirecting these criteria and exploring claims and arguments that are completely irrelevant. The existence of other temples or the development of sexual and reproductive health rights in the UN system do not answer the questions posed by justification criteria. This misdirection is not merely frustrating, poor-quality judicial reasoning. It repeatedly obscures the burdens the limit requires women to bear and sets up an oversimplistic justification-stage where it appears obvious that the justification is constitutional. In many of the cases, women's equality is limited on the basis of arguments that have never been fully interrogated.

The isolating, decontextualising and misdirecting techniques are often employed simultaneously by the courts. Hollowing out the justification criteria may avoid drawing the court into debates on the purpose and efficacy of justification and it can give an aura of judicial objectivity. It does not, however, make the justification-stage neutral or objective but tips the analysis towards permitting women's equality to be limited on the basis of irrelevant and untested claims.

A. Blind to Feminist Strategising

In *Coleman v Court of Appeals of Maryland*,[40] the US Supreme Court bled all context from the limitation claim. It conducted a technical assessment that

[40] *Coleman v Maryland* 556 US 30 (2012).

decoupled the limitation claim from the feminist strategising that explicated the state's choice. Without this context, the Court protected the limitation from any questions on its veracity. This approach to justification operated to constitutionalise the de-prioritisation of women's equality on the basis of ahistorical and dubious claims.

As analysed in chapter four, *Coleman* concerned the constitutionality of the self-care provision in the Family and Medical Leave Act. Under this Act an employee was allowed to take 12 weeks of unpaid leave from work to care for oneself. The self-care provision was part of a larger package of caring protections that also included unpaid leave to care for children, spouses and parents. If an employee was fired for taking this leave, they could sue their employer, and this accountability route was available even if the local-level state was the employer. The State of Maryland argued that local-level state accountability under the Act for the self-care provision was unconstitutional. Section 5 of the Fourteenth Amendment, however, permitted Congress to intrude on the local-level state if the intrusion was targeted to protect and prevent transgressions of equality and did so in a manner that was congruent and proportionate.[41] In *Coleman*, the Court had to assess whether protecting care in the workplace was a justified intrusion under section 5 into the federalist structure of the US.

On a plain reading of the Act, it was not readily apparent how self-care was a proportionate response to prevent inequality against women. There was nothing inherently gendered about people getting sick and needing time off work. Although the self-care provision made no explicit reference to leave for illness related to pregnancy or maternity, this was its underlying purpose.[42] The gender-neutrality of the self-care provision was a reflection of feminist concerns from the 1980s and 90s. Singling out pregnancy for legislative protection, feminists believed, would continue to result in discrimination against women.[43] There was validity to these fears. Despite the prohibition on pregnancy discrimination in the Pregnancy Discrimination Act, passed in 1978, Congress had voluminous evidence that women were still at risk of losing their jobs, including jobs in the public sector, due to pregnancy and maternity.[44] Employers still perceived women as too economically costly to hire and believed that their role was within the home.[45] When drafting the Family and Medical Leave Act, Congress chose to explicitly untie self-care from pregnancy to blunt employer stereotypes against women while still providing women with access to caring protection. A gender-neutral sick leave provision, that protected both men and women, 'avoid[ed]

[41] *City of Boerne v Flores* 521 US 507 (1997) 520.

[42] Laura Kessler, 'The Attachment Gap: Employment Discrimination Law, Women's Cultural Caregiving and the Limits of Economic and Liberal Legal Theory' (2001) 34(1) *University of Michigan Journal of Law Review* 371, 419; *Coleman v Maryland* (n 40) 47–51 (dissenting opinion of Justice Ginsburg).

[43] *Coleman*, ibid 47–51.

[44] Kessler (n 42) 394–400.

[45] *Coleman* (n 40) 59–62.

providing the employers the temptation to discriminate against women'.[46] Justice Ginsberg, in dissent, concluded:

> Congress assiduously avoided a legislative package that, overall, was or would be seen as geared to women only. Congress thereby reduced employers' incentives to prefer men over women, advanced women's economic opportunities, and laid the foundation for a more egalitarian relationship at home and at work.[47]

The context clarifies that the self-care provision in the Act was in place to address women's inequality.

The majority decision of Justice Kennedy in *Coleman* studiously avoided this context and bled it out of the limitation analysis. It applied a formalistic justification analysis to hold that the self-care provisions, which were a well-documented proxy for pregnancy and maternity leave for women, were an unjustified infringement of local-level state immunity. Under the US Supreme Court doctrine, Congress could only intrude when the Act was targeted at redressing inequality. This echoes the purpose analysis under proportionality in that there must be evidence that the Family Leave and Medical Act was directed toward redressing inequality against women. Justice Kennedy concluded that there was no link between self-care and equality. He undertook a plain textual analysis of the Act pointing out that the self-care provision was gender neutral and there was no evidence that states discriminated against men and women in administrating self-care leave.[48] The Court merely noted that self-care could assist with pregnancy-related needs but dismissed the contextual evidence on the broader aims of the provision as 'supposition and conjecture' and characterised it as a 'few fleeting references'.[49] By blinding itself to the feminist political strategising, the Court held there was no nexus between the self-care provision and inequality against women. Without the link to discrimination, opening the state up to liability for not providing self-care leave unconstitutionally abrogated state immunity. A four corners, black-letter and abstract limitation analysis obscured from view the highly relevant context on the aims and purposes of the self-care provision and how it chose to respond to a long history of pregnancy discrimination at work. Although the Court directed the justification-stage to the proper questions and stayed faithful to the objective of each criterion of the limitation analysis, by decontextualising the criteria, the Court permitted restrictions on women's equality rights despite strong evidence that the Act had met the requirements to constitutionally impinge on sovereign immunity of local-level states.

[46] ibid 58 citing HR Rep N0 102-35 pt 1, 27–28 (1991).
[47] ibid 65.
[48] *Coleman* (n 40) 38, 39.
[49] ibid 41.

B. Side-Stepping the Tensions between Religious Freedom and Women's Equality

The justification-stage is exceptionally challenging when women's equality is being limited to protect other constitutional rights. Through a series of statutes and regulations, Sabarimala Temple prohibited women and girls from the ages of 10 to 50 from entering in the belief that these ages aligned with the ages of menstruation. The majority of the Indian Supreme Court analysed this prohibition in *Indian Young Lawyers Association v Kerala* through the prism of the right to religious freedom and belief, holding the ban was unconstitutional.[50] Justice Malhotra, in dissent, was the only judgment that meaningfully evaluated whether the prohibition was consistent with the Indian Constitution's equality guarantees.[51] Her dissent avoided the conflict of rights at the core of this case. It did so by hollowing out the limitation analysis. The justification claims were assessed in isolation from the breach of women's equality and were decontextualised from broader patterns on gender and religious freedom in India. The limitation analysis was also misdirected examining analytically irrelevant information which avoided accounting for the burdens the law placed on women. Both methods created a simple justification-stage which made it seem clear-cut that religious freedom should trump. These techniques, however, also shielded from constitutional view potential contradictions, stigmas and stereotypes embedded in the limitation claims and foreclosed a justification-stage that meaningfully tackled whether limits should be imposed.

Article 14 guaranteed equal protection and benefit of the law. This provision operated in *Indian Young Lawyers Association* more like a justification assessment as the analysis eschewed assessing the equality harms of the impugned law. Under Article 14, Justice Malhotra evaluated whether that law had an intelligible differentia and was rationally connected to the aims it meant to achieve.[52] As outlined in chapter one, for the sake of analytical ease, the Article 14 analysis will be referred to as a justification assessment as the evaluation is centred on the permissibility of treating women differently.

i. Avoiding the Logic of Religion

Indian Young Lawyers Association centred on the constitutionality of limits on women's equality to protect the religious freedom rights of others. This is one of

[50] *Indian Young Lawyers Association v Kerala* (2018) 1 SCC 234.

[51] Article 15 (prohibition on sex discrimination) she concluded, was inapplicable as places of worship were not within the geographic ambit of the non-discrimination provision; ibid [9.2] (dissenting opinion of Justice Malhotra).

[52] Tarunabh Khaitan, 'Equality: Legislative Review Under Article 14' in Sujit Choudhry, Madhav Khosla and Pratap Bhanu Mehta (eds), *The Oxford Handbook of the Indian Constitution* (Oxford University Press, 2016).

the most challenging justification assessments as it was placing limits on a right to protect another right. Justice Malhotra skirted this challenge by examining the value of religious freedom in isolation from the prohibition on women entering the Temple. Religious freedom and protecting religious pluralism, like most competing aims, proffered at the justification-stage, was normatively desirable. The question motivating the justification was not whether this was a worthy objective but whether religious pluralism should be protected at the expense of women's equality. Yet, Justice Malhotra only placed weight on the normative value of right to freedom of religion and belief. There was no investigation into the relationship between the underlying breach, women's equality rights, and the limitation, religious freedom rights. Instead, there were decontextualised statements on the value of religious pluralism. She explained that:

> A balance is required to be struck between the principles of equality and non-discrimination on the one hand, and the protection of the *cherished liberties* of faith, belief, and worship guaranteed by Articles 25 and 26 to persons belonging to all religions in a secular polity, on the other hand. Constitutional morality requires the harmonisation or balancing of all such rights, *to ensure that the religious beliefs of none are obliterated or undermined* (emphasis added).[53]

The limitation, religious pluralism, was the centre of the analysis, as it was religious freedom rights that were the 'cherished liberties' that must not be 'obliterated or undermined'. There was no acknowledgment of women's equality in the constitutional ordering. Neither was there any appreciation of how the prohibition could perpetuate expressive harms on menstruation nor consideration on how it placed constraints on how women were able to exercise their religious beliefs.

The effect of this untethering in *Indian Young Lawyers Association* was to construct a justification-stage where it would be impossible for the court to question whether the religious-based justifications met the intelligible differentia and non-arbitrariness standard. Religion became an inviolable trump at the justification-stage. Faith-based customs and rituals may appear silly, misguided, arbitrary or illogical to non-believers but to those who practice may be elemental. Article 14 frameworks were held as ill-suited and inapplicable to evaluating the religious-based prohibition. Justice Malhotra concluded that 'it is not for the courts to determine which … practices of a faith are to be struck down'.[54] Unless in the most extreme circumstances, like Sati (widow-burning), legal standards on justification could not be brought to bear to assess the religious-based reasons for prohibiting women and girls from entering the Temple. She held the ban did not reach an extreme circumstance. After concluding it was impossible for a court to assess the strength of the limitation, she held the prohibition was a permissible intrusion on women's equality. The contextualisation operated to

[53] *Indian Young Lawyers Association* (n 50) [11.8] (dissenting opinion of Justice Malhotra).
[54] ibid [8.2] (dissenting opinion of Justice Malhotra).

set up an overly simplistic justification assessment that foreclosed an investigation between religion, gender and constitutional ordering.

Assessing religious freedom in the abstract and without any relation to the underlying breach of women's rights obscured from judicial view potential weaknesses in the claims that the prohibition was justified. Menarche and menopause begin at varying ages for girls and women.[55] The age limits of 10 to 50 years old would be both over and under inclusive and arguably not pass the intelligible differentia hurdle. There were other aspects of the ban that may have lacked rationality. The core purpose of the ban was to protect the purity and celibacy of Lord Ayyappa in the form of Naishtika Brahmacharya. The belief that girls and women, 10 to 50 years of age, were a threat to that celibacy, perpetuates, as the concurring opinions on *Indian Young Lawyers Association* observed, prejudicial beliefs on the impurity of menstruation and stigmas on women's sexuality.[56] However, it was not entirely clear if the ban was even located in religious belief. Temple administrators explained that women and girls were banned to protect them from the purported strenuousness of the hike to the Temple during their menstrual periods.[57] If this was the aim of the ban, it would not meet the rationality criteria of Article 14, as it is based on stereotypes on menstruation. There would be no rational connection between physical exercise, menstruation, and entrance to the Temple. In India, Bhatia has observed that sociocultural secular beliefs can 'claim the mantle of religion'.[58] Paying attention to the broader context of the claim of how gender, religion and sociocultural norms have interacted in India meant that there should not be uncritical judicial acceptance that religious beliefs can limit women's equality.[59] Giving carte blanche to limitation claims that were alleged to be grounded in religion at the justification-stage was unwarranted as it ran the risk that gendered secular practices would be constitutionally protected under the guise of religion.

Simply holding that religious beliefs are unassailable elides pertinent questions. The limitation analysis failed to consider whether the prohibition was arbitrary in relation to its objectives and to investigate whether the prohibition was in fact rooted in religious belief. An enriched justification-stage that was sensitive to the relationship between the breach of equality rights and the limitation claim and the broader contextual pattern of women's equality in India would have explored these aspects of the state's justification arguments. Enriching the intelligible differentia and non-arbitrariness standard with a

[55] Amy Lacroix and others, 'Physiology, Menarche' (*National Library of Medicine*, 2023), available at www.ncbi.nlm.nih.gov/books/NBK470216/; World Health Organization, 'Menopause', available at www.who.int/news-room/fact-sheets/detail/menopause.

[56] *Indian Young Lawyers Association* (n 50) [23] (majority opinion of Chief Justice Misra and Justice Khanwilkar); [55] (concurring opinion of Justice Chandrachud).

[57] ibid [23] (majority opinion of Chief Justice Misra and Justice Khanwilkar).

[58] Gautam Bhatia, 'Freedom from Community: Individual Rights, Group Life, State Authority and Religious Freedom Under the Indian Constitution' (2016) 592) *Global Constitutionalism* 351, 362.

[59] ibid.

relational and contextual methodology would have prompted questions on the expressive function of the prohibition and the burdens the prohibition placed on women's religious practices. It would have articulated the costs to women's equality because without knowing the costs how would it ever be possible to determine if the limit was justified? This is not to hold that a relational and contextual methodology would have automatically resulted in women's equality rights trumping the need to protect religious liberty and pluralism. But it would have resulted in a justification assessment that fully accounted for the benefits and detriments of limiting women's equality to protect religious freedom and belief. It is only when this is transparently laid out can the Court come to any determination of the permissibility of the limit. *Indian Young Lawyers Association* is not easy as the Indian Supreme Court had to assess whether one right could constitutionally limit another right. An isolated and decontextualised justification assessment that only examined the strengths of the limitation, religious freedom, flatlined these challenges and avoided the controversaries inherent when rights clash.

ii. Shielding Arbitrariness with Mitigation

Along with decontextualising justification, Justice Malhotra also misdirected the limitation analysis and deviated from the questions the justification frameworks were designed to ask. The appellants in *Indian Young Lawyers Association* argued that the age limit was arbitrary. In response, Justice Malhotra pointed out that women's equality was protected as there were a thousand other temples to Lord Ayyappa, where he had not manifested as Naishtik Brahamachari, that women and girls could enter.[60] The availability of alternative measures did not answer the question on whether the age limits for entrance to Sabarimala Temple were arbitrary. Pointing out the existence of other places of worship only had the effect of minimising the harm of the religious restrictions on women and girls. The misdirected arbitrary analysis in *Indian Young Lawyers Association* itself was decontextualised and formalistic. It assumed women have the freedom of movement to travel and that their religious and spiritual needs can be fulfilled at these other places of worship. Attention to the larger context of women's equality in India would have ensured the justification assessment was sensitive to gendered realities. Studies have shown only 41 per cent of women in India were able to go alone to the market, health facility or places outside their village or community.[61] Women also possess and exercise religious beliefs and for some women their ability to fulfil their religious needs could be negatively impacted by the prohibition on entry to the Sabarimala Temple as they no longer had

[60] *Indian Young Lawyers Association* (n 50) [8.4]–[8.5] (dissenting opinion of Justice Malhotra).
[61] Vidisha Mehta and Harish Sai, 'Freedom of Movement: Studying Women's Mobility in North India' (2021) 6(1) *Urbanisation* S77.

'the freedom to follow their aims and beliefs … to pursue their chosen faith'.[62] It cannot be assumed that other temples where Lord Ayyappa had not manifested as Naishtik Brahamachari would be able to fulfil their religious and spiritual desires. A richer application of justification doctrine would have unearthed the gendered constraints on women's agency and the invisibility of women's right to religious freedom and belief to destabilise claims that women's equality would still be upheld notwithstanding the prohibition.

C. Extending State Control and Distracting from the Gendered Harms

In examining the competing aim in isolation from the precipitating breach of equality and misapplying justification criteria, the UK Supreme Court similarly avoided assessing whether the competing aim met justification standards. This resulted in limits placed on women's equality on the basis of untested arguments. Much like the Temple entry ban, *A and B v Secretary of State for Health* centred on contentious elements of women's sexual and reproductive health. The UK Supreme Court hollowed out the justification-stage to avoid squarely confronting these tensions.[63]

At the time of *A and B* abortion was criminalised in Northern Ireland, unless a woman's or girls' life was endangered or there was a risk of permanent or long-term damage to health. Girls and women in Northern Ireland who did not meet these criteria were forced to remain pregnant, undergo an illegal abortion, with the risk of criminal prosecution, or travel to England to obtain a legal abortion. If women and girls could afford to travel, the National Health Service (NHS) would not fund abortions for Northern Irish women and girls when they sought this service in England. All other women and girls residing in England were entitled to this funding. *A and B* was confined to deciding whether the English NHS funding prohibition was justified under the Human Rights Act and did not assess the underlining criminal prohibition in Northern Ireland.[64] The Court held that there was differential treatment based on geography, as those who normally reside in Northern Ireland were treated differently than those who normally reside in England. This was in breach of Article 8 (the right to private life) in conjunction with Article 14 (non-discrimination). As argued in chapter two, the role of gender was strikingly absent from this analysis. This impacted the justification-stage as the Court examined the limitation claims avoiding any awareness of their meaning and impact on women. This resulted

[62] Cochav Elkayam-Levy, 'Where is God When We Need Her? Women's Right to Freedom of Religion or Belief as Key to Promoting Gender Equality' (2021) 95(5) *Tulane Law Review* 1233.

[63] *A and B v Secretary of State for Health* [2017] UKSC 41.

[64] This was challenged in *Re Northern Ireland Human Rights Commission* [2018] UKSC 27; see also Mairead Enright, Kathryn McNeilly and Fiona de Londras, 'Abortion Activism, Legal Change, and Taking Feminist Law Work Seriously' (2020) *Northern Ireland Law Quarterly* 359.

in a justification-stage that upheld untried claims that it was permissible to limit women's rights.

Lord Wilson employed the traditional four-limb proportionality test to assess whether this difference was justified. Per the UK jurisprudence, the Court had to assess whether:

- the state's objectives were sufficiently important;
- the impugned law was rationally connected to the state's objectives;
- a less intrusive measure could have been used; and
- having regard to these matters and to the severity of the consequences; a fair balance has been struck between the rights of the individuals and the interests of the community.[65]

The state argued that the funding restriction met these standards and was a proportionate response to protect devolution. The Court applied proportionality in a black-letter manner that too readily accepted the veracity of the state's claim, concluding that the funding prohibition was justified under the Human Rights Act. The assessment consisted of only four paragraphs. A limitation analysis enriched with equality via a relational and contextual methodology would have uncovered how the devolution justification reinforced state control over women's bodies. It also would have ensured greater precision in applying proportionality, directing the analysis away from irrelevant lines of inquiry that concealed the harms of the funding ban.

i. The Irrationality of Devolution

The Court did apply all four limbs of proportionality in *A and B* but only the rational connection and balancing limb are relevant for marking out how the justification-stage was hollowed out. Lord Wilson for the majority judgment accepted that the funding prohibition was rationally connected to the sufficiently important objective of protecting devolution. To respect local distinctiveness, to facilitate the peace process in Northern Ireland, to respond to demands for political autonomy and to enhance responsive decision-making, lawmaking powers in select areas of life were invested in legislative bodies in Wales, Northern Ireland and Scotland.[66] Preventing Northern Irish women and girls from securing funding for abortion while in England, would add further loyalty to 'the scheme for health services to be devolved in the interests of securing local provisions to residents in each of our four countries'[67] and protect 'the democratic

[65] *A and B* (n 63) [32].

[66] Kevin Morgan and Geoff Mungham, *Redesigning Democracy: The Welsh Labour Party and Devolution* (Seren Books, 2000) 24; Charlie Jeffery, 'Devolution in the UK: Problems of a Piecemeal Approach to Constitutional Change' (2009) 39(2) *Publius* 289.

[67] *A and B* (n 63) [32].

decision reached in Northern Ireland in relation to abortion services'.[68] Or more simply, burdening women and girls would protect devolution.

A straightforward application of foundational constitutional law principles would reveal the shaky logic in the state's reasoning. The power of legislative decisions are, for the most part, confined to the territorial boundaries of the polity. A decision to criminalise abortion made in Stormont, the Northern Irish legislative body, would apply throughout the borders of Northern Ireland but it would have no force and effect in England, Scotland, or Wales. The legislative bodies for these regions were not bound by Stormont but were free to decide whether abortion should be legal. Devolution was designed to foster pluralism on issues like abortion. Respecting Stormont's decision to criminalise abortion via prohibiting Northern Irish women accessing publicly funded abortions while in England would not be protecting devolution but giving an extraterritorial effect to Stormont's decision. It would allow Stormont to indirectly control policy decisions within English territory. This was Lord Kerr's dissenting argument in *A and B*, stressing the geographic defects in the state's rational connection argument. Funding abortions in England could not undercut devolution as it would not impinge on the delivery of health services in Northern Ireland nor on the legal status of abortion in Northern Ireland.[69]

The dissenting opinion in *A and B* examined the technical workings of devolution to destabilise the state's claims that the limitation was rational, however, this was an incomplete assessment.

Paying attention to the entwined relation and context between devolution and women's equality in sexual and reproductive health would have revealed a hidden darkness to the purported rational connection. The logic of the prohibition was not only seeking to expand respect for Stormont's decisions beyond the border of Northern Ireland but also to restrain women's sexual and reproductive health. Northern Irish women and girls could not escape state coercion of their reproductive choices. As Lord Wilson observed earlier in the judgment, most women and girls do not have sufficient funds to travel to England and to pay for an abortion and only those who had access to between £600 to £2000 could obtain an abortion in England.[70] For many, the prohibition in England acted as a de facto ban on obtaining a legal abortion. It created extraterritorial hurdles to bolster the domestic criminal prohibition by either materially disadvantaging Northern Irish women and girls or forcing them to remain pregnant. The logic of the funding prohibition was rooted in extending state control over women's bodies beyond territorial boundaries. Lord Wilson's surface acceptance of the rationality between devolution and the funding prohibition and Lord Kerr's dissenting black-letter constitutional interrogation missed these undercurrents. The rationality of devolution cannot be assessed in a vacuum, but must be

[68] ibid [35].
[69] ibid [74]–[77], [85].
[70] ibid [5].

placed in *relationship* to the right infringement, that is the differential treatment in health care between English and Northern Irish women and girls in England, and in the *context* of the claim, Northern Irish women and girls trying to obtain their only viable option for legal access to safe abortions. Accounting for the context in 'which the law operates and the technicalities of how the law works in practice' would expose a more pernicious logic to the ban.[71]

ii. Unbalanced Balancing

A and B also turned on the balancing limb of proportionality. This was a misdirected analysis that only tallied the strengths of the competing aims and blatantly ignored the burdens the law placed on Northern Irish women and girls. *A and B* required confronting the incommensurable conundrum. It asked the Court to come to a determination on the normative value of women's equality in sexual and reproductive health against the normative value of devolution. Balancing women's equality against devolution perhaps more than any other step in proportionality, exposed the Court to accusations of exceeding institutional boundaries by adjudicating based on personal ideologies and policy choices.[72] The desire for the justification-stage to be neutral and objective was arguably at its zenith at the balancing stage in *A and B* as abortion was and remains a particularly charged matter for courts.[73] The UK Supreme Court assiduously avoided the overt accounting and weighing required under balancing. Despite Lord Wilson's acceptance earlier in the judgment that the extensive financial and emotional costs the prohibition placed on girls and women from Northern Ireland, this finding was wholly absent from the balancing assessment.[74] Balancing was misdirected along two tracks, neither of which provided any insight into weighing the prohibition against devolution. This misdirection did not achieve neutrality or objectivity. It only created confusion, forestalled transparent debate on normative constitutional ordering and camouflaged the Court's value judgment that a fair balance required Northern Irish women and girls to bear the costs of devolution.

First, the state argued, at the balancing stage it did not possess sufficient resources to fund abortion services for Northern Irish women and girls seeking abortion while in England.[75] The prohibition struck a fair balance between the individual and the community as it protected the limited NHS budget for other needed health services and procedures.[76] Resource constraints is an

[71] Anne Carter, *Proportionality and Facts in Constitutional Adjudication* (Hart Publishing, 2022) ch 2.

[72] Endicott (n 2).

[73] Gauri Pillai, 'Value Driven Separation of Powers' (on file with author); Sandra Fredman, *Comparative Human Rights* (Oxford University Press, 2018) ch 7.

[74] *A and B* (n 63) [5].

[75] ibid [33].

[76] ibid.

oft-repeated justification for limiting equality rights and it is imperative that courts interrogate the veracity of this claim as it is often a smokescreen for inertia, indifference or antagonism.[77] There are many problems with this argument as the state never pleaded that the purpose of the prohibition was to protect resources. Moreover, ring fencing the English health budget to prioritise other health services in England has no positive impact on protecting the democratically made decisions in Northern Ireland. Lord Wilson never pointed out this disjuncture nor did he answer whether costs were sufficient to outweigh women's equality.[78] Although the UK Supreme Court ultimately upheld the prohibition, the public outcry after *A and B* resulted in the state revising the policy and extending the funding, suggesting that the resource constraints arguments lacked credibility.[79] The speedy reversal of the funding policy speaks volumes regarding the Court's failure to use the justification-stage to protect rights from being eroded on the basis of specious and unsubstantiated claims.

Second, the balancing limb investigated the status of abortion under international human rights law.[80] The breadth and scope of abortion rights as developed by UN treaty bodies was a diversion from the central purpose of balancing which is weighing rights against the competing aims. Whether the UN treaty bodies required the state to ensure free access to abortion revealed nothing of the economic, stigmatic and psychological struggles Northern Irish women and girls endured while navigating the funding prohibition, nor did it illuminate any benefits or strengths to protecting devolution. Yet Lord Wilson placed great weight on the state of international human rights law in the balancing exercise. Concluding that the work of the UN treaty bodies 'add background colour to the inquiry into fair balance' but 'material of a far more vivid hue' would be required for the harms of the prohibition to outweigh the benefits of protecting devolution and the democratic decisions of Northern Ireland.[81] Shifting to a black-letter, technical and formalistic analysis on international human rights law allowed the Court to circumvent accounting for the brutality of the prohibition and calculating whether protecting devolution was worth imposing grave harms on Northern Irish women and girls. The balancing stage was converted into a seemingly neutral descriptive analysis on international human rights law. It was as a shield for the Court's determination that devolution must be protected at the cost of Northern Irish women

[77] Samira Shackle, 'Why are Women Being Blamed for Birmingham's Bankruptcy?' *The Guardian* (13 March 2024), available at www.theguardian.com/commentisfree/2024/mar/13/birmingham-council-bankruptcy-equal-pay-women.

[78] *A and B* (n 63) [33].

[79] Jessica Elgot and Henry McDonald, 'Northern Irish Women Win Access to Free Abortions as May Averts Rebellion' *The Guardian* (29 June 2017), available at www.theguardian.com/world/2017/jun/29/rebel-tories-could-back-northern-ireland-abortion-amendment.

[80] *A and B* (n 63) [34]–[35]; Stephen Cragg, 'Abortion, Northern Ireland and the NHS in England: Can Respect for Devolved Government be a Justification for Discrimination' (2017) 4(2) *Journal of International and Comparative Law* 377.

[81] *A and B* (n 63) [35].

and girls' equality in sexual and reproductive health. While this may have permitted the Court to skirt the controversaries around abortion litigation, it also resulted in women's equality being limited without a robust, objective or accurate application of justification frameworks.

D. The Dollars and Cents of Contraception

Affordable access to contraception, like access to safe and legal abortion, is instrumental to women's equality. It was a paradigm shift allowing women to exercise bodily autonomy and control over their lives. Breaking free from cycles of reproduction and care created opportunities for women to pursue education, employment and civic and sociocultural lives. Restrictions on contraception, on the other hand, frustrated 'paths of self-development outside marriage and motherhood'[82] and stymied women's 'social, economic and democratic participation'.[83] Limits to accessing contraception should automatically trigger concerns that this could infringe women's right to equality. Yet in *Hobby Lobby v Burwell*[84] and *Little Sisters of the Poor v Pennsylvania*,[85] Justice Alito in his majority and concurring opinions, isolated, decontextualised and misdirected the state's purpose in protecting women's access to contraception. And in doing so, he trivialised women's equality and ignored glaring realities so as to rollback protections on accessing contraception.

Under the Affordable Care Act, employers were required to include a range of preventive health care measures without any cost-sharing to the employee and under the Women's Health Amendment this required preventive health care measures needed by women. The Health Resources and Service Administration designated contraception as preventive care. In *Hobby Lobby*, a closely held corporation argued that including certain types of contraception in the employer group health plan was a breach of the Religious Freedom and Restoration Act. The corporation in *Hobby Lobby* was looking for accommodation of their religious belief which ultimately was granted and in *Little Sisters of the Poor* the for-profit religious entity was seeking to protect a legal exemption from the contraception mandate which was also ultimately granted.

Turning to the particulars of these cases, per the Religious Freedom and Restoration Act, the state cannot substantially burden the exercise of religious belief unless that burden serves a compelling interest and is the least restrictive

[82] Angela Davis, 'Racism, Birth Control, and Reproductive Rights' in Marlene Gerber Fried (ed), *From Abortion to Reproductive Freedom: Transforming a Movement* (South End Press, 1990) 18.

[83] Lisa Ikemoto, 'Abortion, Contraception and the ACA: The Realignment of Women's Health' (2012) 55 *Howard Law Journal* 731, 738.

[84] *Hobby Lobby v Burwell* 573 US 682 (2014).

[85] *Little Sisters of the Poor v Pennsylvania* 591 US___ (2020).

means for achieving that interest.[86] This justification test has elements of the traditional proportionality analysis, examining the legitimacy of the state's reasons and whether the measure in question was minimally impairing. Despite it being the state advocating for women's equality and other entities seeking to limit that equality, the majority of the US Supreme Court repeated the hollowing out and avoided patterns of Justice Malhotra in *Indian Young Lawyers Association* and Lord Wilson in *A and B*.

i. Removing Gender from Compelling Interest

Much like these cases, *Hobby Lobby* and *Little Sisters of the Poor* drew the US Supreme Court on to sensitive terrain as it had to adjudicate whether incursions into religious liberty were justified to protect women's equality. Justice Alito avoided transparently deciding this question in *Hobby Lobby* by framing the state's compelling interest in material terms. The Religious Freedom and Restoration Act permitted incursion on religion when the state had a compelling interest to do so, and the interest in question was framed as access to cost-free contraception. This focused the analysis on the dollars and cents of contraception. Locating contraception in its historical, political and economic context would have dramatically shifted the state's compelling interest. Siegel and Siegel, tracing the history of the legal regulation of contraception in the US, demonstrated how affordable access was a vital measure to break gendered expectations that confine women to the home and caregiving roles.[87] Flowing from the equality values embedded in the Fourteenth Amendment, the state, they argued, had an interest in ensuring women could secure access to contraception so as to facilitate 'equal opportunities to participate in the worlds of education, employment and politics'.[88] Justice Alito, however, criticised the state, noting that it 'asserts that the contraceptive mandate serves a variety of important interests, but many of these are couched in broad terms, such as promoting "public health" and "gender equality"'.[89] As noted in chapter four, by placing women's equality in scare quotes the Court callously ignored how contraception permitted women to have autonomy over their lives and implied women's equality was only ambiguously connected to contraception. Rather than placing contraception in the broader context of women's struggle to break free of proscribed caring roles, Justice Alito ignored its connection to women's equality.[90]

[86] 107 Stat. 1488, 42 USC §§ 2000bb – 1(a), (b).

[87] Niel Siegel and Reva Siegel, 'Contraception as a Sex Equality Right' (2015) *The Yale Law Journal Forum* 349; Neil Siegel and Reva Siegel, 'Compelling Interests and Contraception' (2015) *Connecticut Law Review* 47(4) 1025.

[88] Siegel and Siegel, 'Contraception as a Sex Equality Right', ibid 356.

[89] *Hobby Lobby* (n 84) 39 (majority opinion of Justice Alito).

[90] Siegel and Siegel, 'Compelling Interests and Contraception' (n 87).

ii. Simplifying the Math of Least Intrusive Measures

Under the Religious Freedom and Restoration Act, the state must demonstrate that there is no less restrictive 'equally effective' means to achieve the compelling interest.[91] Is there another way to ensure access to cost-free contraception that does not entail burdening religious freedom? Framing the compelling interest as purely economic shaped the least restrictive means assessment. It shifted the less restrictive measures analysis away from exploring the efficacy of alternative measures that could protect religious liberty and women's no-cost access to contraception. The analysis was collapsed into a simple mathematical exercise on whether the state or the corporation should shoulder the financial costs. Earlier in *Hobby Lobby*, Justice Alito concluded that under the regulations corporations were forced to either comply in contravention of their religious beliefs or face fines that were repeatedly described as a substantial burden, in the range of $475m per year.[92] On the other side of the equation, Justice Alito, hypothesised that if the compelling interest, cost-free access, was 'of the highest order … it is hard to understand [the state's] argument that it cannot be required under the [Religious Freedom of Restoration Act] to pay *anything* in order to achieve this important goal'.[93] He assumed that the costs of providing contraception 'would be minor when compared with the overall cost of the Affordable Care Act'.[94] Underpinning these calculations is the argument that the financial burdens of rights should be borne by the state and not the individual, or in *Hobby Lobby*, closely held corporations. The math operated to stress the incredulity of the state's arguments to keep the contraception mandate in place. The justification assessment shifted from a rights conflict into a more straightforward objective, neutral and technical calculation on costs burdens. Absent from his discussion, is how removing the contraception mandate would financially burden individual women who would now be materially responsible for the costs of managing their reproductive health. The cost burden is framed only as between the state and the closely held corporation. Justice Alito reiterated this position in his concurring opinion in *Little Sisters of the Poor v Pennsylvania*, stressing that 'Congress could create … a program if it thought that providing cost-free contraception to all woman was a matter of "paramount" concern'.[95]

On a simple reading of Justice Alito's judgments, urging the state to fund contraception was a progressive measure.[96] The UN Committee on the Elimination of All Forms of Discrimination Against Women (CEDAW) regularly

[91] *Hobby Lobby* (n 84) 27 (dissenting opinion of Justice Ginsberg).
[92] ibid 2 (majority opinion of Justice Alito).
[93] ibid 41–42 (majority opinion of Justice Alito).
[94] ibid 41 (majority opinion of Justice Alito).
[95] *Little Sisters of the Poor* (n 85) 15 (concurring opinion of Justice Alito).
[96] Nomi Stolzenberg, 'It's About Money: The Fundamental Contradiction of Hobby Lobby' (2015) 88 *Southern California Law Review*.

recommends that states take positive measures to ensure affordability.[97] The unique context of the US, however, meant urging state funding of contraception under the least intrusive measure of the justification-stage was a chimera. Justice Alito's analysis failed to account for how conservative Republican politicians would, as Gedicks passionately argued, 'walk barefoot over broken glass to keep this from happening'.[98] Conservative Republican lobbyists and lawmakers had been successful in defunding federal contraception programmes for decades and had done 'everything possible to kill' legislation on equality and health care.[99] Any attempt to publicly fund contraception would be 'politically dead on arrival in Congress'.[100] The claim that a federally funding contraception programme was a least intrusive measure to protect religious liberty was deeply disingenuous and devoid of context. It ignored how cases like *Hobby Lobby* and *Little Sisters of the Poor* were linked to a larger antipathy, antagonism and backlash seeking to rollback women's political, social and economic equality.[101] Abstract and unrealistic faith in the political process created an illusion that religious liberty and women's equality could be harmoniously protected. While this cost analysis was obiter in *Hobby Lobby* and in *Little Sisters of the Poor* only discussed in Justice Alito's concurring opinion, it was deeply revealing of how misdirecting the justification-stage to costs and then decontextualising the costs argument directly impacted judicial reasoning. The veneer of objective, neutral and non-controversial math can hide untested claims and pernicious normative reasoning.

Using the broader context of contraception, the compelling interest would be grounded in women's equality rights. The knock-on effect would be to explore whether alternative methods to guarantee contraception access would be as effective as the contraception mandate.[102] This would require confronting the burdens women would shoulder without the protection of the mandate.[103] Women would be expected to navigate multiple layers of government and insurance bureaucracy to access contraception via tax credits, Government subsidies or alternative contraception programmes. If they did not qualify for these alternative hypothetical measures, which themselves were not sufficiently funded to meet the demand for contraception, women would either expend their own resources to manage their reproductive choices or to do without, which could result in unintended pregnancies trapping women in caregiving roles. Bringing a relational and contextual approach anchored in women's equality to least

[97] CEDAW Committee, 'Inquiry Procedure: The Philippines' (2015) CEDAW/C/OP.8/PHL/1 [52].

[98] Frederick Gedicks, 'One Cheer for Hobby Lobby: Improbable Alternative, Truly Strict Scrutiny and Third-Party Employee Burdens' (2015) 38 *Harvard Journal of Law and Gender* 153, 157.

[99] ibid 163.

[100] ibid 162.

[101] American Civil Liberties Union, 'War on Women', available at https://perma.cc/5Y2T-B2QW, as cited in Siegel and Siegel 'Contraception as a Sex Equality Right' (n 87).

[102] Chang and Dai (n 28) 19.

[103] ibid 27–31 (dissenting opinion of Justice Ginsburg).

intrusive measures would also be illuminating. Exploring the relationship between women's equality, religious freedom and sexual and reproductive health would bring to the fore the history of religious belief being used to perpetuate legislation that controlled women's sexuality, limited access to contraception and criminalised abortion.[104] In the modern era, creating broad accommodations and exemptions that include for-profit entities would be a continuation of this lineage, permitting employers to exercise a degree of control over the reproductive autonomy of their employees. By refusing to cover certain forms of contraception, employers stigmatise reproductive choices of employees that the employer did not agree with. Much like *Young Indian Lawyers Association*, *Hobby Lobby* and *Little Sisters of the Poor* drew the US Supreme Court into normatively weighing protecting religious pluralism against women's equality. By taking a misdirected, isolated and decontextualised approach to compelling interest and least intrusive measures analysis, the Court avoided accounting for how the expanded exemption would contribute to women's inequality in public and private life. By stripping the claim of any relational or contextual components there was no counterweight in the justification analysis to query and destabilise the value of protecting religious liberty. The justification assessment in *Hobby Lobby* and *Little Sisters of the Poor* functioned to conceal the limited priority the US Supreme Court placed on women's equality in relation to religious liberty.

IV. MISUNDERSTANDING WOMEN'S INEQUALITY

The justification-stage is being hollowed out. The limitation claims are examined in isolation from the precipitating breach of women's rights and without taking account of the broader context of women's equality. Justification criteria are also misdirected. The analytical questions that the criteria pose are diverted to a completely irrelevant assessment. Both techniques give a veneer of simplicity, objectivity and neutrality to the justification-stage. This is only a veneer. The isolating, decontextualising and misdirecting approaches mask the flaws in justification claim and artificially inflates its strengths. This may avoid the complexities of the justification-stage, but it undercuts the core function of justification as women's equality is limited by arguments that are insufficiently tested.

There is another method whereby courts hollow out the justification-stage. There is a strand of jurisprudence where the courts are not examining the limitation claim in isolation from the breach of women's equality rights. They are

[104] Reva Siegel, 'Reasoning from the Body: A Historical Perspective on Abortion Regulation and Equal Protection' (1992) 44 *Stanford Law Review* 261, 294; Know Your Enemy, 'How They Did it, Part 2: The Christian Rights and *Roe*' (2022), available at https://podcasts.apple.com/co/podcast/how-they-did-it-pt-2-the-christian-right-and-roe/id1462703434?i=1000566704714.

testing the justification claim in relation to women's equality. While on the surface this may appear a positive step to redress the concerns identified above, the relational methodology they employ is highly impoverished. The relationality employed is thin because the courts woefully misunderstand the nature of women's inequality. The complexity of inequality, the cascading forms of disadvantage, its structural nature, its connection to deeply entrenched norms and values disappear from the justification-stage. Courts are adopting a facile understanding of gender-based violence and gender-based poverty exclusively equating these phenomena to physical acts and material deprivation. This misunderstanding matters to the justification-stage. Women's inequality is so deeply engrained in the patterns and rhythms of political, economic, social and cultural life that it is invisible to the proverbial naked eye and accepted as the status quo. This normalcy filters into the justification-stage as inequalities are threaded into arguments that it is permissible to justify limiting women's inequality. Without an accurate understanding of women's inequality – particularly its pervasive and structural nature – the court is unable to test limitation claims, and it becomes impossible to ascertain whether the state seeks to use inequalities against women to justify further inequalities. Much like the isolating, decontextualising and misdirected approach, mis-conceptualising women's inequality sets up a seemingly straightforward, non-controversial justification assessment. However, the aspirations to a fair, balanced, and neutral assessment can operate to preserve the gendered status quo.

A. False Conceptions of Gender-Based Violence

The Violence Against Women's Act (US) created a new civil remedy in federal and local-level state courts under the Civil Rights Act. Victims of violence could sue the perpetrator for financial compensation. At the expressive level, including gender-based violence against women within the remit of the Civil Rights Act communicated that violence was a grave and serious matter of inequality.[105] The remedy also recognised the negative economic dimensions of violence and the failure of more traditional accountability mechanisms to adequately redress gender-based violence. The federal state argued that the Act was constitutional under the Commerce Clause, which allowed Congress to regulate inter-state economic activity, and under section 5 of the Fourteenth Amendment, which permitted Congress to pass legislation to enforce the Equal Protection clause. In *Morrison v US*, the majority of the US Supreme Court disagreed.[106] Much like *A and B* and *Coleman*, this case pitted women's equality against federalism. And similar to these cases, the US Supreme Court brought a high degree of

[105] Five Four Pod, '*US v Morrison*', available at www.fivefourpod.com/episodes/us-v-morrison/.
[106] *Morrison v US* 529 US 598 (2000).

formalism and abstraction to the justification-stage by examining the limitation criteria in relation to an inaccurate understanding of gender-based violence.

i. Mistaking the Relationship between Violence and Trade

The Court placed untenable definitional boundaries on gender-based violence against women. This exaggerated the dangers that the Violence Against Women Act posed to the federalist structure of the US and blinded the Court to the relationship between gender-based violence and the Commerce Clause. The US Constitution leaves the regulation of trade to the local-level state. Under the Commerce Clause of the Constitution, Congress may regulate inter-state commercial activity. Per the doctrinal evolution of this Clause, the state could justify violating federalism, if it could establish that there was a substantial relationship between gender-based violence against women and intra-state commerce.[107] The majority opinion of Chief Justice Rehnquist concluded, without any meaningful analysis, that 'gender-motivated crimes of violence are not, in any sense of the phrase, economic activity'.[108] The links between gender-based violence, economic activity and inter-state borders were seen as minimal or attenuated. Gender-based violence was conceptualised as non-economic and the civil remedy was unconstitutionally encroaching on the local-level state sphere in relation to trade. The Court repeatedly connected violence to criminal and family law which implicitly perceived gender-based violence as finite and individualised physical incidents. By adopting a limited understanding of violence, the Court was unable to identify the local-level state's assumption that violence was simply physical acts that had no relation to or impact on economics. Without unearthing this misconception, it was then simple for the Court to conclude that the civil remedy in the Violence Against Women Act did not fit within the constitutional permitted exemptions to federalism.

Morrison avoided reckoning with the systemic nature of violence. It is not an isolated abhorrent act but part of a grave and far-reaching pattern. Violence against women is not accidental but a powerful tool of oppression and domination, an extreme form of inequality against women, and as such is not contained or confined but cuts across all areas of life. Gender-based violence against women is part of a web of gender power relations, norms and institutional structures that enforce 'gender roles or prevent, discourage or punish what is considered unacceptable female behaviour'.[109] Identifying the structural inequality at the heart of gender-based violence against women clarifies that it manifests in multiple forms, including economic gender-based violence.[110] Weissman argued that

[107] ibid 609.
[108] ibid 613.
[109] CEDAW Committee, 'General Recommendation No 35 on Gender-Based Violence Against Women' (2017) CEDAW/C/GC/35 [19], [10].
[110] European Institute for Gender Equality, 'Understanding Economic Violence Against Women', available at https://eige.europa.eu/sites/default/files/documents/EIGE_Factsheet_EconomicViolence.pdf.

gender-based violence against women is 'often specifically economic in purpose and … deliberately designed to prevent a woman's economic independence'.[111] Gender-based violence aims to perpetuate women's subordination including economic subordination. Justice Souter, in dissent, observed that gender-based violence cost the US economy $3bn per year.[112] Unsurprisingly, the massive economic impact of violence was not contained by territorial boundaries but spilled across local-level state borders. Incidents of violence and the chilling effect of violence inhibited women from taking up employment opportunities that would require travel across local-level state boundaries.[113] Gender-based violence negatively impacted women's labour force participation resulting in greater health problems, higher absenteeism from work, lower productivity and under- and unemployment.[114] This in turn reduced the supply and demand for inter-state goods and services.[115] Gender-based violence against women was enmeshed with inter-state commerce. It was only by adopting a limited and inaccurate understanding of violence and ignoring the cascading gendered impacts of violence on women's equal participation in the economy that the majority of the Court in *Morrison* was able to conclude the Violence Against Women Act was not justified under the Commerce Clause.

ii. Mistaking the Systemic Failures to Redress Violence

Mis-conceptualising women's inequality also impacted the Court's assessment of section 5 of the Fourteenth Amendment and severed the relationship between violence and the US Constitution. Women who experience gender-based violence repeatedly reported being brutalised and re-traumatised by the criminal law process.[116] The failures of criminal justice were well documented. Gender prejudice and stereotypes resulted in lackadaisical police investigations.[117] Criminal trials 'inappropriately focus on the behaviour and credibility of the victims' and punishments for gender-based violence against women were 'unacceptably lenient'.[118] Due to gender discrimination, women were routinely denied equal protection of the law and, in response,[119] Congress created a civil remedy under the Violence Against Women Act as an alternative accountability route.

[111] Deborah Weissman, 'Gender-Based Violence as Judicial Anomaly: Between "The Truly National and the Truly Local"' (2001) *Boston College Law Review* 1081, 1102–03.
[112] *Morrison* (n 106) 632.
[113] Weissman (n 111) 1090.
[114] ibid 1091.
[115] *Morrison* (n 106) 636.
[116] Weissman (n 111) 1092.
[117] *Morrison* (n 106) 620.
[118] ibid.
[119] Julie Goldschied, '*United States v. Morrison* and the Civil Rights Remedy of Violence against Women Act: A Civil Rights Law Struck Down in the Name of Federalism' (2000) 86(1) *Cornell Law Review* 109, 118.

As outlined above, section 5 of the Fourteenth Amendment can only be used by Congress to create this civil remedy, if it was a congruent and proportional measure to prevent, deter or correct violations of women's equality rights.[120] The majority in *Morrison* concluded that the civil remedy was not proportionate as it targeted private actors who had committed gender-based violence against women and not the public officials who perpetuated gender bias when seeking accountability for that violence.[121] This position reasserted the sharp divisions between private and public and located violence within the private sphere. It also sought to place firm boundaries on what constituted violence and failed to see violence as a continuum that included inadequate accountability mechanisms. Gender-based violence against women cannot be so neatly defined. As Bunch observed in her ground-breaking article on violence against women, it is 'profoundly political. It results from the structural relationships of power, domination, and privilege … Violence against women is central to maintaining those political relations at home, at work and in all public spheres'.[122] The Court failed to grasp that violence committed by private actors was connected to larger patterns of gender subordination and oppression committed by other public actors. It did not recognise that the interplay between private and public actors was responsible for the ongoing harms of gender-based violence. As Weismann noted, 'it was the very intersection of gender-motivated violence by private actors with the states' failure to provide equal protection of the laws which underlay the need for a federal civil rights action'.[123] Permitting civil remedies under the Violence Against Women Act was a step to tackle this synergy by destabilising impunity for violence by private actors and this could spill over to the culture that underpins discrimination by public actors. Placing violence in its context of subordination against women marks a clear path for connecting the civil remedy to the Equal Protection Clause. It is only by adopting a narrow understanding of gender-based violence, ignoring its structural dimensions, that the Court was able to cut the Violence Against Women Act from the Fourteenth Amendment.

B. Demonising Gendered Social Benefit Dependency

The UK Supreme Court was equally blind to the structural roots of women's economic inequality and held in *SG and others v Secretary of State for Work and Pension*,[124] *DA and others v Secretary of State for Work and Pensions*,[125]

[120] *Boerne* (n 41).
[121] *Morrison* (n 106) 626.
[122] Charlotte Bunch, 'Women's Rights as Human Rights: Towards a Re-Vision of Human Rights' (1990) 12 *Human Rights Quarterly* 486, 491.
[123] Weissman (n 111) 1105.
[124] *SG* (n 8) 16.
[125] *DA and others v Secretary of State for Work and Pensions* [2019] UKSC 21.

and *SC and others v Secretary of State for Work and Pensions*[126] that a series of benefit reforms which disproportionately imposed income poverty on women were a legitimate way to discipline the individual wayward behaviour of women. The Court placed its misunderstanding of gendered economic inequality in relation to the state's aim. In doing so, it failed to expose gendered stereotypes on poverty that were ingrained into these aims. The Court ended up using inequality against women to justify inequality against women undercutting the function of the justification-stage to root out this circularity.

The benefit cap, limiting the amount of social benefits any individual could claim; the work conditionalities, the requirement to find a specific number of hours in the formal labour market to escape the cap; and the two-child limit, restricting access to the subsistence child benefits to the first two children, were all implemented to reduce public spending. The state had taken on £850bn in debt from bailing out the banks in response to the 2008 economic crash.[127] All of these reforms disproportionately impacted women. The gendered division in care meant women relied more on social benefits and the gendered structures of the labour market created obstacles to women finding employment. In *SG, DA* and *SC*, the UK Supreme Court held the cap, work conditionalities and two-child limit were prima facie an infringement of women's equality rights under the Human Rights Act. The state responded with similar justification rationale in all three cases. First, the state sought to make fiscal savings; second, it wanted to incentivise women to make certain choices such as moving to smaller accommodation, entering the paid labour force or reflecting on the financial readiness to have children; and third, the state wanted to improve benefit fairness by not rewarding non-working people with benefits that would exceed the income of the average working person.[128] As argued in chapter four, the UK Supreme Court employed a light-touch review in these cases, uncritically accepting the state's arguments. A searching analysis would have revealed faulty logic as, the state's own assessment showed, there was no rationality between income poverty and incentivising behaviour.[129] Enriching the justification-stage via a relational and contextual approach, particularly the legitimate aims limb of proportionality, would also have revealed how a misunderstanding of women's inequality hid gender myths embedded in the purpose of the reforms.

[126] *SC and others v Secretary of State for Work and Pensions* [2021] UKSC 26.

[127] Meghan Campbell, 'The Proportionality of an Economic Crisis' in Shreya Atrey and Sandra Fredman (eds), *Exponential Inequalities* (Oxford University Press, 2022).

[128] *SG* (n 8) [63], [66]; *DA* (n 125) [7]–[8]; *SC* (n 126) [191], [193], [208].

[129] House of Lords Economic Affairs Committee, 'Universal Credit Isn't Working: Proposals for Reform' (HL 2019–21, 105) 3.

i. Shielding Gendered Illegitimate Aims

The first limb of proportionality is often glossed over by courts, but it does serve an important function of filtering out aims that lack a degree of legitimacy. Little attention has been paid to deriving an analytical framework for filtering out legitimate and non-legitimate reasons for limiting rights. Barak argues that the aims must be consistent with the values of a constitutional democracy and while the boundaries of what compromises constitutional values may be amorphous and nebulous, there is general agreement that a law whose purposes is discriminatory would not be proper or legitimate.[130] Competing policy aims cannot be antithetical to the right to be protected.[131] With respect to the incentivising behaviour and welfare fairness, the legitimacy of these goals in *SG*, *DA* and *SC* is inconsistent with the values of liberal democracies as it is based on discriminatory stereotypes that women's poverty is rooted in individual moral failings.

Regardless of whether the manifestly without reasonable foundation test (*SG* and *DA*) or the four-limb proportionality test (*SC*) was used, the Court accepted after a cursory analysis the importance and significance of the state's objectives. Lord Hughes in his concurring opinion in *SG* held:

> It is agreed on all sides that the scheme has legitimate aims. At the very least, the principal aim of discouraging benefit dependence and encouraging work is agreed to be legitimate. For my part I agree that at a time of national economic crisis it was also legitimate to seek to reduce the overall expense on benefits, and that establishing a different balance between those who worked and paid taxes and those who did not was a further legitimate aim.[132]

In the abstract, helping women in poverty enter paid work and crafting a fair benefit system appear legitimate. This is akin to *Indian Young Lawyers Association* as the aim of protecting religious pluralism examined in isolation from the breach of women's equality was entirely worthy and important. In *SG*, *SC* and *DA*, the UK Supreme Court did undertake a relational approach as it explored these aims in relation to women's equality. But it examined the wrong relationship as it fundamentally misunderstood women's equality. It was therefore unable to see the stereotypes that the reforms were built on and ultimately unable to test out the legitimacy of the purpose in pursuing the benefit's reforms.

As argued in chapter two, the Court in *SG*, *DA* and *SC* skirted investigating the breach of women's equality rights. However, the Court's description of the reforms and its extensive citation of the state's rationale for the cap, work conditionalities and two-child limit imply agreement that women's poverty is rooted in individual moral failings and poor decision-making. The judgments across

[130] Barak (n 37) ch 9.
[131] Tsakyrakis, 'An Assault on Human Rights' (2003) (n 4) 487.
[132] *SG* (n 8) [135].

these decisions explain that the current welfare system has disincentive effects and perpetuates welfare dependency. Citing the Minister's comments at a Public Bill Committee meeting, the *SG* judgment noted that the aim of the reforms was to push 'working people on low incomes ... to cope with difficult circumstances, ... they had to live within their means'.[133] Lord Reed in *SG* explained that it was 'important to make efforts to assist those capable of working to find work: effort 'which can include the removal of financial disincentives' and that there was a 'perception that the benefits system has been excessively generous to some recipients'.[134] In *SC*, he cited the Treasury's Impact Assessment warning that the 'current benefit structure ... removes the need for families ... to consider whether they can afford to support additional children' and the two-child limit represents a 'desire to ensure families in receipt of benefits are encouraged to make financial decisions supporting themselves solely through work'.[135] Taking these statements together, they locate women's economic inequality in their own behaviour. Women live in poverty due to their resistance to employment, their inability to budget, their failure to secure a job or have a 'prudent' number of children. Women were work-shy, benefit-scroungers who were living lives of luxury by leaching off hard-working people.[136] The reforms were aimed to correct women's misbehaviour. As Cohen-Rimer explained, the reforms reflect a belief that individuals are responsible for their dire straits and they 'need to be "fixed" ... for poverty to be alleviated'.[137]

The legitimacy of imposing income inequality on women to achieve benefits fairness and to incentivise behaviours would crumble when the purpose of the reforms is put in the context of a more accurate understanding of women's poverty. Gendered economic inequality is a function of cultural norms and institutions.[138] Unequal pay and the concentration of women in jobs that were undervalued were but two examples of the structural nature of women's poverty. Gender norms on caring forced women into part-time work which is lower paid and precarious and thus for many women, working in the formal labour market would not break the cycles of poverty.[139] Lady Hale was cognisant of these forces, in dissent, observing that women with caring duties 'will face considerable difficulties in finding suitable work that will fit with her childcare arrangements'.[140]

[133] ibid [35].
[134] ibid [65].
[135] *SC* (n 126) [14].
[136] Meghan Campbell, 'The Austerity of Lone Motherhood: Discrimination Law and Benefit Reform' (2021) 41(4) *OJLS* 1197.
[137] Yael Cohen-Rimer, 'What's Choice Got To Do With It? Addressing the Pitfalls of Using Choice-Architecture Discourse Within Poverty Law' (2023) 86(4) *MLR* 951, 953.
[138] UN Working Group on Discrimination Against Women and Girls, 'Gendered Inequalities of Poverty: Feminist and Human Rights-Based Approaches' (2023) A/HRC/53/39.
[139] Trade Union Congress, 'The Motherhood Pay Penalty' (2016), available at www.tuc.org.uk/sites/default/files/MotherhoodPayPenalty.pdf.
[140] *DA* (n 125) [145].

The exorbitant costs of childcare can force women out of the labour market[141] and the effort, skill and responsibility women expended on taking care of their own children was not recognised as work under the reforms. In 2018, it was estimated that all of women's unpaid care work amounted to £352bn,[142] yet the benefit reforms refused to recognise this as socially valuable work that should be supported. Understanding that women's poverty is rooted in structural discrimination and placing that understanding in relation to the state's objectives, the legitimacy of these aims is highly questionable as they wrongly seek to correct behaviours that are not located in individual actions. There is a cruelty to the state's objectives as it sought to punish women for circumstances and choices beyond their control. By accepting these aims as legitimate, the UK Supreme Court perpetuated these gendered myths on women's poverty. Kumm observed that aims do not have legitimacy simply because majoritarian political processes desire that aim.[143] By failing to challenge pernicious ideologies on women's economic inequality, the Court did just that and failed to ensure that the state's limitation arguments meet the required justification threshold.

V. CONCLUSION

The justification-stage is being hollowed out. Through a series of techniques – isolating, decontextualising, misdirecting and misunderstanding – the criteria are devoid of any content. These methodologies are used to construct a justification-stage that does not draw the court into controversial decision-making. It also, however, undercuts the central purpose of justification as isolating, decontextualising, misdirecting and misunderstanding makes it impossible to interrogate whether limitation claims meet the requisite level of coherency, persuasiveness and veracity. This has resulted in women's equality being constitutionally limited on the basis of dubious, speculative and stigmatic arguments. Digging more deeply into how justification frameworks have malfunctioned in the practice of adjudication across different jurisdictions helpfully reorients debates that have dominated justification. The hollowing out of justification is not tied to any specific limitation test. The solution lies not in devising new tests or tinkering with existing frameworks. It requires enriching justification with women's equality. The parameters of this approach and how it can work in practice are explored in the next chapter.

[141] Work and Pensions Committee, 'Universal Credit: Childcare' (HC 2017–19, 1771); Women's Budget Group, 'The Female Face of Poverty' (2018), available at http://wbg.org.uk/wp-content/uploads/2018/08/FINAL-Female-Face-of-Poverty.pdf.

[142] Kate Andersen, *Welfare the Works for Women? Mothers' Experiences of the Conditionality Within Universal Credit* (Bristol University Press, 2023).

[143] Kumm (n 14) 62.

6

Enriching Justification

I. INTRODUCTION

WOMEN'S SUBSTANTIVE EQUALITY is the motivating force that can breathe life into the justification assessment. Justification reasoning, as argued in chapter two, can pervert the equality-stage, pushing into the shadows the severity and gravity of inequality against women. Equality reasoning does not harm the justification-stage but enriches it. This is the asymmetry between the equality-stage and the justification-stage as equality cuts across both stages whereas justification is confined to the one. Justification frameworks, at their heart, are analytical tests to help courts assess the constitutional priority, on one hand of competing rights and interests and, on the other, women's equality. There are a range of relations and contexts that can be utilised to explore any limitation claim. This chapter argues that a relational and contextual approach anchored in women's equality can immeasurably enrich the justification-stage. It should always be employed when assessing the constitutionality of limits to women's equality. This means that courts should explore whether a limitation is sufficiently legitimate, rational, necessary or balanced by bringing the limitation into a *relationship* with the underlying breach of women's equality and each limitation claim can be examined within the broader *context* of women's equality. Is it justified to prohibit women's employment in hotels and bars to protect them from being exploited at work? Testing the limitation in a relation to the breach of women's equality in employment and against a contextual backdrop of gendered activism would enrich the justification-stage. It would expose illogical assumptions in the justification claim on the availability of better forms of work and uncover how the limitation arguments were entwined with negative gendered cultural stereotypes on women who work in hotels and bars. Enriching justification in this manner adopts established feminist methodologies and takes the novel step to extend and adapt them to the limitation analysis.

As marked out in chapter five, courts often uncritically accept arguments that women's equality must be given lesser priority. They do so by avoiding using justification tests. In part, it is theorised that this was to protect the courts from wading into controversaries that would expose it to critiques of judicial overreach. This comes, however, at a cost. Women's equality has been limited on the basis of dubious, speculative and flimsy arguments that grossly misunderstand the nature of women's inequality. Developing a new justification test to redress these problems is needlessly hubristic as it is difficult to envision breaking away from the stronghold that proportionality or proportionality-like reasoning has over the justification-stage. A more constructive way forward is to sharpen the application of justification criteria via a relational and contextual approach that is anchored in the commitment to women's substantive equality. This methodology can correct against current wrong turns in the jurisprudence and, at the same time, give courts a workable set of tools to assess the permissibility of the proposed limit to women's equality rights.

Women's equality is a multi-dimensional concept. It seeks to end gendered material and social disadvantage, stereotypes, stigmas, prejudice, negative cultural attitudes, violence, oppression, neglect and exclusion. Equality touches upon all aspects of life and manifests in creative, transformative, innovative and responsive ways. At the same time, justification claims are themselves shaped by an array of political, legal, economic, social and cultural factors. To enrich the justification-stage, to use equality to test whether limitation arguments meet the required threshold, relationality and contextuality play an important directive role. The complexities of both women's equality and justification means there will be a plethora of relationships and contexts at stake in any given case. Without seeking to straitjacket the justification-stage, this methodology directs the court to consider when analysing proposed limits to women's rights: the relationship between the limit and the specific breach of women's rights and the meaning of the limit in the broader context of women's equality. These relations and contexts anchored in women's equality must always be harnessed to the established justification test and utilised to ascertain whether the justification is permissible. There may be other relations and contexts that are illuminating. For example, in cases where women's equality is limited due to a fiscal crisis or budget constraints, understanding the economic events that precipitated the crisis can be instructive in assessing whether the limit is balanced.[1] The relevancy of other relations and contexts will be a function of the unique factual-legal matrix of the case. But regardless of the specifics of the case, the limitation argument's relationship with the breach of women's equality and the broader context of women's equality is inherently relevant to the justification-stage assessment. Much like a high intensity review, argued for in chapter four, this relevancy demonstrates respect for the constitutional nature of women's equality. It asks pertinent questions from the perspective of those being asked to bear the burden of the justification. This approach does not require the court to exceed institutional boundaries, as it does not require courts to impose its own view on constitutional priorities. It simply requires that court to explore in a sophisticated manner whether the established justification criteria have been

[1] Meghan Campbell, 'The Proportionality of an Economic Crisis' in Shreya Atrey and Sandra Fredman (eds), *Exponential Inequalities* (Oxford University Press, 2022).

met. A strength of this approach is that in many cases it deflates any purported controversaries in determining whether normative precedence should be given to women's equality.

Justification is riddled with conceptual conundrums and controversies. Advocating for a relational and contextual methodology in the context of women's claims to equality appears to be adding further unnecessary layers of complexity. This would be a misunderstanding of both the purpose of the justification-stage and how a relational and contextual approach functions. Justification is inherently a relational exercise, as it brings two competing objectives into dialogue with each other. Paying attention to the breach of women's equality rights at the justification-stage, is simply making explicit an inherent function of justification and moreover it helpfully throws a light on whether the aim is legitimate, the means are rationally connected, necessary and proportionally balanced. Similarly, investigating the nature of context and the function its serves at the justification-stage, clarifies that gendered contextualism can reveal hidden or difficult to spot meanings embedded in a justification claim. This methodology, rather than derailing the justification-stage, enhances the core function of justification as it tests the veracity, strength and persuasiveness of limitation claims.

The chapter proceeds as follows. Section II introduces a relational and contextual methodology at the justification-stage. It takes an interdisciplinary approach investigating feminist relational theory. With respect to context, it draws on anthropology, intellectual history, linguistics and literary criticism. It then moves to consider how these methodological approaches can be translated and adapted to the justification-stage. Section III examines jurisprudence from South Africa, India and Canada and argues that applying the relational and contextual approach ensures that only exact, convincing limitations of due weight and significance are constitutionally permitted to limit women's equality. The chapter concludes with reflecting on how the relational and contextual approach anchored in women's equality can respond to future challenges.

II. THE TOOLS OF RELATIONALITY AND CONTEXTUALISM

The justification-stage, as marked out in chapter five, can devolve into a formalistic and mechanistic exercise that isolates, decontextualises, misdirects and misunderstands the application of justification criteria. A relational and contextual approach anchored in women's equality can act as a corrective. Justification criteria should be explored in relation to the specific breach of women's equality and tested against the broader context of women's equality. The methodology proposed in this chapter can enrich the justification harmoniously achieving the twin aspirations of the limitation analysis: a rigorous assessment that forensically tests out justification claims while also protecting against the justification-stage from devolving into wholly subjective moral reasoning.

At first glance, it might appear that relationality and contextuality are superfluous or redundant as the analytical heavy lifting is done by women's substantive equality. It is equality that is the normative anchor of the proposed enrichment of the justification-stage. Canadian legal feminist scholar and now current justice on the Supreme Court of Canada, Justice Sheliah Martin, observed the need for equality to shape the justification-stage:

> The division between breach and limit is intended to protect the integrity and strength of the right, but there should be no insistence on false symmetry. There should not be watertight compartments because the section 1 [justification] analysis needs to flow backwards into a review of the purpose of equality rights.[2]

There is a lack of specificity on the 'flow' between equality and justification. In a similar vein, Jackson, in beginning to chart the relationship between equality and justification, argued that a 'conscientiously applied' proportionality framework can 'generate insights into the nature and structure of inequality that might otherwise elude judges'.[3] Samuels also argues that the proportionality should be applied in a way consistent with feminist legal methods.[4] But there has yet to be a clear articulation of how equality can precisely enrich the justification-stage. This is very much needed, as uncovered in chapter five, courts can misunderstand women's equality at the justification-stage, latching onto thin and inaccurate conceptions. Simply calling for equality to be utilised at justification runs the risk of replicating these misunderstandings. Moreover, the justification-stage is not a second equality analysis and care must be taken to prevent the limitation analysis from developing into an evaluation of how the impugned law breaches the concept of equality. Relationality and contextuality are key. To adopt the metaphor from the Introduction, relationality and contextuality are the hammers to test the limit against the anvil of substantive equality. They direct the analysis to the relevant aspects and components of women's substantive equality that can shed light on whether the limitation claim meets the required justification criteria. This is a holistic assessment that does not place a sharp delineation between relational or contextual. This chapter builds upon Martin, Jackson and Samuels' observations. It develops a more fully fleshed out methodological approach that marks out how women's equality rights can positively shape the justification-stage.

Relational and contextual are ubiquitous concepts in legal reasoning, especially feminist legal methodologies. Despite their centrality, these are elusive legal concepts that defy a simple meaning and can, at first glance, appear to needlessly complicate the already difficult task of justifying equality rights.

[2] Sheilah Martin, 'Balancing Individual Rights to Equality and Social Goals' (2001) 80 *The Canadian Bar Review* 299, 365.

[3] Vicki Jackson, 'Proportionality and Equality' in Vicki Jackson and Mark Tushnet (eds), *Proportionality: New Frontiers, New Challenges* (Cambridge University Press, 2017) 171.

[4] Harriet Samuels, 'Feminizing Human Rights Adjudication: Feminist Legal Methods and Proportionality Principle' (2013) 21 *Feminist Legal Studies* 39, 44–7.

Relationality, and especially contextualism, can be conceptually incoherent, lacking needed boundaries and definitions. LaCapra, an intellectual historian, noted that contexts are contestable and the search for context can be endlessly regressive.[5] This is because there is no authoritative or objective formula for determining whether 'one context or set of contexts is particularly significant'.[6] Judges can latch onto widely diverging relations and contexts, resulting in the justification-stage losing any claim to certainty, predictability or objectivity. The act of identifying a relevant set of relations or contexts can also too readily be shaped by individual concerns, beliefs, ideologies or predilections. Seemingly the proposed methodology could result in an analytical free-for-all. There have been numerous critiques that the balancing stage of the proportionality test creates an impossible relationship of weighing incommensurables.[7] The relationship between the costs of a breach of women's equality and the strengths of the competing objective cannot be balanced out by any legal framework. The argument would go that adopting a relational and contextual approach to the entire justification-stage results is a wholly subjective moral exercise and confuses the limitation analysis. At the same time, there might be concerns that requiring a relational and contextual approach anchored in women's equality places a metaphorical straitjacket on judicial reasoning. It demands a specific type of reasoning that may appear to restrain the justification-stage from examining all relevant facets to a limitation argument. An interdisciplinary investigation into the conceptualisation of 'relational' and 'contextual' provides insights into how the strengths of this proposed legal methodology can be directed towards enriching the justification-stage rather than derailing or constraining the limitation analysis.

A. Justification is Relational

There is a strand of jurisprudence, as analysed in chapter five, that examined justification claims in the abstract and divorced from the precipitating breach of women's equality rights. In *Indian Young Lawyers Association v Kerala*, in dissent in the Indian Supreme Court, Justice Malhotra examined the claim that religious freedom required limits on women's equality in a way that was divorced from the breach of women's rights.[8] Only the strengths of protecting religious freedom were examined at the justification-stage, the costs to women's equality were not accounted for. In a similar vein, in *A and B v Secretary of State for Health*, the majority explored the rationality of using devolution to

[5] Dominick LaCapra, 'Intellectual History and Its Ways' (1992) *The American Historical Review* 425, 430.
[6] ibid.
[7] See chapter five.
[8] *Indian Young Lawyers Association v Kerala* [2018] 9 SCR 561.

justify breaches of women's equality rights without any awareness of women's sexual and reproductive health.[9] This formalistic application of justification criteria resulted, in these cases, in women's equality being limited on the basis of speculative arguments as limitation claims were never really tested. The justification-stage must move away from being a pro forma checklist applied in a vacuum. The relationality strand of the proposed methodological approach to the justification-stage prevents flimsy arguments eliding limitation requirements. But what does it mean to adopt a relational methodology to the justification-stage and how does it enrich the justification analysis? This subsection seeks to answer this question by examining feminist relational theory.

Individuals experience the world in a relational manner. This sentence has a degree of dissonance. The word 'individual' connotes single, separate or distinct from a group.[10] Yet as John Donne, the seventeenth century English poet, famously wrote, 'no man is an island'.[11] This is a paradox at the heart of the human experience. Human beings are both individuals with unique qualities and features but are also part of and formed by relations, groups and communities. No person is a disconnected individual, but is 'shaped by and acting in and through relationships'.[12] As Nedelsky explained, 'relationships are central to people's lives – to who we are, to the capacities we are able to develop, to what we value, what we suffer and what we are able to enjoy'.[13] Relationships are how humans both interact with and make sense of the world. They are ubiquitous, spanning across the life cycle. Ranging from 'intimate to global',[14] including parents, teachers, friends, lovers, partners, co-workers, landlords, employers, medical professionals, regulators, financial institutions, the state and international organisations. Relationships are not exclusively between individuals but are between individuals and social, economic, cultural and political structures. Moreover, intrapersonal relationships are inevitably shaped by miso and macro relations.[15] Relations can be good and bad as they simultaneously enhance and constrain what people are able to be, what they are able to do and the choices they are able to make.[16]

The western liberal tradition, however, severed the synergy between individuals and relations. It conceived of human beings as atomised individuals who

[9] *A and B v Secretary of State for Health* [2017] UKSC 41.

[10] 'individual, adj and n' (*Oxford English Dictionary Online*), available at www.oed.com/search/dictionary/?scope=Entries&q=individual.

[11] John Donne, 'Mediations XVII' in Henry Alford (ed), *The Works of John Donne Volume III* (Parker, 1839) 574–75.

[12] Christine Koggel, Ami Harbin and Jennifer Llewellyn, 'Feminist Relational Theory' (2022) 18(1) *Journal of Global Ethics* 1.

[13] Jennifer Nedelsky, 'A Relational Approach to Law and Its Core Concepts' in Deborah Brake (ed), *The Oxford Handbook of Feminism and Law in the United States* (Oxford University Press, 2023) 57.

[14] ibid 59.

[15] ibid.

[16] Koggel, Harbin and Llewellyn (n 12).

operate rationally to maximise their control and use of material resources.[17] This understanding had strong implications for gender power relations. Despite beliefs in the power of the individual or the utility of the individual as an analytical device, human beings were still created and sustained through relationships. To preserve western liberal theorising, these relations were ignored, excluded and denigrated. This division between the individual and the relational strongly mapped with gender. Men were the independent individuals operating in the public space and women were the relational actors performing caring work in the home. Law rarefied this division. Men acting in the public space were the subject of law and women acting in the private space were ignored by law. This ignorance of relations had severe consequences for women. Feminist relational legal theorists have uncovered how law, by ignoring the relational nature of human existence, has been used to reinforce relationships of constraint and in doing so perpetuated gender and other hierarchies.[18] Women are 'embodied with categories such as "mother", "wife" and "date"' and there are a 'host of expectations about the roles of women within those relations'.[19] These relational assumptions 'drive the logic of judicial decision that have a real impact upon women's lives, and they often validate and enforce a gendered structure of relationships'.[20] Failing to identify an employment relationship between a domestic worker and her employer because the work was performed in a private home operated to exclude women from labour laws and compounded gender and as well, in many cases, racial and class subordination.[21] Failing to identify de facto intimate partner unions as relations of mutual dependency and support was used to exclude these unions from marital property laws. Due to pervasive gender norms, not recognising these relations compounded women's economic precarity.[22] Feminist relational theory also challenged assumptions within relational sets, for example, that the provision of care work to children, parents or partners is rooted in love and therefore could not be demanding or exhausting work.

Theorising on women's exclusion, feminist relational theory called for a transformation and advocated for understanding 'the relational dimension of human experience [as] central to law'.[23] Feminist relational theory brushes against the grain of dominant legal paradigms. By paying close attention to all

[17] Sandra Fredman, 'Discrimination' in Peter Cane and Mark Tushnet (eds), *The Oxford Handbook of Legal Studies* (Oxford University Press, 2003).

[18] Koggel, Harbin and Llewellyn (n 12).

[19] ibid.

[20] Catherine Albiston, Tonya Brito and Jane Larson, 'Feminism in Relation' (2002) 17(1) *Wisconsin Women's Law Journal* 1, 4.

[21] *Mahlangu v Ministry of Labour* [2020] ZACC 24.

[22] UN Committee on the Elimination of Discrimination Against Women (CEDAW), 'General Recommendation No 29 on the economic consequences of marriage, family relation and their dissolution' (2013) CEDAW/C/GC/29.

[23] Nedelsky (n 13) 59.

relationships of power 'at all levels of personal, local, regional, national and global' it is possible to 'uncovers the role of norms, structures and powers'.[24] Albiston, Brito and Larson warn that 'differences in social power can become invisible when courts (and scholars) refuse to engage in relational … analysis'.[25] Much work has been done, particularly by Nedelesky, to develop a more relational understanding of law. She has evolved a legal concept of autonomy that moves away from individualistic conceptions. Arguing that autonomy must be rooted in relations and laws that further autonomy must construct relationships that facilitate agency and choice.[26] Work continues to be done, using feminist relational theory, to uncover the power dimensions of relationships, and to map how a variety of laws and legal concepts reifies intersecting power relations of subordination. This points the way forward to reconstructing power, relationships and law to enhance well-being via a relational understanding of humanity.

Acknowledging that the central importance of relations to how individuals interact with each other and the world may not readily appear to be a key to enriching the justification-stage when adjudicating claims for women's equality. How do the insights of feminist relational theory assist in determining if making fiscal savings is legitimate? Or if restricting abortion or contraception access is necessary to protect devolution or religious pluralism? Legitimacy is, so the thinking goes, exclusively an assessment on moral or philosophical conceptions of the public good and necessity is solely a practical investigation into alternative measures. Any insights from feminist relational theory appear irrelevant to these assessments. But only examining the legitimacy or necessity claims in isolation from the precipitating breach of women's equality rights is to ignore how limitation arguments are embedded in a polycentric web of other relations. The objective in imposing income poverty on women by revoking equal pay agreements as in *Newfoundland (Treasury Board) v NAPE*[27] or by reforming benefits as in *SC v Secretary of State for Work and Pensions*,[28] *SG v Secretary of State for Work and Pensions*[29] and *DA and DS v Secretary of State for Work and Pensions*[30] created entwined relationships between individual women, the needs of others in the community and domestic and international financial institutions. The justification-stage in these cases determined the ordering of the relationship between women, the community and the state and created power hierarchies between different sets. Limits to rights seeks to create power hierarchies between women's equality and other aims and objectives. Feminist relational theory serves as an important reminder that the justification-stage is relational for the simple fact that it creates relationships between women's equality and other objectives.

[24] Koggel, Harbin and Llewellyn (n 12) 7.
[25] Albiston, Brito and Larson (n 20) 2 (footnotes omitted).
[26] Nedelsky (n 13).
[27] *Newfoundland (Treasury Board) v NAPE* [2004] 3 SCR 381.
[28] *SC and others v Secretary of State for Work and Pensions* [2021] UKSC 26.
[29] *SG and others v Secretary of State for Work and Pensions* [2015] UKSC 16.
[30] *DA and others v Secretary of State for Work and Pensions* [2019] UKSC 21.

The application of the various limbs of justification frameworks, thus, cannot be conducted in a manner that is disconnected from these relationships as the legitimacy or necessity criteria only make sense when considered within its relationship to women's equality. Ignoring these relationships dangerously inflates the value of the limitation as most justification claims at first glance appear laudable. It is only by examining the limitation claims in tandem with women's right to equality can the justification-stage perform its function of rigorously testing the veracity of these claims. For example, a relationality approach to justification in *Indian Young Lawyers Association* would not examine the value in protecting religious freedom in isolation from the breach of women's equality. It would direct the Indian Supreme Court to ask questions on the rationality of the limit, investigating whether sociocultural assumptions and stereotypes on menstruation and women's sexuality had become cloaked in religiosity. Or in *A and B*, a relational rational connection analysis would bring to the fore that the logic of the funding prohibition on abortion was not about protecting devolution but bolstering the domestic criminal prohibition and extending state control over women's bodies beyond territorial boundaries, as Northern Irish women and girls could not even travel to England to escape the force of criminalisation.

Examining the limbs of the justification test in relation to the underlying breach of women's equality enriches the justification-stage. First, it directs the justification analysis to specific elements of women's equality. It is not the all-encompassing concept of equality that is used to test the limitation arguments but a narrower subset. It is the aspects of equality that are relevant to the breach of women's rights. For example, in assessing whether it is legitimate to protect sociocultural traditions at the expense of the right, the legitimacy is not tested writ large against women's equality. The legitimacy assessment can focus the dimensions of equality violated by the breach. In *Independent Thought v Union of India*, the Indian Supreme Court's legitimacy analysis zeroed in on the relationship between the value of preserving the tradition and the equality dimensions raised by that tradition which legally condoned men sexually assaulting girls.[31] This moored the assessment to the specifics of the case, preventing it from drifting into an unrestrained analysis on the tensions between women's equality and customary traditions. Relationality provides more guidance and certainty to how substantive equality can enrich the justification-stage.

Second, relational theory does not accept the design and value of relationships as innate or given. It relentlessly pokes and prods at relationships, questioning how the configuration of relationships can break cyclic relations of oppression. It is this methodological inquisitiveness that can be brought to the justification-stage. Relationality does not accept at face-value that the social inclusion of women in poverty is of less value than curbing public expenditure.

[31] *Independent Thought v Union of India* [2017] 13 SCR 821.

It questions hierarchies that are sought to be enforced via the justification-stage. Bringing a relational approach to the justification-stage sharpens the analysis and, in many cases, exposes flaws in limitation reasoning. This is marked out in more detail in the analysis below in Section III.

B. Justification is Contextual

The relational approach is supported and entwined around a contextual justification-stage. Feminist relational theory stresses context. Davies explains that a relational view of rights requires an understanding of rights that is 'contextual and deeply social'[32] and Nedlesky explained 'relational feminism offers a lens of analysis that highlights context'.[33] While the relational is contextual, it is still required to pin down what contextualism means. Sheppard, when advocating for a contextual approach to assessing whether there has been a breach of the right to equality, explained that

> A contextual approach to … equality requires a broad-ranging inquiry to embrace the voices and stories of exclusion and discrimination, information about institutional policies, practices, and the systemic dynamics of exclusion, and knowledge of the larger social and structural realities of inequality.[34]

Contextualism rejects conceptualising rights in formalistic or abstract terms and is 'more sensitive to the reality of the dilemma posed by the particular facts'.[35] Justice Wilson of the Supreme Court of Canada advocated that

> real lives, contemporary women's lives, should not only be taken seriously but should be regarded as primary in interpreting constitutional guarantees which impact … on women's equality. Experiences must not be shoehorned to fit within constitutional guarantees.[36]

At the equality-stage, context prevents the law from demanding women conform to preconceived conceptions on how inequalities should manifest and allows the richness, complexity, contradictions and messiness of reality to shape women's right to equality. Importantly, in Justice Wilson's understanding, not all contexts are relevant to the equality-stage. She places primacy on the context of women's lives. It is their understanding of disadvantage, exclusion, oppression, prejudice and stereotyping that should inform assessment of any breach of section 15 of the Charter.

32 Margaret Davies, 'Persons, Property and Community' (2012) 2(2) *feminists@law* 1, 17.
33 Nedelsky (n 13) 61.
34 Colleen Sheppard, *Inclusive Equality: The Relational Dimensions of Systemic Discrimination in Canada* (McGill-Queen's University Press, 2011) 66.
35 *Edmonton Journal v Alberta (Attorney General)* [1989] 2 SCR 1326 [52].
36 Bertha Wilson, 'Women, the Family and the Constitutional Protection of Privacy' (1992) 17 *Queen's Law Journal* 5, 13.

These insights should not be confined to the equality-stage but can also enrich the justification-stage.

At the justification-stage, context is also a vital tool, as it can be directed to interrogate whether the limitation claims meet the threshold required by justification tests. As marked out in chapter five, the failure to undertake a contextual approach has impoverished the justification-stage. Ignoring the context in which the law was drafted, particularly feminist legislative strategy, blinded the US Supreme Court in *Coleman v Maryland* to the link between justifications for infringing on federalism and the self-care provision in the Family Leave and Medical Act.[37] Or avoiding the broader context of Northern Irish women and girls' sexual and reproductive health rights prevented the UK Supreme Court in *A and B* from accurately weighing the value of devolution against the harms imposed on women and girls. At its broadest a contextual approach to justification directs the court to investigate a wide array of factors, experiences, stories, facts and dynamics that go beyond the four-corners of the justification argument. A contextual methodology is a recognition that the justification-stage is not a sterile analysis and that limitation claims are not proposed in a vacuum. Justifications are embedded in a wide range of broader context sets. This chapter argues that contexts anchored in women's equality must always enrich the limitation stage.

This imperative springs from the nebulous nature of context. Unlike a relational approach which is contained by the legal-factual matrix of the claim, the contextual approach to the justification is seemingly unbounded and infinite. There is no pre-determined formula to identifying context. If it is relevant to assessing whether a justification is legitimate, rational, necessary or balanced it should be drawn into and utilised in the limitation analysis. Courts can latch onto widely different ideas of what constitutes a relevant context. A recent decision from the Canadian Supreme Court highlights the potential pitfalls of contextualism. In *R v Sharma*, the Court had to determine whether a legislative restriction on conditional sentencing was a breach of section 15 on the basis of race.[38] The majority opinion, which found no infringement of equality rights, assessed the restriction on conditional sentences in the 'broader context of sentencing law' and the role of Parliament in determining repercussions for criminal acts.[39] The dissenting opinion, on the other hand, found an unjustified violation of equality rights by examining the historical and contemporary context of Indigenous offenders and the tragic history of colonialism in Canada. The same legal-factual matrix but diverging contexts. This is illustrative of the central challenge to the contextual approach to the justification-stage. How can courts identify the context relevant to testing the veracity of the state's limitation arguments? And despite differences across cases and across jurisdictions

[37] *Coleman v Maryland* 556 US 30 (2012).
[38] *R v Sharma* 2022 SCC 39.
[39] ibid [60].

on how rights are justified, is there any context that is inherently relevant to assessing the permissibility of limits to women's equality? By stretching across disciplinary boundaries to define context and examine its paradoxes, this section seeks to answer these questions. It makes the case for how the justification-stage must take account of the larger context of women's equality. Drawing on Justice Wilson's insight from the equality-stage, the justification-stage must give primacy to women's context of what the limitation means to their lives. It is this context that enriches the limitation analysis.

i. The Simplicity of Context

Context is treated as obvious or a function of common sense or conventional wisdom.[40] The apparentness of context means judgments rarely openly reflect on how the relevant context is defined, selected and used. There is an unspoken assumption that context is 'self-evident, as a given attribute in the world, something that is stable, clear and sufficient'.[41] Dilley, a social anthropologist, noted how surprising it is given the importance of context how very little attention has been paid to what is context.[42] At its heart context is a heuristic device that reveals 'hidden meanings and deeper understandings'.[43] Dilley explained that context is 'a set of connections construed as relevant to someone, to something or to a particular problem, and this process yields an explanation, a sense, an interpretation for the object so connected'.[44] Context is a device to reveal, through understanding connections, the meaning and values that infuse a text, claim, narrative, event, experience, situation or circumstances. These meanings are not always readily apparent, and context is a tool to uncover these difficult to detect understandings. The analytical purpose of context aligns with the core purpose of the justification-stage. Both are geared towards uncovering and exploring meaning. A contextual application of the limitation frameworks, particularly one anchored in women's substantive equality, as argued below, guarantees a richer, more thorough investigation into the veracity and strength of justification claims.

ii. The Challenge of Context

The simplicity of context belies its challenges. Exploring these challenges helps to understand why the broader context of women's equality is an inherently relevant context when considering justifications that limit that equality.

[40] Roy Dilley, 'The Problem of Context' in Roy Dilley (eds), *The Problem of Context: Perspectives from Social Anthropology and Elsewhere* (Berghahn Books, 1999) 2.
[41] ibid.
[42] ibid.
[43] ibid 3.
[44] ibid.

Understanding context as connection implies that there is also disconnection, that there are irrelevant contexts. There are choices to be made in identifying and using context. There is a choice in what is an important, significant and illuminating context and what is consigned as useless, extraneous and irrelevant. Judgments can stress certain contextual backdrops and ignore others at the justification-stage. The absence of common concepts or common perspectives can result in contextual babelism where courts speak at cross purposes choosing different contextual elements. *Sharma*, discussed above from the Canadian Supreme Court, is an example of this contextual chaos. Decisions as to context are never neutral but are reflective of power relations. Courts can put on contextual blinders and refuse to engage with contexts regardless of how relevant they may be to understand the legitimacy, rationality, necessity and balance of limitation claims. For example, in *Coleman* and *A and B*, the US and UK Supreme Court avoided using feminist contexts to assess the veracity of limitation claims. In these cases, contextual choices excluded women from the justification-stage and ejected women's understanding of how the limitation claims would burden their lives. Developing a contextual methodology to the justification-stage must be cognisant of how context is an exercise in power. Including the broader context of women's equality at the justification-stage is an important tool for recognising women as full constitutional subjects and not consigning gender understandings to the margins of the constitution.

Furthermore, context is infinite. The connections needed to make sense can extend forever and in a myriad of directions: cultural, social, political, religious, economic, ecological, historic, linguistic, gendered, racial, temporal, to name but a few. There are critiques that context is 'unmasterable' and 'boundless'.[45] Dilley observed that

> there is no limit to its contents, it is unsaturable and is always open to further description; any definition of context can itself be contextualised by means of a new context, and the process is open to infinite regression.[46]

From a legal perspective, this is problematic as it creates deep uncertainty as to what is or isn't relevant to assessing justification claims and creates too much space for judges' preferences, biases and ideologies to shape a contextual analysis of limitation claims. Dilley playfully explains that in law context is only ever limited by the lawyers' imagination, the client's finances and the patience of the court.[47]

The impossibility of controlling context, of creating a definitive contextual checklist or formula is not fatal to contextualism. Culler, a prominent literary

[45] Jonathan Culler, *On Deconstruction: They and Criticism After Structuralism* (Cornell University Press 1983) 123; Dilley (n 40) 22.
[46] Dilley (n 40) 22.
[47] ibid 36.

academic critic, warned against 'impetuous nihilism'.[48] The aim is not to seek an objective determinative context but to recognise its living nature. It can be contested, chaotic, competing. Different decision-makers, different interpreters, different geographies, different temporalities, different linguistic, sociocultural, political, economic cultures will create and inspire 'further connections, correlations and contexts'.[49] Context is a dynamic and changeable concept since it 'undergoes a continuous process of structuring and re-structuring the flow of incoming and out-going information as regards the production and processing of language in context'.[50] At first glance, this understanding of context is unhelpful for the justification-stage as courts must come to definite determination. The infinity of contextualism should be a prompt for judicial transparency, a core value that the justification test, like proportionality, seek to further and enhance.[51] In sum, flowing from the challenges of contextualism, courts must approach context with a heightened awareness of the power of contextualism, the paradoxes of infinite meaning and sensitivity to articulations and connections.

iii. Contextualism in Justification

The quagmires of context point towards the need to always bring the context of women's equality to the justification-stage. First, contextualism is a process of inclusion and exclusion. The justification-stage is an analytical process where courts determine if women's equality should be given constitutional priority. Both processes involve the creation of hierarchies. Excluding the context of women's equality from the justification-stage cements women's exclusion from the law. It signifies that only non-gendered contexts are relevant to limitation rationales. Ignoring the context of women's equality holds that the disadvantage, stigma, marginalisation and constraints women bear are analytically irrelevant to assessing whether a purpose is legitimate or whether the infringement of their rights is necessary. This is illogical and somewhat absurd. It also denigrates gendered understanding of the limit and ultimately weakens the justification analysis. Refusing to consider the context of women's equality epistemically deprivileges women from the justification-stage and is part of the lineage, analysed in chapter four, of pushing women out of the constitutional project. Much like a searching and probing justification-stage, a contextual analysis rooted in women's equality demonstrates respect for the fundamental nature and normative significance of women's constitutional right to equality.

[48] Culler (n 45) 133.

[49] ibid 134.

[50] Anita Fetzer, 'Contexts in Interaction: Relating Pragmatic Wastebaskets' in Rita Finkbeiner, Jorg Meibauer and Petra Schumacher (eds), *What is Context? Linguistic Approaches and Challenges* (John Benjamins Publishing Company, 2012) 108.

[51] Alec Stone Sweet and Jud Mathews, *Proportionality Balancing and Constitutional Governance: A Comparative and Global Approach* (Cambridge University Press, 2019) ch 1.

Second, the relevant contexts will always be a function of the unique features of the claim, but women's equality is automatically relevant. Always holding that women's equality is a relevant context is another method for recognising the importance of women's equality and aligns the justification-stage with constitutional norms and values. It also is a tool that assists courts in determining whether the limitation arguments have met the justification burden as it can test whether there are hidden gendered meanings in the limitation claim such that the claim does not meet the criteria. For example, in assessing whether incentivising individuals into work is a legitimate aim the justification stage is immensely enriched in placing that aim in the broader context of gendered welfare dependency revealing how the aim in built on gendered stereotypes against women in poverty. It would be impossible to identify this lack of legitimacy without a contextual methodology that examines broader understandings of women's equality. As marked out in chapter five, ignorance, neglect and even antagonism towards women regularly underpin claims that the limitation is justified. Enriching the justification-stage with the context of women's equality can redress these problems.

This is not to hold that other contexts are irrelevant or also cannot assist at the justification-stage. When women's equality is limited due to a fiscal crisis, understanding the origins of that crisis can be valuable context in understanding whether it is constitutionally permissible to require women to bear the brunt of recovery measures. Or when assessing whether religious liberty or pluralism is sufficient to limit women's equality, understanding the role of religion in the state and of the status of the religious denomination can throw light on the justification arguments. A degree of judicial discretion is needed to ensure courts can draw on relevant connections to give meaning to limitation claims, but women's equality is an inherently relevant context when assessing purported limits to that equality.

Third, contextualism also gives a direction to the justification-stage. It may seem odd to make this claim as context has been described as amorphous. Yet, at the justification-stage it can provide a needed steer as to what aspects of equality should be drawn upon to test the limitation claim. Turning back to *Independent Thought*, the law in question was a criminal exemption for marital rape for men who: (i) committed sexual assault; (ii) was married to the girl; and (iii) she was aged 15 to 18. The Court had to determine whether the exemption, which was in place to protect sociocultural traditions, was a permissible limit on women's equality. A contextual approach anchored in women's equality would direct the court to examine the broader inequality harms of early forced marriage and sexual violence against all women and girls. It steers it to specific contexts of women's equality. This pinpointed context would then destabilise the claims that retaining the exemption is on balance worth the cascading and reinforcing harms against girls. Simply arguing for the court to test the justification against women's equality would leave it unclear what aspects of equality were relevant and, as argued in chapter five, courts repeatedly misunderstand women's equality. The contextual approach provides a direction to the enriching process. Context is not a firm steer, as this would undercut its flexibility, but a gentle push towards gendered facts, experiences, voices and understandings that are relevant in revealing difficult to detect or hidden flaws in the justification. Furthermore, on a more practical level, different jurisdictions have different understandings of equality. Some adopt a very nuanced and sophisticated understanding and some a thin one. Enriching justification with equality could result in the misunderstandings identified in chapter five being replicated. For example, by conceptualising gender-based violence as individualised physical acts, the US Supreme Court failed to see how creating a civil remedy to redress this violence was a justified intrusion into federalism.[52] A direction that the justification should be contextual could address this problem as it can steer the justification analysis beyond the limited understanding of the right to equality some courts employ. In this case, it would steer the Court to equality contexts such as the economic impacts of gender-based violence and the accountability gaps.

In determining whether women should bear equality burdens to achieve other communal objectives, the relationship between the breach of equality and the objectives, as well as the broader context of women's equality should enrich in the limitation analysis. Feminist legal methodologies are well suited to the justification-stage as its aims echo the central purposes of the limitation analysis grappling with 'real-life dilemmas posed by human conflict' and 'underlying political and moral considerations'.[53] Moreover, gendered understandings of the limitation claims are highly relevant to assessing if those claims are constitutionally justified, as it is women who must bear the real life consequences of those claims. The relational and contextual methodology requires applying justification criteria against an understanding of where women's equality has been achieved in the state and where women's equality has fallen short. Ultimately, this approach is taking the 'women question', an established feminist legal methodology of asking 'the gender implications of a social practice or rule' to the justification-stage.[54]

III. THE ANVIL OF WOMEN'S SUBSTANTIVE EQUALITY

Having sketched out the proposed methodology, the chapter now turns to investigate how it could work in the practice of adjudication. Women's equality is the anvil on which the court can test whether a purported justification meets constitutional muster with relationality and contextuality being the tools to use on the anvil. This does not mean the justification-stage collapses into a covert reiteration of the equality-stage analysis. Rather, the court can draw on a

[52] *US v Morrison* 529 US 598 (2000).
[53] Katharine Bartlett, 'Feminist Legal Methods' (1990) 103(4) *Harvard Law Review* 829.
[54] ibid 837.

relational and contextual understanding of women's equality to assess whether an aim is legitimate, evaluate whether a justification is rational, explore whether a measure is necessary and determine if there is balance between the aim and women's equality rights. A relational and contextual approach to the justification enriches the analysis because it creates a sophisticated synergy between the limitation and women's equality. This synergy can be used to explore whether limitations are accurate, persuasive and coherent enough to justify imposing constitutional limits on women's equality rights. This is not an unconstrained analysis but is directly shaped by the lived realities of women who are being asked to bear burdens.

There are glimmers of this proposed methodology in the jurisprudence, but it could be more fully embraced to strengthen the limitation analysis. Given the challenges of this methodology, outlined above, courts must be transparent in articulating the relations and context that inform the justification-stage. This final section marks out how this methodology can be more fully developed and how it enriches the justification-stage. Although not all jurisdictions employ a proportionality framework, this section organises the analysis around the four limbs of that test as the courts in this study invariably draw on one limb or another when assessing the permissibility of limits to women's equality.

A. Legitimate Aims

The initial step for many justification tests centres on assessing the legitimacy, importance, properness or compelling nature of the state objective in limiting women's equality. This step is often glossed over with courts uncritically accepting the state's claim that it aims have the requisite level of seriousness.[55] In part, this may stem from the difficulty of articulating a coherent theory of what constitutes a legitimate aim in a constitutional democracy.[56] While the boundaries of legitimacy may be opaque, aims that are built upon or perpetuate women's inequality cannot claim any degree of importance. However, at first glance, it may not be apparent that the aim is twisted around inequality, as most aims proffered at the justification-stage have a veneer of legitimacy.

The relationship between the breach of women's equality rights and the aims, as well as the broader context of women's equality, can be drawn upon to brush against the grain of the competing goals to expose purposes that lack legitimacy. This section examines where courts are successfully using the proposed methodology to enrich the justification-stage while also pointing out where it can be further brought to bear.

[55] Anne Peters, 'A Plea for Proportionality: A Reply to Yun-chien Chang and Xin Dai' (2021) 19(3) *International Journal of Constitutional Law* 1135, 1138.

[56] Stavros Tsakyrakis, 'Proportionality: An Assault on Human Rights?' (2009) 7(3) *International Journal of Constitutional Law* 468, 482.

i. The Illegitimacy of Continuing Patriarchal Historical Traditions

The precise application of the relational and contextual approach to the legitimacy limb of the justification-stage will be a function of the specific factual-legal matrix of the claim. However, there are common patterns that are worth exploring as these patterns mark out the strength of the enriched methodology. Many of the laws that encroach on women's equality have a long antecedent. The state argues the law is legitimate notwithstanding its impact on women's equality as the law aims to preserve historical practices or customary traditions. The historical context of women's political legal, sociocultural and economic status at the time the law was brought into place or at its zenith, can clarify whether the law has the required legitimacy. This approach exposes how the importance of the state's purpose is premised on a patriarchal historical reality that is outdated and no longer fits with modern aspirations for gender equal societies.

Decisions from the South African Constitutional Court and Indian Supreme Court use the historical context and the relationship between the breach and the purpose of the law to explicate why the law does not serve a compelling goal. Apartheid era legislation mandated that the laws that governed succession for Black persons was governed by 'Black law and custom' and the customary law of succession, which Black people were legally forced to use, contained the principle of male primogeniture. In *Bhe v Khayelitsha*, the South African Constitutional Court held this was unfair discrimination against women.[57] The Court then had to determine if male primogeniture was a justifiable limit 'in an open and democratic society based on human dignity, equality and freedom'.[58] The South African Constitutional Court has been critiqued for failing to develop the role of the section 36 limitation clause in the context of equality rights.[59] The justification-stage is often cursory and there is only a nominal application of the section 36 requirements. This provision echoes the traditional four-part proportionality analysis requiring the Court to examine inter alia 'the importance of the purpose of limiting the right'. The concurring limitation analysis of Justice Ngcobo in *Bhe* stands out, as it takes nascent steps towards fully employing this methodology. His judgment examined the *relationship* between the purpose of the limit (preserving socio-cultural traditions) and the breach of women's equality (material and recognition harms of being barred from inheriting) as well as the broader *context* (women's economic roles in both the past and in the present).

In the past, within traditional African societies, there was a sharply defined gender division of labour between men and women. These gender relations, Justice Ncgobo noted, were 'developed in the context of a traditional

[57] *Bhe v Khayelitsha* [2004] ZACC 17.

[58] Section 36 of the South African Constitution.

[59] Cathi Alberty and Beth Goldblatt, 'Equality' in Stu Woolman and Michael Bishop (eds), *Constitutional Law of South Africa*, available at https://constitutionallawofsouthafrica.co.za/.

society which was based on subsistence agricultural economy characterised by a self-sufficient family organisation'.[60] The male head of the family unit had obligations towards women within his family unit to provide food, shelter and clothing.[61] Male primogeniture's purpose was to support and strengthen these social and economic arrangements. This context helps explain an original, more benign purpose to the exclusion of women from inheriting. In contemporary times, modes of living in South Africa had radically changed. More and more women were participating in economic activity and the relational bonds between members of a family unit and tribal community had weakened under the pressure of market capitalism.[62] Succession rules that favoured men had a justifiable purpose within a past gendered social structure but as that structure no longer existed, the legitimate objectives of male primogeniture also crumbled away. As evidence of the multitudinous nature of context, this gendered investigation into context not only enriched the section 36 limitation analysis but also was instrumental in developing the role of customary and Indigenous law in the South African Constitution, specifically conceptualising the value and significance of this body of law in the post-apartheid era.[63] With respect to relationality, the relationship between the purpose of the limit and the breach of women's equality rights highlights the seismic shifts across time in women's roles in society and brings into sharp focus that the contemporary objective was to cast women in socially and economically subordinate roles. Justice Ngcobo concluded that 'whatever role the rule of male primogeniture had played in traditional society, it can no longer be justified in the present day and age'.[64] It was through an enriching justification with women's equality via a relational and contextual approach that the South African Constitutional Court was able to identify how male primogeniture lacked legitimacy.

The Indian Supreme Court also stressed that laws which treated women and girls unequally in marriage cannot rest their legitimacy in a patriarchal past understanding of gender relations and it did so by implicitly adopting a relational and contextual approach to the justification-stage. In *Independent Thought v Union of India*,[65] the Court had to assess whether criminal exemptions to child rape within marriage breached Article 14 of the Constitution and in *Joseph Shine v Union of India*,[66] it had to decide whether the criminalisation of certain forms of adultery were similarly in breach. The Indian Supreme Court does not draw sharp distinctions between the equality-stage and the justification-stage. The jurisprudence on Article 14 would direct the Court to

[60] *Bhe* (n 57) [188].
[61] ibid [162]–[164], [188]–[189].
[62] ibid [189].
[63] Sanele Sibanda and Tshepo Bogosi Mosaka, '*Bhe v Magistrate, Khayelitsha*: A Cultural Conundrum, Fanonian Alienation and An Elusive Constitutional Oneness' (2015) *Acta Juridica* 256.
[64] *Bhe* (n 57) [190].
[65] *Independent Thought* (n 31).
[66] *Joseph Shine v Union of India* (2019) 3 SCC 39.

assessing whether these laws suffered from a lack of intelligible differentia or suffered from arbitrariness. However, in the judgments in *Independent Thought* and *Joseph Shine*, the Court assessed whether these laws had a legitimate or worthy purpose. The Court has not explicitly adopted the four-part proportionality test.[67] It framed the legitimacy analysis in terms of 'constitutionality morality', which is a broader concept than legitimacy under the proportionality test.[68] However, the lynchpin of the limitation analysis in these cases was whether custom and tradition were sufficiently important reasons to justify treating women and girls differently. The Court concluded the illegitimacy of the aims in *Independent Thought* and *Joseph Shine* through a relational and contextual assessment anchored in women's equality.

Turning to *Independent Thought* to examine how this approach enriched the justification-stage, the age of consent in the Indian Penal Code was 18 years old. Anyone who has sexual activity, even consensually, with a minor was guilty of rape. There was one exception. If a girl, aged 15 to 18, who was married and had non-consensual sex with her husband, he was not guilty of any crime.[69] The state justified the differential treatment for married girls as an 'age old tradition' that 'must be respected and not destroyed'.[70] Under a formalistic and abstract legitimacy assessment, this aim does not appear problematic. Protecting cultural traditions, particularly in light of the homogenising power of globalisation, was highly desirable. A relational analysis, however, destabilised the properness or worthiness of the customary tradition. It was not the legitimacy of maintaining a broad, unspecified or abstract custom that must be justified, but the worthiness of maintaining a tradition that permitted a man to sexually assault a girl. The relation between the breach of women's equality and the limit directed the justification-stage and prevented it from being sidetracked into an unfocused analysis on the abstract tensions between equality and customary traditions. Moreover, putting the aim of the measure in relation to breach clarified that the purpose could never be held to be constitutionally legitimate. Its aim was to maintain a tradition that denied personhood to girls. Kumm observed that 'there is nothing inherently wrong with traditions [or] convention … but there are many traditions [or] conventions … that merely reflect and perpetuate prejudices towards certain groups, defined in terms of class, race, ethnicity, religion, gender, or sexual orientation'.[71] If tradition and custom was used to justify

[67] Aparna Chandra, 'Limitation Analysis by the Indian Supreme Court' in Mordechai Kremitzer, Talya Steiner and Andrej Lang (eds), *Proportionality in Action: Comparative and Empirical Perspectives on the Judicial Practice* (Cambridge University Press, 2020) 488–92.

[68] Nakul Nayak, 'Constitutional Morality: An Indian Framework' (2023) 71 *The American Journal of Comparative Law* 354; Abhinav Chandrachud, 'The Many Meanings of Constitutional Morality' (18 January 2020), available at https://papers.ssrn.com/sol3/papers.cfm?abstract_id=3521665.

[69] Section 375(2) of the Indian Penal Code.

[70] *Independent Thought* (n 31) [81] (opinion of Justice Lakur).

[71] Mattias Kumm, 'The Idea of Socratic Contestation and the Right to Justifications: The Point of Rights-Based Proportionality Review' (2010) 4(2) *Law and Ethics of Human Rights* 142, 159.

violating women's equality rights, that tradition has to be 'linked to plausible policy concerns that qualify as reasons that legitimately restrict [the] rights of others'.[72] In *Independent Thought* the state only sought to preserve the past to maintain a historic tradition. However, if the core purpose of that tradition was to severely oppress women and girls, the law which codified that tradition could not be legitimate.

The context of the law also supported this conclusion. Justice Lokur in his concurring opinion, held that the Court cannot come to the justification-stage

> with the blinkered visions of days gone by but with the social realities of today. Traditions that may have been acceptable at some historical point of time are not cast in stone. If times and situations change, so must views, traditions and conventions.[73]

This was implicitly embracing the proposed enriched methodology as Justice Lokur recognised that the justification claims cannot be assessed in isolation. He examined past understandings of women's legal and social position in marriage, contrasting them with modern conceptions to conclude that the criminal exemption to the marital rape of girls did not have a proper purpose. Justice Lokur noted that marital rape exemptions were a manifestation of a history that denied the autonomy of girls and women in marriage. The exemptions were premised on 'the out-dated notion that a wife is no more than a subservient chattel of her husband'.[74] In the modern era, there has been a legal and policy rejection of these gendered attitudes towards women and girls. In his opinion, Justice Lokur canvassed contemporary measures to prohibit and eliminate early forced marriage, the criminalisation of child sexual abuse and the recognition of children's rights.[75] The broader legal context was unequivocable that girls possess rights and that the synergy of early forced marriage and the marital rape exemption denied girls bodily autonomy, increased the risk of violence, poverty, early pregnancy, maternal mortality and, stymies education and employment opportunities, and deprives them of 'leading a youthful life'.[76] Legal permission for men to sexually assault girls could no longer be deemed legitimate 'even if sanctified by tradition and custom' as today it was a highly 'undesirable practice'.[77] Women's equality enriched the justification-stage. A gendered contextualism lens directed the Court to elements or aspects of that equality which were relevant to explicating why preserving the sociocultural tradition was no longer legitimate. This included women's historical legal inequality in marriage, the equal rights of girls and the equality impacts of early forced marriage and these contexts provided the tools to uncover how the law's purpose was not constitutionally proper.

[72] ibid.
[73] *Independent Thought* (n 31) [86] (opinion of Justice Lakur).
[74] ibid [71] (opinion of Justice Lakur).
[75] ibid [18], [20], [35], [44], [45] (opinion of Justice Lakur).
[76] ibid [41], [79] (opinion of Justice Gupta).
[77] ibid [57] (opinion of Justice Lakur).

Justice Chandrachud adopted a similar approach to assessing whether the criminalisation of adultery could be justified in *Joseph Shine*. Section 497 of the Indian Penal Code criminalised men who engaged in sexual intercourse with another man's wife. No criminal culpability was attached to women who committed adultery nor to a married man who slept with a woman who was not married. Justice Chandrachud held that in assessing the permissibility of criminalising adultery, the assessment 'cannot be construed in isolation' and the law must be placed in the historical context 'of the institutions and values which have forced women to a shackled existence so far'.[78] The purpose of the law in *Joseph Shine*, much like *Independent Thought*, was to protect the husband's proprietary interest in his wife and to prevent aggrieved husbands from seeking vigilante retribution.[79] The law was passed in the 1860s when women had 'no rights of independence of their husbands and were treated as chattel or property of their husbands'.[80] The sexual double standard in the Indian Penal Code reflected Victorian era morality which permitted and expected men to control women's sexuality. In the modern era, this aim was blatantly discriminatory against women and Barak has noted that 'a law whose only purpose is to discriminate' is not a law with a proper purpose.[81] Using feminist and legal scholarship, Justice Chandrachud traced evolving understanding of gender, sexuality and marriage. A law which aimed to deprive women of autonomy over their sexuality did not have a purpose that 'square[s] with today's constitutional morality'.[82] Justice Malhotra in her concurring opinion came to a similar conclusion:

> A law which could have been justified at the time of its enactment with the passage of time may become out-dated and discriminatory with the evolution of society and changed circumstances. What may have once been a perfectly valid legislation … may become obsolete and archaic. The historical background in which Section 497 was framed, is no longer relevant in contemporary society.[83]

ii. Unearthing Illegitimate Purposes via Substantive Equality

The synergy of the gendered contextual history and the contemporary relationship between the underlying breach and the competing aim can test out whether a law has the required legitimacy to justifiably infringe women's equality rights. The justification-stage also needs to place the seemingly proper aim in relation and context of women's equality to test whether it devalues, trivialises,

[78] *Joseph Shine* (n 66) [2] (concurring opinion of Justice Chandrachud).
[79] ibid [6] (opinion of Justice Nairman).
[80] ibid [12.2] (concurring opinion of Justice Malhotra).
[81] Aaron Barak, *Proportionality: Constitutional Rights and Their Limitations* (Cambridge University Press, 2012) 251.
[82] *Joseph Shine* (n 66) [23] (opinion of Justice Nairman).
[83] ibid [13] (concurring opinion of Justice Malhotra).

objectifies, demeans, disparages, excludes, silences, dominates and marginalises women.

Courts are taking tentative steps towards adopting this methodology to the legitimacy limb of the justification-stage, particularly with respect to misrecognition harms embedded in the competing objective, less so in relation to systemic harms. These arguments are explored below.

a. The Illegitimacy of Gender Stereotypes

Misrecognition harms against women are pervasive and persistent and infiltrate all aspects of life, including the justification-stage.[84] The limitation analysis should question how the purpose echoes stereotypes, stigmas or negative cultural attitudes towards women by examining the aim in relation to the breach and broader contextual sociocultural gendered patterns. It can evaluate whether the aim reflects 'institutionalised patterns of cultural value [that] constitute women as inferior, excluded … or simply invisible'.[85] If the aim is built upon gendered recognition harms it lacks legitimacy, and the infringement of women's equality rights cannot be justified.

The dissent in *S v Jordan* in the South African Constitutional Court drew on the relational and contextual approach to the justification-stage to flush out how the purpose of a law on sex work was built upon gendered stereotypes that stigmatised women. The law, which only criminalised sex workers and not the purchasers of sex, was held by Justices O'Regan and Sachs to be constitutionally unfair discrimination against women. They then had to determine whether the law could be justified under the section 36 limitation clause.[86] The lynchpin of their assessment was the 'important purpose' factor as their analysis was centred on whether the state had a proper or compelling reason for exclusively criminalising sex workers. The dissent started with a relational approach anchoring the legitimacy analysis in the breach of women's equality. Justices O'Regan and Sachs held that 'it is the difference between the treatment of patrons and prostitutes … which must be justified'.[87] A common problem at the justification-stage, as identified in chapter five, was the legitimacy analysis being isolated and decontextualised into a wide-sweeping assessment. Although Justice Ngcobo in his majority judgment did not find a breach of equality rights and did not explicitly conduct a section 36, in *obiter* he conducted a highly isolated and decontextualised limitation analysis. Reshaping the justification-stage into an assessment on the criminalisation of commercial sex writ large.[88]

[84] Rebecca Cook and Simone Cusack, *Gender Stereotyping: Transnational Legal Perspective* (University of Pennsylvania Press, 2010) chapter 1.

[85] Nancy Fraser, 'Feminist Politics in the Age of Recognition: A Two-Dimensional Approach to Gender Justice' (2007) *Studies in Social Justice* 23. 31.

[86] *S v Jordan* [2002] ZACC 22.

[87] ibid [95].

[88] ibid [26], [30].

The relational and contextual approach would direct the legitimacy assessment away from evaluating the properness of criminalising sex work into a targeted question on the legitimacy of criminalising one side of the transaction. What purpose does the law serve when it only targeted women as morally blameworthy and not men? By directing the legitimacy assessment to the breach of women's equality, this inevitably led to the conclusion that the law was seeking to buttress gender subordination. Justices O'Regan and Sachs observed that 'wherever the conduct of prostitutes is treated as the primary criminal offense, it seems that the patterns of gender inequality and illegitimate double standards relating to male and female sexuality will be reinforced'.[89] By engaging in commercial non-procreative sex outside of marriage, sex workers were deviating from moral or acceptable sexual behaviour.[90] This threatened men's control over women and, as Nussbaum has argued, sex workers must then be 'controlled and condemned'.[91] The broader context of gendered sexual relations pinpointed that the purpose of the law in *Jordan* was to castigate this supposed transgression. And thus, it could not be deemed legitimate and could not, according to the dissent, be a justifiable limit to women's equality.

A different range of gender myths were proffered by the Indian Government in *Ministry of Defence v Babita Puniya* to justify employment prohibitions.[92] Women were barred from permanent commissions in the Indian Army. There were multiple aims underscoring this prohibition. The army sought to protect women from 'the inherent dangers [of] serving in the army, adverse conditions of service which include an absence of privacy in field and insurgency area, maternity issues and child care'.[93] Furthermore, women would not be able to meet the physical fitness needed for combat, women would not be able to cope with the lack of privacy or hygiene and women's presence in the field would impact on the male environment.[94] Service in the army with a permanent commission required personal sacrifice, long separation from family and frequent transferring which would interfere with women's caring roles.[95] For the totality of these reasons, women were prohibited from these positions.

The Indian Supreme Court did not take the army's aims at face-value but explored how they refracted gender recognition harms. Much like in *Independent Thought* and *Joseph Shine*, the Court did not explicitly adopt the four-part proportionality assessment, but the Article 14 analysis touched upon the legitimacy of these reasons for restricting women's equality in employment. Justice Chandrachud for the Court concluded that 'arguments found on

[89] ibid [97].

[90] Martha Nussbaum, 'Whether from Reason or Prejudice: Taking Money for Bodily Services' (1998) *The Journal of Legal Studies* 693, 707.

[91] ibid.

[92] *Defence v Babita Puniya* [2020] 3 SCR 833.

[93] ibid [23].

[94] ibid [35].

[95] ibid.

the physical strengths and weaknesses of men and women and on assumptions about women in the social context of marriage and family do not constitute a valid constitutional basis for denying equal opportunity to women officers'.[96] The enriched justification methodology could have gone a step further. It could have more explicitly relied on a broader context of women's equality at work, teasing out how the prohibition is a continuation of long-standing beliefs that women were physically unfit, were unable to endure harsh conditions and were disruptive to male working environments. The army sought to perpetuate myths that women were simultaneously weak and sexually dangerous. The purpose of the prohibition was to strengthen and extend the web of cultural attitudes that hold that women's primary place is within the home caring for children and this role should be prioritised over work in the labour market. These aims were blatant gendered stereotypes and were not sufficiently legitimate to justify restricting women's equality at work. In *Babita Puniya* and *Jordan*, the aims could be framed as normatively valuable – criminalising morally contentious practices or protecting women from harm – but a relational and contextual methodology centred on women's equality can lay bare how these aims were a camouflage for objectives that sought to demean women.

b. The Illegitimacy of Gendered Structures

A relational and contextual assessment can also be employed to explore whether the objective of the law is a continuation of oppressive gendered structures and systems. Inequality is not the result of isolated acts or omissions. Iris Marion Young explained oppression is 'embedded in unquestioned norms, habits, and symbols, in the assumption underlying institutional rules and collective consequences of following those rules'.[97] The architecture of systems and institutions are premised on men's living patterns which operate to disadvantage, exclude, oppress, dominate and stigmatise women. The purpose of laws that breach women's rights can be to bolster these gendered structures. A relational and contextual methodology anchored in women's equality can identify how the objective of the law seeks to further structural inequality against women.

In *Quebec v Alliance du personnel professional et technique de la santé and des services sociaux*[98] employers had to conduct pay audits every five years, but women were statutorily barred from retroactive compensation for any unequal pay between the audits. This was held by the majority of the Supreme Court of Canada to be a breach of section 15. Justice Abella for the majority then employed the *Oakes* proportionality test to assess whether this breach was constitutionally permissible. The state claimed that limiting retroactive pay had a pressing

[96] ibid [54].

[97] Iris Marion Young, *Justice and The Politics of Difference* (Princeton University Press, 1990) 5.

[98] *Quebec v Alliance du personnel professional et technique de la santé and des services sociaux* [2018] 1 SCR 464.

and substantive objective as it was a 'realistic' measure designed to encourage employers to comply with the equal pay laws.[99] The Court accepted that 'encouraging increased employer compliance' through 'lightening the burden' was legitimate, although the majority ultimately concluded that the restriction was not minimally impairing.[100] An enriched approach to the justification-stage would have defeated the justification claim at the first limb of the *Oakes* proportionality test.

The aim was not simply to encourage equal pay, as this is a laudable objective, but to achieve this objective by restricting women's right to receive equal pay. The objective, therefore, perpetuated structures that conceptualise women's equal pay either as optional or a negotiating tool which employers could weaponise to evade paying women for the work they perform. Analysing the broader context of equal pay in Canada would reveal a long history of employers failing to meet equal pay duties. Empirical data indicated that employers were unaware of the law, misunderstood their obligations, lacked the resources to implement the law and, more nefariously, intentionally underpaid women.[101] Encouraging employer compliance via restricting retroactive pay continued this tradition and vested power to the employer. Chief Justice McLachlin in her dissenting opinion in *Centrale de syndicats du Quebec v Quebec*,[102] a companion case to *Alliance*, commented on the properness of employer compliance as an aim at the justification-stage. She noted that accepting this objective

> would be to accept that obeying pay equity laws is an option that can be negotiated and that the very segment that perpetuate systemic pay inequities – the employers – should be able to perpetuate them as the price of accepting the law.[103]

It added another brick to employment structures that frustrate women's equality at work. This aim diluted women's equality as it framed it as discretionary or voluntary and accepted that employers must be bribed and cajoled to comply with the law. This purpose cannot be accepted as legitimate.

In a similar vein in *Centrale*, a relational and contextual approach to the first limb of the proportionality test would have exposed the structural inequalities embedded in the state's purpose. Work traditionally performed by women has been chronically undervalued. In these workplaces, there were rarely male comparators to easily demonstrate the extent of the unequal pay. Despite legal requirements to ensure equal pay, Quebec had delayed in devising a methodology to implement this duty in workplaces dominated by women and prohibited

[99] ibid [47].
[100] ibid [48].
[101] Parbudyal Singh and Ping Peng, 'Canada's Bold Experiment with Pay Equity' (2010) 25(7) *Gender in Management* 570; Judith McDonald and Robert Thornton, 'Have Pay Equity Laws in Canada Helped Women? A Synthetic-Control Approach' (2016) 46(4) *American Review of Canadian Studies* 452.
[102] *Centrale de syndicats du Quebec v Quebec* [2018] 1 SCR 522.
[103] ibid [157].

retroactive pay during the period of delay. This delay was held to be a breach of the section 15 equality rights and the state argued in *Centrale* that it was justified. More specifically, the state held the delay had a legitimate purpose as the goal was to find 'the right approach'.[104] A relational and contextual assessment of this objective would explore how these objectives reinforced economic structures that devalued work traditionally performed by women. Women cluster in caring, cleaning, catering, cashiering and clerical work, and since women performed this labour for free in the home it has remained undervalued in the market.[105] There needed to be a comprehensive structural re-evaluation of the effort, skills and responsibilities needed to perform this type of work. In *Centrale*, the aim, that it was too difficult to undertake this structural review, that it was too challenging to redress the synergy of the pay inequalities and gender job segregation, was a defeatist objective. It denied the possibility of women's equality at work. It continued to place the burden of difference on women and accepted the continued existence of systems that punish them for working in industries that deviate from the male experience. The aim legitimated structures that forgive women's unequal pay. Justice Abella for the majority, however, accepted this was a legitimate aim and concluded the delay met the other requirements under the *Oakes* proportionality test.

An enriched approach to justification examines not only women's historical subordination or gender stereotypes but pays careful attention to how objectives reinforce and legitimate structures that oppress women and ensures these purposes do not cross the justification threshold.

B. Rational Connection

The enriched methodology can be brought to bear with respect to the rationality limb of justification. This is because states put forward an argument that the law or policy which limits women's equality is a rational measure to achieve the competing legitimate aim without reflecting on whether the rational connection is built upon gendered assumptions. Ignorance of women's lives and even antagonism towards women's choices can be masked by the purported logic and reason of a justification. Rationality can be deeply gendered. It was the conceptual basis for depriving women of equal rights. For large swaths of history, women were deemed irrational and thus could not enjoy any form of legal personhood.[106] Unsurprisingly, rationality was, and remains, coded, with male perspectives, and is influenced by gender power and privilege.[107] Feminist scholars working

[104] ibid [43].

[105] Sandra Fredman, *Discrimination Law*, 3rd edn (Clarendon, 2022) chapter 2.

[106] Sandra Fredman, *Women and the Law* (Oxford University Press, 1997) 3–5.

[107] Karen Jones, 'Gender and Rationality' in Alfred Male and Piers Rawling (eds), *The Oxford Handbook of Rationality* (Oxford University Press, 2004).

across disciplines have painstakingly unpicked how rationality can be deployed to reinforce gender hierarchies against women[108] and more specifically, how the legal concept of rationality have been used to cement women's inequality.[109] But vestiges of biased conceptions of reasonableness remain, including at the justification-stage. To women who lack autonomy, arguments that excluding them from legal protections is a logical way to protect individual choice ring hollow. Or to women who are in financially precarious situations, arguments that prohibitions on working in a lucrative industry is a rational measure to enhance their dignity appear disingenuous. Testing the rationality of the limitation arguments against the relationship between the limit and the specific breach of women's equality rights and the broader context of women's equality can ensure that justifications that are distorted by gender bias are not given constitutional imprimatur.

i. The Rationality of the Labour Market

Using the logic of protecting women from exploitation, the state of Maharashtra in India banned dancing in certain hospitality establishments. Prohibitions on dancing disproportionately impacted on women who were the predominant dancers. These types of working bans were a violation of women's equality and part of a long global history that has sought to legally restrict women's economic opportunities and participation. The Indian Supreme Court in *State of Maharashtra v Indian Hotel Restaurant and Association* had to determine whether the dancing prohibition was in breach of Article 14 of the Indian Constitution. This would require the Court to assess whether the prohibition had an intelligible differentia and was arbitrary. Placing the logic of the ban on the anvil of women's equality – more specifically in relation to the underlying breach of women's equality and in the broader context of women's employment and employment activism in India – would mark out how the supposed rationality of the ban operated to push women into more risky and exploitative work.

The state argued that dancing in restaurants, hotels and bars capitalised on the poverty of vulnerable women and was a front for trafficking and prostitution.[110] The aim of the ban was to protect women from exploitation and violence. At the justification-stage, the Court needed to investigate whether there was a rational link between the dancing ban and women's safety at work. The prohibition, the state argued, would positively contribute to the 'larger issues of the dignity of women' and 'the destructions of environments and circumstances where it is

[108] ibid.

[109] Fredman (n 106); Patricia Smith (ed), *Feminist Jurisprudence* (Oxford University Press, 1993); Ratna Kapur, *Gender Alterity and Human Rights: Freedom in a Fishbowl* (Edward-Elgar, 2018).

[110] *State of Maharashtra v Indian Hotel and Restaurant Association* (2013) 8 SCC 519 [4], [10], [43], [48], [55], [57], [64].

profitable to keep women vulnerable'.[111] At first glance, there was a compelling rational connection between the state's legitimate objectives, protecting women from being exploited, and prohibiting a type of dancing that has a track record of poor working conditions.[112] The logic of the justification-stage, prohibiting dance – protecting women, rested on an overly simplistic reasoning that failed to account for the gendered nature of the labour market.

The logic of the ban was based on two propositions, if dancing was prohibited it would: (i) easily channel women into other jobs, such as at call centres; and (ii) that these other forms of employment were better for women.[113] Taking the second proposition, that dancing was a lesser form of work that was exploitative, for most women in India, to work was to work in precarious, low or no wage, low-status work.[114] A study examining trends between 1983 and 2018 found that women's working conditions have remained poor with women concentrated in agricultural labour, lower wage jobs, the informal sector and unpaid family work.[115] Dancing was part of a large pattern of inequality in work, nor was it a markedly more oppressive form of work. The larger context would expose the gendered restraints of the labour market. Many women reported that dancing was a way to gain financial security and independence as opposed to other forms of work, such as domestic work or factory work, which they described as exploitative.[116] For many women, choosing between working as a dancer or working in a factory, farm or private home was a choice between bad and worse. Dancing was a logical choice within a system that restricted women's opportunities and was permeated with unjust working conditions. The rationality of the ban failed to give due weight to gendered realities. It ignored women's decision-making and was deeply paternalistic, in that it co-opted women's agency to navigate patriarchal institutions. Moreover, the rationality of the ban failed to respond to women's needs, as the women working in the dancing industry wanted better working conditions and terms, including unionising, to protect them at work, rather than a prohibition which would limit their ability to economically support themselves.[117]

Building upon this, the first proposition also falters against a relational and contextual assessment anchored in women's equality. The rationality of the ban presumed that women who dance could find another form of income. Many of the women who danced did not have formal education or training, many were

[111] ibid [43].
[112] Anna Morcom, *Illicit Worlds of Indian Dance: Cultures of Exclusion* (Oxford University Press, 2013).
[113] *Indian Hotel and Restaurant Association* (n 110) [77].
[114] Pallavi Gupta and Satyanarayan Kothe, 'Gender Discrimination and the Biased Indian Labour Market: Evidence from the National Sample Survey' (2024) 35 *World Development Perspectives* 100613.
[115] S Sundari, 'Structural Changes and Quality of Women's Labour in India' (2020) 63 *The Indian Journal of Labour Economics* 689.
[116] *Indian Hotel and Restaurant Association* (n 110) [78].
[117] Morcom (n 112) ch 5.

supporting their children and families, and they could not simply transition to other forms of employment in call centres or factories.[118] The ban eliminated their only viable source of income. It was estimated it made 75,000 women unemployed and forced many of these women into sex work which greatly increased their risk of being subjected to violence and exploitation.[119] The ban, in practice, achieved the exact opposite of its intended aims because of its deeply flawed rationality.

These arguments were put before the Indian Supreme Court.[120] Ultimately, with respect to the gender equality dimensions of *Indian Hotel and Restaurant Association*, the Court concluded there was no evidence that dancing was connected to trafficking in women and thus concluded the ban was arbitrary as it was designed to ameliorate a problem that did not exist.[121] However, the judgment could have gone further, using the proposed enriched approach to justification to more directly confront the gendered rational flaws in the state's limitation arguments.

ii. The Rationality of Marriage

The justifications for legal restrictions on de facto intimate partner unions also suffered from a lack of rationality when those limitations are placed in relationship to the breach of equality and context of women's equality within marriage. In the Canadian and South African apex courts, the argument was made that the restrictions were a rational measure to protect individual autonomy as the law did not impose a property regime on individuals who had chosen not to enter a formal marriage. A relational and contextual assessment of the rational connection for the exclusion would reveal that the limit was based on the logic of preserving male power.

Choice and autonomy in intimate partner relations were and remain connected to gender power relations. Due to stubborn and deeply engrained gender norms, in and outside of the home, women lack economic and social power within intimate partner relations. This negatively impacts their bargaining power and hampers their ability to insist on legal relationships that reflect their needs, wishes and desires. Justice Madlanga in *Bwanya v Master of the High Court* in the South African Constitutional Court noted that in a society 'dominated by men in virtually all areas of human endeavour … a woman may have to be content with what in essence is the man's choice'[122] and if some women are 'desirous of getting married, [she] cannot because their men partner's choice is not to get married. And there is nothing the women's partner

[118] ibid.
[119] ibid 147.
[120] *Indian Hotel and Restaurant Association* (n 110) [71]–[85].
[121] ibid [105].
[122] *Bwanya v Master of the High Court* [2021] ZACC 51 [63].

can do about it'.[123] The South African Constitutional Court came to a similar conclusion in *Women's Legal Centre Trust v President of the Republic of South Africa*.[124] Muslim marriages were excluded from legal recognition. The Court found this disproportionately impacted on Muslim women who 'due to disparity in their respective bargaining powers' were unable to insist that they also be married in a manner that guaranteed their marriages would be legally protected.[125] Justice Abella, in dissent in the Canadian Supreme Court, similarly explained in *Quebec v A*, 'one member of a couple can decide to refuse to marry or enter a civil union and thereby deprive the other of the benefit of needed support when the relationship ends'.[126] Her analysis was gender neutral, but the evidence was consistent that it was women who were economically worse-off upon relationship breakdown.[127] As evidenced by the facts in *Quebec v A*, 'Ms. A consistently wanted to marry, but Mr. B refused' and that refusal 'depriv[ed] Ms. A of access to the possibility of spousal support at the end of the relationship'.[128]

The gendered realities of marriage and intimate partner unions matter not just in assessing whether the legal restrictions on certain forms of unions were a violation of women's equality rights but instrumental in rigorously assessing the rationality of the justifications for breaching these rights. Legal restrictions are repeatedly justified as a rational legal intervention to enhance individual autonomy and choice.[129] The rationality of this limitation was premised on equality within marriage where parties are able to arrive at a mutually acceptable decision as to how to legally govern their relationship yet due to gender power imbalances, autonomy-based limits on women's equality translate to a justification that was premised on preserving and protecting those imbalances. A relational and contextual analysis that paid close attention to women's agency and the constraints on that agency would point towards the rational connection of the ban was not protecting choices but preserving a gendered status quo. In *Bwanya, Women's Legal Centre Trust* and *Quebec v A*, the relevant judgments tangentially questioned grounding limitation in the rationality of choice,[130] although all could have been more explicitly unpacked via an enriched justification assessment on how the justifications were premised on untenable assumptions on women's agency within marriage and how the justifications arguments were used to cement male power.

[123] ibid [88].
[124] *Women's Legal Centre Trust v President of the Republic of South Africa* [2022] ZACC 23.
[125] ibid [47].
[126] *Quebec v A* [2013] 1 SCR 61 [375].
[127] CEDAW (n 22) [4].
[128] *Quebec v A* (n 126) [375].
[129] *Nova Scotia (Attorney General) v Walsh* [2002] 4 SCR 325 [43]; *Volks v Robinson* [2005] ZACC 2 [91]–[93].
[130] *Bwanya* (n 122) [16], [60]–[69],[93]; *Women's Legal Centre Trust* (n 124) [47], [55], [56]; *Quebec v A* (n 126) [335], [359].

C. Necessity

Another common justification criterion is necessity. Least intrusive or minimally impairing, as the necessity criterion is often referred to, requires courts to assess whether it is necessary to treat women unequally to achieve the aim or whether there are other measures that could secure the state's goal without breaching women's equality rights. This requires considering hypothetical measures and then evaluating the feasibility of these different measures to flush out if the state's decision to burden women is truly necessary.[131] A relational and contextual assessment anchored in women's equality can provide insights into alternative possibilities and the likely efficacy of these possibilities, and in many cases can throw into sharp relief the absurdity of claiming the only way to achieve a competing goal is to violate women's equality.

i. The Necessity of Social Benefit Reforms

Turning to the jurisprudence analysed in chapter five, applying a relational and contextual assessment to the benefit reform cases, *SG* and *SC*, in the UK, would bring to the fore a range of alternative measures that the UK Supreme Court should have explored with the state. Lord Reed in the judgments in *SG* and *SC* accepted that disproportionately imposing income poverty on women through a series of reforms that restricted access to social welfare on women was necessary. Repeatedly throughout the judgments, he accepted these reforms as 'inevitable' implying that there were no other alternatives to achieve the Government's aims – balancing the budget, incentivising certain behaviours or welfare fairness – other than violating women's equality rights.[132] In *SG*, in assessing the necessity of the benefit cap, which capped the amount of benefits women could claim, he accepted the state's assessment of necessity. He explained 'the Government has made a judgment, endorsed by Parliament' that setting the cap at any other level 'would be less effective in achieving its aims'.[133] A relational and contextual assessment would explore the necessity of the reforms in light of their relationship to the breach of women's equality and the broader context of gender-based poverty in the UK.

The Court in *SG* and *SC* could have drawn on the broader context of women's equality, particularly feminist economic theory, which seeks to simultaneously protect women's rights and achieve economic security. The Court could have explored alternatives that were consistent with feminist economic theory. This context would have destabilised the necessity of the reforms as it would have questioned whether austerity was a logical or kneejerk response to any

[131] Stone Sweet and Mathews (n 51) 47.
[132] *SG* (n 29) [61], [76], [96]; *SC* (n 28) [195], [199].
[133] *SG* (n 29) [69].

fiscal crisis.[134] It would have then canvassed alternatives that reflect economic priorities that centre the value of care, cooperation and relationships such as a strong investment in social care or increasing tax revenue. The Women's Budget Group argued that a financial transactions tax at only 0.01 per cent would raise approximately £25 billion per year in revenues, alleviating the need for discriminatory welfare cuts.[135] A contextual limitation analysis enriched with equality could bring feminist legal imaginations and utopias to the necessity limb.[136] It could provide new ways of seeing, new ways of doing, new ways of being that push the state beyond the straitjacket of typical gendered responses to economic and social problems. Courts are often accused of overstepping their institutional boundaries at the necessity limb.[137] The relational and contextual approach did not require the Court in *SG* and *SC* to become a court of economic theory. Nor does it set up an insurmountable burden as it may be that the state could persuasively rebut any claims that these other measures would have been effective in achieving the competing objectives. An enriched approach to justification, however, does require the UK Supreme Court to probe and investigate least invasive measures and in doing that it can draw on a relational and contextual understanding of women's substantive equality to identify alternatives.

ii. The Necessity of Gendered Prohibitions at Work

With respect to women's safety from violence, the Indian Supreme Court drew on the relational and contextual approach to flush out gendered stereotypes in the state's necessity arguments and point out the possibility of other measures. In *Anuj Garg v Hotel Association of India*, the state claimed that it was necessary to prohibit women from working in premises that served alcohol to protect them from violence.[138] The Indian Supreme Court, using Article 14, conducted a loose proportionality analysis, to assess whether this prohibition was constitutionally justified. The state argued the prohibition was necessary to protect women from violence at work. Placing this limitation claim in relation to the underlying breach, gendered restrictions on economic opportunities, it became apparent that the necessity of the prohibition was based on romantic paternalistic attitudes that used protection as a pretext to deprive women of agency, lock them in the home and confine them to traditional gendered roles. Bringing the

[134] Mark Blyth, *Austerity: The History of a Dangerous Idea* (Oxford University Press, 2013) ch 3.

[135] UK Women's Budget Group, 'The Gender Impact Assessment of the Coalition Government Budget June 2010' (2010), available at https://wbg.org.uk/wp-content/uploads/2016/12/RRB_Reports_12_956432831.pdf.

[136] Mary Mossman, 'Feminism and Legal Method: The Difference It Makes' (1987) 3 *Wisconsin Women's Law Journal* 147; Susan Himmelweit, 'Feminist Economics: Why All Economists Should Be Feminist Economists' in Lilliann Fischer and others (eds), *Rethinking Economics* (Routledge, 2017).

[137] Stone Sweet and Mathews (n 51) 47.

[138] *Anuj Garg v Hotel Association of India* (2008) 3 SCC 1.

necessity of the prohibition into relationship with the breach, necessity would only be made out if women are conceptualised as the weaker and inferior sex. The broader context of violence against women in India was also instructive when testing the necessity of the prohibition. Justice Sinha noted that there was a barrage of other measures that could be employed to keep women safe that did not require reinforcing gender stereotypes.[139] A relational and contextual approach that explored how the necessity of the measure in relation to the expressive harms of the prohibition and context of innovations in redressing gender-based violence marked out how the measure was not required to achieve women's equality at work.

In a similar vein, in *India Hotel and Restaurant Association* the state also argued the necessity of prohibiting women from dancing at certain establishments to protect women from sexual violence. As argued above, the justification faltered on rationality as the prohibition on dancing did not protect women but pushed them into economic destitution. It also would not pass muster under a relational and contextual necessity assessment. In this case, the relevant context was both the gendered stigmas against women who danced and the voice of women who danced. It was these aspects of women's equality that would undercut any claim that the prohibition was necessary.

The ban was preceded by a strong public discourse on women who dance in hospitality. Different advocacy groups argued that women who dance in bars were lazy and earned high salaries from men who should be investing their money into the family.[140] Women who danced were femme fatales who threatened the traditional family. This negative cultural attitude towards women was reflected in the state's arguments in *Indian Hotel and Restaurants Association* as it described women who dance as 'young girls desirous of earning easy money being attracted to such dance bars and getting involved in immoral activities'.[141] In response to this negative cultural discourse, women dancers formed a collective organisation and were advocating for a range of measures to improve working conditions including the distribution of tips, dress codes, rules of conduct and the recognition of dancing as a profession.[142] There were alternatives that would have protected women from violence at work that did not require prohibiting their employment. The broader context marked out how women were drawing on the structural and participation dimensions of substantive equality to construct a new way of seeing women at work. The state's decision to pursue prohibition rather than these other measures is telling as it indicated that the prohibition was in place to punish women who were perceived as morally or socially deviant. Enriching justification with women's equality by identifying the

[139] ibid [41].
[140] *Indian Hotel and Restaurant Association* (n 110) [20], [44], [55]; Morcom (n 112) 147.
[141] *Indian Hotel and Restaurant Association* (n 110) [12].
[142] Morcom (n 112) 160–65.

broader gendered context of the prohibition not only marked out alternatives but flushed out insidious and discriminatory objectives. This echoes Jackson's observations on how a justification-stage can be utilised to detect inequalities that can be difficult to detect on a plain reading of the state's limitation claims.[143] These necessity arguments were put before the Indian Supreme Court but were not fully drawn upon in the Court's conclusions. A missed opportunity to build a sophisticated justification jurisprudence.

iii. The Necessity of Protecting Autonomy in Marriage

The majority of the Canadian Supreme Court repeatedly held that excluding de facto intimate partner unions was not a breach of equality rights but the dissenting opinions in *Nova Scotia (Attorney General) v Walsh* and *Quebec v A* came to the opposite conclusion and proceeded to a limitation analysis under section 1 of the Charter. The state argued that the purpose of the exclusion was to protect individual choices and that the only method for ensuring the law did not impose legal consequences on individuals regardless of their personal choices was to restrict the application of marital property laws.[144] Furthermore, the impact of exclusion was minimal as women could pursue other legal remedies if they were destitute at relationship breakdown. Measures to mitigate the negative impact on women's equality rights properly belong within the balancing limb of the justification-stage where there is meant to be a holistic assessment of whether the costs to women's equality are worth achieving the competing legitimate aim. Yet, in many judgments, mitigation measures were assessed under necessity, perhaps reflecting how necessity in practice becomes a broad assessment of alternatives. A relational and contextual assessment would expose the flaws in these mitigation measures.

Women could either enter a contractual relationship with their partner to protect their economic interests or go to court and argue their partner was unjustly enriched from their labour.[145] Putting the contractual route in relation to the underlying breach reveals that this measure was an illusion. Women did not have the bargaining power within the relationship to demand that the relationship be legally recognised as a marriage nor would they have the power to insist on a contract to protect their interests.[146] The unjust enrichment argument also would not withstand a contextual scrutiny. Its feasibility depends on the willingness of courts to give monetary weight to care labour. Women must persuade courts that the work they performed in the home was of economic

[143] Jackson (n 3) 171.
[144] *Quebec v A* (n 126) [375].
[145] *Walsh* (n 129) [164]–[169].
[146] See *Sithole v Sithole* [2021] ZACC 7 [38].

value and not simply expressions of love or nurturing.[147] Kumaraguru warns that judicial actors steeped in gender stereotypes would likely struggle to see unpaid care work as 'true labour deserving of wages'.[148] This warning has rung true as the evidence was that lower courts undervalued care work and failed to recognise how caring work underpinned the acquisition of financial assets.[149] The judicial role under the necessity limb was not to blindly accept assertions that there are no other measures that could possibly achieve the competing objective or that mitigation measures that soften the inequality against women were feasible. The relational and contextual approach would direct the courts to explore how alternatives interact with the underlying breach of women's rights and the broader gendered context of the claim, giving courts tools to fulfil its function at the justification-stage.

D. Balancing

Balancing is the justification criteria that attracts the most attention and raises the most consternation. As argued in chapter five, judgments repeatedly misdirect balancing, oversimplifying and outright ignoring the harms women are expected to bear. Enriching justification with equality via relationality and contextualism demands a full accounting of the strengths and weaknesses of the competing objectives and the extent of the inequality. This proposed methodology gives the court tools to balance these incommensurables as it permits the court to explore whether the purported benefits are not only accurate but also more starkly exposes whether those benefits are worth pursuing inequality against women.

i. Gender Balancing at Work

Is it worth restricting the scope of equal rights to ensure greater compliance with the diluted gender pay obligation? As argued above, in *Alliance*, the justification-stage should have ended at the legitimate aim limb as enriching justification with equality would not accept aims that bolster structural gender inequality against women. However, it is worth exploring how a relational and contextual methodology would strengthen the balancing limb of the *Oakes* proportionality analysis. On one hand, the state claimed, based on pure speculation, that the benefits of restricting the breadth of the obligation will enhance employer

[147] Wendy McKeen, 'The Wages for Housework Campaign: Its Contribution to Feminist Politics in the Area of Social Welfare in Canada' (1994) *Canadian Review of Social Policy* 21.

[148] Yanitra Kumaraguru, 'Wages for Housework: A Step Towards Equality at First Glance, A Step Away at Second?' (*Feminist Perspectives*, 19 April 2022), available at https://www.kcl.ac.uk/wages-for-housework-a-step-towards-equality-at-first-glance-a-step-away-at-second.

[149] Regina Graycar, 'Matrimonial Property Law Reform and Equality for Women: Discourses in Discord?' (1995) 25 *Victoria University of Wellington Law Review* 9.

compliance with equal pay laws and on the other hand, women were required to legally accept being paid unequally for years on end. The majority judgment stressed, under the balancing assessment, that the state's claims on compliance were not based on evidence, whereas the negative impact of unequal pay on women was well documented.[150] The empirical imbalance could not be the basis for limiting women's rights. Justice Abella went a step further in *Alliance* and explicitly adopted the relational and contextual approach grounded in women's equality in balancing these interests and rights. She held that lowering 'the bar in the hope of compliance strikes me … as being inconsistent with respect for substantive equality'.[151] Unfortunately, Justice Abella did not unpack the role of the substantive equality in balancing. This can leave it vague as to how and why substantive equality enriches the balancing limb of the *Oakes* test. Women's equality at work is a broad field and the inequalities underpinning the pay gap are multi-fold. Relationality and contextualism can guide the justification-stage to the aspects of women's equality at work that are most able to enrich assessing if the limitation was balanced.

With respect to bringing the justification claim that the law is balanced in relation to the breach of women's equality rights, on one hand, the law perpetuated significant gendered material and expressive harms as it communicated to employers that their intransigence on women's equality will be rewarded and on the other hand, there was only a hope that reducing the obligation would enhance long-term compliance. Teasing out the relationship between the limit and women's equality more starkly showed the imbalance. With respect to the broader context of women's equality at work, the analysis could be directed to the failing legislative history of ending gendered pay inequalities and employer failure to comply with legal obligations. This contextual analysis would have demonstrated how this objective was part of a larger pattern of conceptualising women's equal pay as voluntary, charitable or ignorable. Weighing this against purely speculative claims would have bolstered Justice Abella's conclusion that the aim was deeply inconsistent with women's substantive equality.

ii. Gender Balancing in Early Forced Marriage

Lastly, *Independent Thought* was a strong example of using a relational and contextual approach to balancing. Much like *Alliance*, as argued above, the objective in exempting marital rape for girls between the ages of 15 and 18 did not have a proper purpose. Although balancing was not explicitly part of the justification framework, the Indian Supreme Court in *Independent Thought* implicitly adopted an enriched methodology to balancing, and this case is part of a line of jurisprudence moving towards the four-part proportionality limitation test.[152]

[150] *Alliance* (n 98) [53].
[151] ibid [54].
[152] Chandra (n 67).

The state held the exemption was justified as it was part of a long-standing sociocultural tradition that was worthy of constitutional protection.[153] It pointed out the harms in revoking the exemption. Due to the slow pace of economic and educational development, criminalising the marital rape of girls would criminalise large swathes of people.[154] The Court did not accept this accounting of the pros and cons of the exemption at face-value but placed these arguments in relation to the breach and the broader context of sexual violence and early forced marriage for girls in India. There were an estimated 23 million girl brides and one in five marriages were early forced marriage.[155] When girls are married, Justice Gupta observed that a crucial stage in girls' development was thwarted, and they were denied agency to create their own lives.[156] They were often isolated which breaks bonds of friendship, family and community and blocks educational and future employment opportunities. Due to the synergy of gender and age, girls have little autonomy within early forced marriage and were at increased risk of all forms of violence and had limited ability to control their sexual autonomy and reproduction. Girls in early forced marriage were at a greater risk of sexually transmitted infections, early pregnancy, maternal morbidity and mortality. There were strong intersectional dimensions to early forced marriage and it reinforced other vectors of inequality. Girls from poor, uneducated, rural areas and Scheduled Castes and Scheduled Tribes were more likely to be forced into marriage.[157] Justice Lokur concluded that

> looking at the impact of early marriage from a rights perspective, it can said that the key concerns are denial of childhood and adolescence, curtailment of personal freedom, deprivation of opportunities to develop a full sense of selfhood and educational opportunity.[158]

He also examined the broader context of sexual violence. The justification analysis combed through judicial decisions on sexual violence, noting that this violence inflicted severe physical and mental injuries and damaged self-esteem and dignity.[159]

This relational and contextual approach anchored in women's equality was able to thoroughly identify the gendered harms of the law, and these harms were weighed against the value of preserving tradition. Justice Lokir held:

> we have been adverted to the wealth of documentary material which goes to show that an early forced marriage and sexual intercourse at an early age could have detrimental effects on the girl child … therefore the practice of early forced marriage … even if sanctified by tradition and custom may yet be an undesirable

[153] *Independent Thought* (n 31) [68] (concurring opinion of Justice Gupta).
[154] ibid [49], [68] (concurring opinion of Justice Gupta).
[155] ibid [72] (concurring opinion of Justice Gupta).
[156] ibid [37] (concurring opinion of Justice Gupta).
[157] ibid [13] (concurring opinion of Justice Lokur).
[158] ibid [12] (concurring opinion of Justice Lokur).
[159] ibid [67] (concurring opinion of Justice Lokur).

> practice today … Should this traditional practice still continue? We do not think so and the sooner it is given up, it would be in the best interest of the girl child and for society as a whole.[160]

The Court did not conduct a formalistic or mechanical balancing exercise, nor did it misdirect the analysis to an irrelevant assessment. It squarely confronted the strength of benefits of protecting sociocultural traditions in relation to the harms of legally permitting sexual violence against girls and against the broader context of the rights violations inherent in early forced marriage. The totality of these grievous harms emphasised how the benefits of the exemption were minimal against practices that perpetuated severe inequalities against women and girls. Notably, in both *Alliance* and *Independent Thought*, a relational and contextual assessment would calm fears that balancing is unprincipled weighing of incommensurables or that it inappropriately draws courts into legislative or executive decision-making spaces. This proposed methodology provided a logic to balancing and while the task of balancing is never easy, a relational and contextual approach stabilised the role of the court while simultaneously ensuring there was a comprehensive weighing of the costs and benefits of pursing an aim that breaches women's equality rights.

IV. CONCLUSION

Women's equality enriches the justification-stage. The justification-stage must test the veracity of a justification in relation to the specific breach of women's equality and within the broader context of women's equality. Relationality and contextualism are prominent feminist legal methodologies that are designed to test relational power hierarchies and reveal hidden meanings. This chapter harnesses the strengths of feminist relationality and contextualism and translates and adapts them to the justification-stage. The proposed approach captures that justifications create hierarchies between rights and other objectives and that justifications are created within political, economic, historic, social and cultural contexts. Limitation claims cannot be analysed in isolation from the specific breach of women's equality, nor can they be divorced from the broader context of women's equality. To assess the legitimacy of the justification, say achieving long-term compliance with equal pay laws, the court must examine this objective in light of the breach, restricting retroactive pay, and the broader context, a long history of employer intransience in complying with duties to end gendered pay inequalities. In a similar vein, assessing the rationality of an employment prohibition aimed at protecting women's safety at work, requires placing the logic of the justification in relation to the breach of women's rights, restricting limited opportunities for economic independence, and the broader context, the

[160] ibid [87] (concurring opinion of Justice Lokur).

lack of good quality employment for women writ large and the sociocultural demonisation of women who perform this type of work. To strain the metaphor, women's equality is the anvil upon which to test the legitimacy, rationality, necessity and balance of a justification claim and relationality and contextualism are the tools to direct the court to the aspects of women's equality that are relevant for testing the justification claim. While there may be a host of other relations and contexts that can illuminate whether a justification meets the limitation criteria, the relationship between the limit and the breach of women's rights and the broader context of women's equality is automatically and always relevant. This approach ensures that the justification-stage does not undercut the constitutional significance of women's equality, and it shows respect for the women who are being asked to bear the consequences of the limitation. Moreover, their perspective, their understanding of their own equality brings rich analytical insights into the strength of limitation claims, exposing weaknesses. Enriching justification with women's equality ensures that women's rights are limited only when the justification thresholds are met.

In applying this methodology, the courts not only guarantee justification serves its function of protecting rights but also respecting institutional boundaries. In the cases analysed above, the courts were not over-stepping and taking on the role of the executive or legislative body. They were performing their assigned function in the separation of powers by not accepting limitation claims at face-value but rigorously testing them. The relational and contextual approaches anchored in women's equality can also operate to deflate fears of judicial over-reach. This methodology unearths flaws making it objectively clear and certain that the limitation claims do not have the required strength to constitutionally limit women's rights and thereby protecting the court against critiques that it is imposing its own constitutional priorities.

However, not all cases may be so straightforward. Yet, even in these cases equality can enrich the justification-stage. For example, if the courts must assess whether a law that criminalises all aspects of sex work, but the selling of sex (essentially exempting women from criminal sanction) was a justifiable limit to women's equality, the proposed methodology would bring forth contested relations and contexts all anchored in women's equality. With respect to the legitimacy or rationality of criminalising sex work, on one hand, a relational and contextual methodology would identify how some feminists conceptualise sex work as a form of violence against women that objectifies, exploits and demeans.[161] It would thus be legitimate and rational to criminalise all aspects of the sex work, except selling, to protect women from violence. On the other hand, a relational and contextual approach would tease out how criminalisation can increase risks of violence. To appease the purchasers of sex, who seek

[161] UN Special Rapporteur on violence against women and girls, its causes and consequences, 'Prostitution and Violence against Women and Girls' (2024) A/HRC/56/48.

to evade criminal sanction, sex workers would be pushed into more dangerous practices.[162] Furthermore, many women advocate for sex work as a form of bodily autonomy and a type of employment that offers women a chance to escape economic destitution.[163] This relational and contextual analysis would question whether criminalisation was necessary or the least intrusive measure. Each of these competing relations and contexts are anchored in women's equality, but here there is no consensus on whether women's equality is hindered or protected by criminalising the purchase of sex. In part this reflects the heterogeneity of feminism. An array of identity characteristics, experiences, circumstances or positionality can result in differing beliefs on how women's equality can be respected, protected and fulfilled. This holds true for many contemporary issues of women's equality, from polygamy to wealth concentration, to climate change. At first glance, it would appear the relational and contextual methodology would add little to the justification-stage and could be discarded. This, however, would be a mistake. The methodology developed in this chapter would bring the needed transparency for the courts to make an accurate determination. There would be a full canvassing of the strengths and weaknesses and then it would be a matter of judgment for the court whether the limitation met the constitutional requirements.

It may appear disappointing or even to be an evasion to hold that the relational and contextual approach does not offer a concrete answer in cases like the hypothetical criminalisation of sex work. But justification is messy. It is trying to untangle where constitutional priorities should lie. The relational and contextual approach acknowledges this chaos, this complexity rather than avoiding it or flatlining it. It accepts that justification is not formalistic, mathematical or mechanical and that there is space for weighing and valuing competing relations and contexts that are anchored in equality. In squarely confronting that this methodology can pull in opposite directions, the court is still not exceeding its bounds. It is not indulging in unprincipled moral reasoning but testing the boundaries of the justification criteria in a sophisticated manner. Exploring how this methodology works in cases like sex work is also an important reminder that this approach does not foreclose limiting women's rights. But it does enrich it. The strengths of this approach – its respect for the constitutional nature of women's equality; its drive for greater transparency; its ability to measure the strength of limitation claims – would result in a more consistent and in-depth application of justification frameworks. By fully engaging with the relational and contextual approach, even in hard cases, the court will engage with how justification can replicate or dismantle gendered disadvantage, stigmas, structures and exclusions.

[162] *Canada (Attorney General) v Bedford* 2013 SCC 72.

[163] Christine Overall, 'What's Wrong With Prostitution: Evaluating Sex Work' 17(4) *Signs: Journal of Women in Culture and Society* 705; Nussbaum (n 90).

To conclude by looking back and looking forward. Women's equality plays three important functions with respect to justification. It can ring-fence the determination of whether there has been a breach of women's equality rights to protect against justification concepts warping the analysis. Equality guides the calibration of the justification-stage pointing the limitation analysis towards a stringent standard of review. Lastly, equality enriches justification criteria so the justification-stage is not a mechanical exercise but is one that is alive to the relationships and context between the limit and those who must bear the consequences of the limit. The normative claims on how equality matters to justification are built upon the comparative doctrinal analysis that pierced through assumptions on how justification worked in practice. There remain, however, many more questions to explore. Does this proposed asymmetrical relationship between equality and justification hold true for other grounds of discrimination? Would it work with respect to justifying racial inequality, disability inequality or gender identity inequality? Women often seek to secure their equality through other rights. Abortion rights, for example, are rarely litigated on equality grounds but more often in relation to privacy or security of the person. Do the claims made in this monograph have any salience when a different right is at stake at the justification-stage? Reflecting on the future from a comparative perspective, not all jurisdictions adopt a two-stage approach to women's equality, as advocated for in the monograph, nor do all apex courts in the current political climate appear open to embracing the protecting, guiding and enriching function equality can play at the justification-stage. How can these normative claims be made real and embedded into court praxis? Much like the feminist lawmakers did in *Coleman*, this requires careful legal and political strategising tailored to the unique legal, sociocultural and political pathologies of the jurisdiction. This monograph only offers the first step and much remains to be considered. But importantly it does signal out that women's equality matters to justification.

Appendix

Canada

Section 15 of the Canadian Charter of Rights and Freedoms

(1) Every individual is equal before and under the law and has the right to the equal protection and equal benefit of the law without discrimination and, in particular, without discrimination based on race, national or ethnic origin, colour, religion, sex, age or mental or physical disability.

(2) Section (1) does not preclude any law, program or activity that has as its object the amelioration of conditions of disadvantaged individuals or groups including those that are disadvantaged because of race, national or ethnic origin, colour, religion, sex, age or mental or physical disability.

Section 1 of the Canadian Charter of Rights and Freedoms

The *Canadian Charter of Rights and Freedoms* guarantees the rights and freedoms set out in it subject only to such reasonable limits prescribed by law as can be demonstrably justified in a free and democratic society.

India

Article 14 of the Indian Constitution

The State shall not deny to any person equality before the law or the equal protection of the laws within the territory of India.

South Africa

Section 9 of the South African Constitution

(1) Everyone is equal before the law and has the right to equal protection and benefit of the law.

(2) Equality includes the full and equal enjoyment of all rights and freedoms. To promote the achievement of equality, legislative and other measures designed to protect or advance persons, or categories of persons, disadvantaged by unfair discrimination may be taken.

(3) The state may not unfairly discriminate directly or indirectly against anyone on one or more grounds, including race, gender, sex, pregnancy, marital status, ethnic or social origin, colour, sexual orientation, age, disability, religion, conscience, belief, culture, language and birth.

(4) No person may unfairly discriminate directly or indirectly against anyone on one or more grounds in terms of subsection (3). National legislation must be enacted to prevent or prohibit unfair discrimination.

(5) Discrimination on one or more of the grounds listed in subsection (3) is unfair unless it is established that the discrimination is fair.

Section 36 of the South African Constitution

(1) The rights in the Bill of Rights may be limited only in terms of law of general application to the extent that the limitation is reasonable and justifiable in an open and democratic society based on human dignity, equality and freedom, taking into account all relevant factors, including—

(a) the nature of the right;
(b) the importance of the purpose of the limitation;
(c) the nature and extent of the limitation;
(d) the relation between the limitation and its purpose; and
(e) less restrictive means to achieve the purpose.

(2) Except as provided in subsection (1) or in any other provision of the Constitution, no law may limit any right entrenched in the Bill of Rights.

United Kingdom

Article 14 of the Human Rights Act 1998

The enjoyment of the rights and freedoms set forth in this Convention shall be secured without discrimination on any ground such as sex, race, colour, language, religion, political or other opinion, national or social origin, association with a national minority, property, birth or other status.

United States

Fourteenth Amendment

(1) All persons born or naturalized in the United States, and subject to the jurisdiction thereof, are citizens of the United States and of the State wherein they reside. No State shall make or enforce any law which shall abridge the privileges or immunities of citizens of the United States; nor shall any State deprive any person of life, liberty, or property, without due process of law; nor deny to any person within its jurisdiction the equal protection of the laws.

(5) The Congress shall have power to enforce, by appropriate legislation, the provisions of this article.

Index

www.ingramcontent.com/pod-product-compliance
Ingram Content Group UK Ltd.
Pitfield, Milton Keynes, MK11 3LW, UK
UKHW020810290926
15470UKWH00003B/1060

9 781509 967872